FRANK SINATRA

a celebration by Derek Jewell

with a film commentary by George Perry

Little, Brown and Company

Boston   Toronto

*For the people of St Joseph Medical Center,
Burbank, California
and Hughes and Mala Miller*

Library of Congress Catalog Card no. 85-81197

First American Edition

Printed in Great Britain

Picture Acknowledgements:
Associated Press: 16BL, 101, 119; BBC Hulton/
Bettmann Archive: 45BR, 53B; Camera Press:
29B, Jerry Watson 20BR, 127, Ray Johnson 121,
Terry O'Neill 111, David Sutton 109, Bob
Willoughby 93T; Culver Pictures: Half Title, 8BL,
11T, 35, 42T, 43TR, C, 45BL, 50TL, BR, 57TL,
58T,C, 59B; The Frank Driggs Collection: 31, 32–
3, 40–1, 41T,B, 46, 67; The Kobal Collection: 38,
45TR, 49L,R, 54TR, 62, 71BL, 150, 152, 153, 154,
155, 156, 157, 159, 160, 161, 162, 163, 164, 165,
166, 167, 168, 169, 170, 171, 172, 173, 174, 176,
177, 178, 179, 192, Ted Allan: 98, 175, Gene
Trindl: 78; Peter Martin: 36; The Ted Nunn
Collection: Endpapers; The Official Elvis Presley
Fan Club of Great Britain: 92; Neal Peters: 23;
The Photo Source/Keystone © 1981 Images
Bettina Cirone: 141; Pictorial Parade: 9, 16TL,
20TL, 27L,R, 28T, 34, 45TL, 47, 50TR, 51B, 53T,
54B, 55, 58B, Frank Edwards © Fotos

International: 19, 114, 125, D. Hammond: 51CR,
89T, Joanne Jacino: 11B, Bob V. Noble © Fotos
International: 131, Pictorial Press: 30, 57BL, BR,
64, 87BC,B, Globe Photos: 82R, 96B, Ted Allan:
93B, John Hamilton: 97, Marty Mills: 96T, Don
Ornitz: 80B, Phil Stern: 94, 95, 103, Bob
Willoughby: 82B, William Woodfield: 80T, 81, 85,
90; Popperfoto: 29T, 68, 71TL, TR,BR, 76, 87TC,
104L, 124T, Jeff Slocomb Photography: 118B,
UPI: 135T,B; David Redfern: Frontispiece, 12T,
122, 148; David Redfern Photography/William
Gottlieb: 24, 57TR; Rex Features: 51TR, 71CL,
CR, 82TL, 106–7, 108, 118T, Globe Photos: 51TL,
Sipa/Alain Morvan: 130B; Frank Spooner
Pictures/Gamma/John T. Barr: 124B; Syndication
International: 12B, 16TR, 50BL, 126, 134; John
Topham Library: 6, 21, 42–3, 43TL, 54TL, 61,
72B, 75, 104R, 105T,R,B, 110, 130T, 137B; UPI/
Bettmann Archive: 8TL, R, 15, 44, 52, 59T, 72T,
79, 86, 87T, 89B, 129, 137TL.

CONTENTS

*'A voice for all seasons,
a man for all dreams'*

1 OVERTURE

IT WOULD BE A CONVENIENT, BUT QUITE unconvincing, fancy if one could say of Francis Albert Sinatra that it is incredible to find him entering the eighth decade of his turbulent life. The fact is, however, that we are not in the least surprised, for he has grown older in very public fashion. He was not even 50 years of age before he was singing about the September of his years, almost glorying in vanished youth with recordings of songs bearing titles like *Once Upon a Time, Last Night When We Were Young, How Old Am I* and the classic *It Was a Very Good Year*. We whose lives have been indelibly marked by his songs have not always thanked him as he has reminded us of our own aging. He has retired once at 55, come out of retirement two years later, switched political allegiances from mid-left to mid-right as so many people do later in life, and proceeded to sing all over the globe deep into the 1980s. We have watched the face and form grow puffier, have read about hair transplants and arthritic joints, and have wished that he would not always be quite so remote from those who have helped to make him rich and famous and, on occasions, that he would desist from being quite so filthy-tempered.

And yet, as he passes 70, none of those negative thoughts matters particularly to the millions of fans in the generation – and perhaps two generations – who hold him in an affection which superficially seems almost irrational. That army of admirers would scorn those rebels who do not wish to celebrate Sinatra's life and work, or even that perhaps more substantial faction which would applaud his work but not always his life. There can be, in my view, no argument about the esteem in which his artistic achievement should be held. He is the greatest popular singer the world has ever known, probably its most compelling entertainer; and popular music, as its name suggests, means more to most people than any other kind of music. It is the classless glue which has helped to stick western society together for all of the century in which he and

I have lived. It is, too, and always has been, even before the age of twentieth century mass communication, a cave of treasures in which is stored our experiences of war and peace, the good and bad times and the in-between, our hopes and fears, our memories of love, hate, partings and reunions, our sexual and spiritual aspirations, our ambivalence about death, the myths and fantasies which have sustained our very existence. Sinatra more than any other single mortal in the history of music is the keeper of the keys to that cave of treasures. This is remarkable not only because he is not a composer in the normal sense of the word, simply a performer, but also because he appears to have a lot going against him, as well as for him, as a human being.

Although the essence of what Oliver Cromwell told the Dutch artist Peter Lely is well enough known, the precise words are often misquoted, so a reminder is perhaps not amiss. 'I desire you would use all your skill to paint my picture truly like me,' the Lord Protector of the Commonwealth said, 'and not flatter me at all; but remark all these roughnesses, pimples, warts, and everything as you see me, otherwise I will never pay a farthing for it.' Those will be the guiding principles of this book, even though it is a celebration, since who would pay a farthing were they not? On his track record so far, however, Sinatra himself is unlikely to applaud the 'warts and everything' approach. At this stage only a single illustration is needed. One of his closest friends, Sammy Davis Junior, a member of the notorious Clan of the late 1950s and 1960s, dared to say during the course of a television interview: 'I love Frank, but there are many things he does that there is no excuse for. I don't care if you are the most talented person in the world. It does not give you the right to step on people and treat them rotten. This is what he does occasionally.' No more than the self-evident truth, it might be claimed, but Sinatra appears to demand absolute loyalty and respect from his associates.

Sinatramania is getting off the ground as the mid-1940s approach. It matters not whether the fans are battling to get his name on a piece of paper, as they were when he sang at Ebbets Field in New York, a baseball park, in aid of the 1944 Red Cross War Fund, or lining up outside a theatre, or simply wanting to gaze at their idol tinkling the piano keys in a typical publicity shot of the period . . . the galvanising effect he had in all circumstances on females was spectacular.

Davis had to wait in humiliation before he was restored to favour, publicly, at a Los Angeles charity show. It is illustrative of the niceties and shades of Sinatra's code that other remarks by Davis, Dean Martin and fellow-sycophants come within the category of OK jokes, as with Davis's description of the Clan as 'just an ordinary bunch of guys who get together once a year and take over the whole world.' Sinatra and his friends have always liked to act big, talk big and play it big.

An inability to endure criticism is, though, scarcely a rarity among those of vast talents. The strikes against Sinatra bite deeper. His mean streak, which has involved him in fights, physical and verbal, throughout his life seems never totally to have been softened even with age and, paradoxically, has burned most malevolently when life has gone best for him. His ego appears unbelievably inflated at times. His actions and words have often seemed recklessly foolish, sometimes in the direst of bad taste – and although it is true that he may have been misquoted on occasions, I have heard enough of his outbursts personally to know that he has not been over-harshly judged on that score.

What kind of man is it who says when the 'richer or poorer' section arrives during his fourth marriage ceremony. 'No, no, richer, richer'; or in public, during his act at The Sands in Las Vegas, four weeks after his wedding to Mia Farrow, a young woman 30 years his junior, when she herself was sitting at a ringside table, 'Maybe you wondered why I finally got married. Well, I finally found a broad I could cheat on', a quip which according to the eyewitness columnist quoted by biographer Tony Scaduto, made her cry; or, yet again in public at Las Vegas, this time at Caesar's Palace on 22 May 1974, toasting his first grandchild from the stage, 'I wish her one hundred times the fun I've had and one hundred times as many guys as I've had broads'?

The answer to the question is, of course, the kind of man who is like Frank Sinatra. For

9

astonishingly, the yahoo air which overhangs such words can almost be dispelled when you examine other evidence. Of that same granddaughter he would say only three months later: 'All I ask is that Nancy never lets the child grow up and see *The Kissing Bandit*, a picture I made some years ago. I've been trying to change my name ever since!' That shows as much of a gift for self-deprecation as, at other times, he has demonstrated wit whose cutting edge does not detract from its humour. The kind of gutter Press treatment he has had to endure throughout his life makes the classic Sinatra epigram about newspaper columnists music to most people's ears: 'All day long they lie in the sun. And after the sun goes down, they lie some more.' Similarly, he's had his share of tacky women. Of the one who claimed she had broken with him because his sex tastes were kinkier even than hers, he said: 'Hell hath no fury like a hustler with a literary agent.' The heart warms to its very cockles when Sinatra delivers lines like these, just as it responds to the myriad stories of his acts of kindness – many of them deliberately kept quiet until they have leaked out with the years – his gargantuan efforts for charities and his well-documented defiant stands for underdogs and victims of bigotry at various times in his life.

An important feature of Sinatra, as is by now surely becoming evident, is that the man is a welter of paradoxes. Yet nothing of his complexity, or its effect upon his listeners and his public standing, could conceivably have been known at the outset of his career as an entertainer when, almost from the moment in his mid-20s that he was exposed to American audiences of any significant size, he began to have the most extraordinary effect upon young women and to win the grudging admiration of many men. One of the earliest bemused observers of Sinatra was a writer for *The New Yorker*, E. J. Kahn Junior, who persuaded that eminent magazine to publish a long profile of the singer, already using the word *phenomenon*

in the title. Later the material was brushed up into a book called *The Voice: The Story of an American Phenomenon* which is rather a collector's item these days, even down to its mistakes. Kahn thought Sinatra was born in 1917, not 1915, for instance, but he got a great deal more right than wrong, pointing out that the adulation poured on Sinatra was not without precedent. He notes that women had keeled over listening to Franz Liszt playing the piano, had kissed the seams of Johann Strauss's coat, wept on seeing Paderewski's red hair, and been so overcome by the sight of the long golden locks of an improbably named Norwegian violinist, Ole Bull, that they removed the horse from the shafts of his carriage and pulled it around New York themselves. There was also the matter of the mayhem at Rudolph Valentino's funeral. The difference, however, as Kahn was at pains to point out, lay in the motivation. The worship directed at most of these gentlemen was, Kahn surmised, scarcely platonic; it might even be termed romantic or, more acutely still, lustful. By contrast, few of Sinatra's fans appeared to have designs on him. They honestly enjoyed and approved the fact that he'd married his childhood sweetheart, Nancy Barbato, seeing her as a cross between elder sister and godmother.

Of course there were a few facets of the phenomenon which this assessment omitted: the swooning, the screaming, the nervous paralysis, the high jinks whereby girls would pay vast sums for his cigarette butts or might bribe hotel maids to let them snuggle down between the sheets he had used at night before the bed linen was changed – and the peeing. Here it was, the urinating phenomenon, two whole decades before The Beatles. As it was graphically expressed by an usher at the Paramount Theatre in New York, where the most famous Sinatra riot of 30,000 fans took place in 1944: 'That Sinatra hits those girls right in the kidneys.' Kahn was not over-concerned about all this. The Sinatra boom was reported

by him with extreme good nature; no striking of moral attitudes or shock-horror philosophising. It was no accident, surely, that his book was entitled *The Voice*. That was the thing which marked Sinatra out – the amazing effect which that voice had.

Certainly it was the voice (and its effect) which mattered to me. When I first fell under Sinatra's spell, at around 17, in 1945, towards the end of the Second World War, as I waited to go to Oxford University, I was neither a girl nor a homosexual. So the swooning and scratching of the American teenage bobbysoxers of that time was irrelevant to me, if not virtually unknown. I'd read a bit or two about crowd scenes in America, but little news of that kind made the four-page British newspapers then. So it must have been the voice, heard on the blessed American Forces Network of those years, which got to me. Come to think of it, Mr Kahn wasn't the only one to use those two words as if they were identification enough.

Chief among Sinatra's nicknames at the time was, in fact, *The Voice*. They painted it on the nose fuselages of some American bombers around then. The planes were flown by men too. The point is a serious one. From the beginning, Sinatra's fans included a substantial number of males – a fact central to his evolution into a world idol, as we shall discover – and they undoubtedly included me.

The reasons were simple. I liked his sound. Even then, he was better than any of his rivals, more open, lighter and less mannered of tone, giving a personal stamp to a song like no one else I'd ever heard, making you feel he was singing only to you even if you weren't female. Very soon, too, up at Oxford, he was to become my ally, in the unparalleled way that he has been an ally all my life in musical terms – and the ally of all those other millions of men who share some at least of my feelings about him. The first Sinatra record I bought was a 78 on which *The Charm of You* was coupled with *I*

Fall In Love Too Easily. I swiftly discovered that this was a surefire aid to breaking the ice in the affairs of late adolescence. The words, like many others in popular song, were pretty mushy. *The Charm of You is comparable to a Christmas tree with toys, to little girls and boys when first they see the tree . . . .* Never mind. They seemed to do the trick every time and, in Sinatra's mouth, they really did have the ring of the finest poetry. What was more, he sounded, incredibly, as if he actually *believed* them. How true this was became apparent when the words on the other side of the 78 helped as well. *I fall in love too easily, I fall in love too fast, I fall in love too terribly hard for ever love to last . . .* and this appeared to say we should both (the girl and I) get on with things (although the relative innocence of the time debarred us from many actions which would simply be shrugged at today) without worrying too much if the whole affair came to an end in a week or two. That proposition

seemed to suit quite a number of the men and women around Oxford at the time.

I retain my affection for those early Sinatra songs still (others included *Nancy, I Couldn't Sleep a Wink Last Night, This Is a Lovely Way to Spend an Evening*) even though my critical faculties compel me to admit that the over-rich orchestrations of Axel Stordahl, all weeping strings and sweeping harps, were later to be improved upon by the bitter-sweet arrangements of Nelson Riddle and Don Costa. And these examples of Sinatra's hold upon me, seeing him as musical friend, supporter and sympathiser, were only the beginning of his spell. By the time I was out of undergraduate and National Service days, and into the arms of both career and bride, a new Sinatra had arisen. He was more mature, more dangerous, more scarred and infinitely more swinging and more affecting. So now his songs were the accompaniment to the blissful early and then middle years of marriage.

12

If we felt happy or wanted to be happier, we would play *Come Fly With Me* in the arrangement of Billy May, or *Our Love Is Here To Stay*, *South of The Border* and *Witchcraft* as conceived by Nelson Riddle; if our mood was more mellow, we might turn to *Little Girl Blue* or *The One That Got Away* (again, Riddle's arrangements) or the Gordon Jenkins version of *Autumn Leaves*; and if we were really downcast – or if we felt we wanted to empathise with Sinatra's suffering, since we were well aware by now of the hell of his affair with Ava Gardner and the mixture of pain and pleasure he seemed compulsively to cook up for himself – we'd go to that darkest of songs, *I'm a Fool To Want You*, perhaps the greatest arrangement Axel Stordahl ever did, or later to classics like Riddle's peerless chart-topper, *One For My Baby*, or the 1959 Gordon Jenkins gloss on *I'll Never Smile Again*, the touching song which had done so much to set the young singer on his way back in 1940.

The point need scarcely be laboured. Sinatra had given me the songs of youth. As we both grew older, even though I trailed him by well over a decade, he offered the songs of experience. Many were songs for the present, a few looked forward, far more looked backward, and still more could not be dated in this fashion at all. They were never-ending songs, frozen in time. Happy or sad, triumphant or humiliated, extrovert or darkly inturned – these were songs for all seasons of my life, throughout my life, somehow never seeming old-fashioned and certainly not just a cause for nostalgia, even though nostalgia was part of the charm as one's children grew up and sought their independent pleasures. My experience of identification with what Sinatra has sung down the years is, of course, shared by multitudes of other people, both famous and unknown. One terrifying version of the death of Marilyn Monroe (accident . . . suicide . . . even murder?) has her, on the last night of her life, offended by a call from Bobby Kennedy and Peter Lawford inviting her to a party 'with a couple of hookers', and trying to sleep *while a stack of Sinatra records played.* In fact, she scarcely awoke, making just one further telephone call – in a voice furred with the bucketing syncopation of sleeping-pill stupor—before being found many hours later dead, in the nude. How many other souls, in the depths of depression as well as when elated, will not similarly have sought communion with the voice they knew so well? This intense sense of identification between audience and artist is one of the roots of Sinatra's greatness.

Even before he had begun seriously to suffer for his art (which he did first in the late 1940s and early 1950s), when his voice and his way of using it were most of what he had to offer, he could reach out to the most unexpected corners of the world. At my Oxford college, Wadham, I met in 1946 a Russian under-graduate called Alexander (Shura) Shiwarg, born of a businessman father in Harbin, Manchuria, who became one of our set although I lost touch with him after university. He was a remarkable and mysterious fellow, who had been studying medicine in Hong Kong when the Japanese overran it in 1941. Although the holder of a Russian passport, he joined the British army (rare if not unique) and his fighting career on the streets of Hong Kong lasted just 18 days before he was thrown into a prison camp until 1945. I again met, and had dinner with, Shiwarg in the spring of 1985 after a hiatus of 40 years and when he heard I was writing about Sinatra he exploded with laughter:

'Amazing. That takes me back all the way to 1945. When I got out of prison camp, I was desperate for news. We'd heard nothing reliable for years, only rumours of victories and defeats, and hearing names like Roosevelt and Churchill spat out by Japanese guards, and then there was talk about some terrifying explosion – that was Hiroshima, of course. So I wandered down to the waterfront looking for people who could speak English and I found a British submarine mother ship and I asked the sailors, "What's been happening? What's been happening?" And they said, "Frankie Sinatra, that's what." And I thought it must be some damn Pacific atoll I'd missed the name of, like Iwojima, but they soon put me right. "He's an American singer, a kid just like us, and girls swoon and go crazy when he sings, and sometimes he doesn't even have to sing."

'I couldn't believe it. I was shattered. Just as I thought the brave new world was congealing like scabs on the wounds of war, all these people could talk about was Frankie Sinatra. Anyway, they put some records on an old windup gramophone and I heard him, and Bing Crosby too doing *Don't Fence Me In*, and that became the theme song of my liberation. I still get goosepimples today if I hear it – but can you beat that damned Sinatra? More important to these kids than the war, and they were English too!'

In 1975 I remember Sinatra singing at a concert in the Royal Albert Hall, London, with various princesses present as well as two of his ex-wives, Ava Gardner and Mia Farrow. As he produced the words of *Didn't We* . . . . 'This time we almost made it, didn't we?' . . . it occurred to me that he might have been singing it almost directly for the gamine, Mia Farrow. Perhaps this was only an illusion, but the impression was heightened by known history. He produced that blackly pessimistic *I'm a Fool To Want You* back in 1951 when he was driven mad by Ava Gardner and his career was at its absolute nadir. Not too much later were to come *Little Girl Blue*, *A Foggy Day* and, later still, *In the Wee Small Hours of the Morning*, sadness heaped on sadness. Sinatra has always managed, by some alchemy, to transform personal pain and joy into masterpieces of the art he practises. He sings his autobiography, you might say, and by still further magic it is *our* autobiography too.

Again, I recall an occasion when that feeling came home to me most vividly. It was once

more at the Royal Albert Hall, in September 1978, and he sat hunched in the half-light at one point, cigarette glowing in his fingers, a 32-piece string section behind him, telling us (from *The One That Got Away*) that 'the road gets rougher, it's lonelier and tougher', that 'suddenly you're older'. The sense of audience response to those bleak words, mingling with the sudden strings which sustained them, was so powerful it was damn near physical. Sinatra was opening up the bank of memory, making so many in the audience recall what they'd done or failed to do with their lives, where they'd been proud or ashamed, how they'd laughed or wept. This was time destroyed then recreated by one man's style in performance, a phenomenon which can happen in popular music as in no other art form. Why else do you think audiences respond to *My Way*, that Sinatra anthem whose self-indulgent tone has enraged so many critics, and seems at times to have become a tedious trademark even to the man himself? Listen to what Sinatra is saying; like 'I've had my share of losing'. Too true, old chum, the audience is thinking – and haven't we all? Sinatra sings for himself and for us; the fusion is complete.

The irony, as we extend our focus to take in the musical techniques and the artistic context of Sinatra's singing, is that he would never have been able to achieve this position of symbol for a generation had it not been for the invention of the microphone not too long after he was born. There are still, I suppose, some people (including critics) who believe that the microphone is an adjunct we should somehow be ashamed of using, that singers whose voices are amplified are inherently lower in worth than singers whose voices are not. But the true value of the microphone is that it enables singers to search for subtlety and meaning, to colour their interpretations with the finest shades of dynamics and emotion, to take audiences into their confidence by singing in a natural, conversational way.

Sinatra seized upon the possibilities of the

14

microphone like no other singer of his time, not even the fabled first 'crooner', Bing Crosby, and he was never in doubt as to precisely what it meant to him. 'Many singers never learned to use one. They never understood, and still don't, that a microphone is their instrument,' he once said, magisterially, to the readers of *Life* magazine in a piece called 'The Secrets of My Success'. Watch as well as listen to Sinatra at work to understand the full meaning of this. Hear the careful snap and precision of his diction, see him changing the distance of the mike from his mouth, which achieves a continual effect of light and shade in his songs, apart from softening the impact of noisy consonants, stretched vowels or repeated sibilants, and also disguises the moments when Sinatra has to breathe in. Not that he's ever had any trouble about that. He learned his pure legato line from endlessly watching how Tommy Dorsey achieved smoothness in his trombone playing; Sinatra has always gone into training before major tours or seasons, cutting down on liquor and smokes, running and – as Gene Kelly among many others has stressed – swimming

underwater for lengthy periods to expand and toughen his lungs. In the spring of 1985 he finally gave up smoking after 50 years.

The classic essay on Sinatra and his contemporaries – all of them working in the Afro-American idiom loosely this century called 'popular' – is to be found in the introduction to *The Great American Popular Singers* by Henry Pleasants. This delightful and erudite American writes so beautifully and with such insight that his work deserves to be read in full. But his argument can be summarised fairly straightforwardedly.

When opera was invented in Italy in the late sixteenth century the ideal was *bel canto*; a declamatory style, expressive and full of variety, in which music supported a poetic text. Large orchestras, together with the perversion of operatic style into seeking ever greater volume and brilliance, overshadowed this early tradition from the seventeenth century onwards. Singers concentrated on tone rather than meaning, on sheer volume rather than dynamics, producing from the chest rather than the head, the sound reverberating to the very

Wedding cakes are wedding cakes, and Frank Sinatra has tasted four of his own. In descending order (left), and starting with his second cake and bride, the women he married are: Ava Gardner (1951), Mia Farrow (1966) and Barbara Marx (1976).

16

last row of distant galleries. The age of boomers and belters lasted until the microphone arrived (even Al Jolson was more in the line of Caruso than anyone else) and it together with radio broadcasting freed singers again to concentrate on meaning, on intimacy, on conversing with their audiences instead of haranguing them.

Sinatra's natural baritone, light at first, growing darker and deeper with the years, was ideally matched with the microphone. He could place the meaning of lyrics first – even though he can tastelessly change lyrics too, a trick which once made a furious Cole Porter, wheelchair-bound, demand to be removed from a Hollywood studio party as Sinatra fiddled with an acknowledged Porter classic. By contrast the composer Alec Wilder thought he improved *melodically* on the original of George Gershwin's *I've Got a Crush On You* in his version of 1947. Sinatra, with mike, could certainly choose whether to attack the words or ride easy with them, sometimes letting his vocal range be stretched to its limits. He has never seemed to care if he's occasionally caught out straining to achieve a note. It's part of what he is, his naturalness, and it can immeasurably add to the sense of desperation and crisis in his more melancholy ballads.

The truth of the matter is that Sinatra pours so much of himself into all his best performances that his version of many songs becomes the definitive one, the yardstick by which every other singer's interpretation is judged. He has been called America's poet laureate, and that in a sense is true, for although other men and women have *composed* what he sings, his is the final touch which gives songs their completeness, the shapes and colours by which we remember them. In the words of Sammy Cahn, who with Jule Styne dates back to the early days of *I Fall In Love Too Easily* and *What Makes The Sunset*: 'I don't sit down to write a Sinatra song. I write a song, then he sings it, and *HE* makes it a Sinatra song.' A few other singers coming up with Sinatra in the 1940s were beginning, like him, to stamp themselves unforgettably on particular songs – Ella Fitzgerald with *A-Tisket, A-Tasket*, Judy Garland with *Over The Rainbow*, Hoagy Carmichael with his own *Hong Kong Blues* – but the idea of the performance being more important than what is performed, the singer superseding the song, to which we have become so used in the age of rock'n'roll, was still relatively novel when Sinatra was in his twenties. He defined the art, set others copying it, and as with most other moves he made in his early life knew exactly what he was about. He was well aware, very early, that he had to be different from Bing. 'I decided to experiment a little and come up with something different,' he told readers of *Life* magazine in 1965. 'What I finally hit on was more the bel canto Italian school of singing. I had to stay in better shape because I had to *SING* more.' Bel canto, you will observe – and he hadn't even read Henry Pleasants!

His definition may have been a little loose; but his dedication to the forthright melodic warmth so typical of Italian singing, combined with the conversational intimacy which marks crooning, was demonstrably firm from the earliest days. He was equally sure, at his beginning, of the artists he admired and felt he could learn from. In the American magazine *Ebony* in 1958 he wrote of Billie Holiday: 'Every major pop singer in the US during her generation has been touched by her genius. She was the single greatest musical influence on me.' Billie Holiday, whose jazz background was even stronger than Sinatra's, refashioned, redefined and recreated songs just as he did. She was perhaps the one who encouraged him more than any other to shade his work with a swinging tinge of improvisation and jazz feeling. He has, over and over, been voted the favourite singer of jazz musicians.

You must have noticed that so far I have been talking of Sinatra only as a singer, which seems a glaring omission when the man has appeared in 57 movies. Even more of an omis-

As soon as Sinatra began to appear in early films like *Higher and Higher*, he made it straight into teenage magazines like *Movie Fan* – and posed pictures like that below, 'with a young admirer' as the caption sweetly put it, were commonplace. The line of his movies has so far run on until 1980; en route, in 1971 (right), Sinatra was on hand to take an award at the annual Oscar ceremonies.

sion does it seem when one remembers that Sinatra's whole career was rekindled from ashes in 1954 by his appearance in *From Here To Eternity* and the Oscar awarded for his performance as Angelo Maggio. Sinatra is, without doubt, majestic singer *and* formidable film actor *and* supreme entertainer.

I do not intend to ignore his films. I will deal with them when they are milestones or especially illustrative of the man, but the detailed information is provided in George Perry's excellent filmography. It is not only my view that Sinatra's film career has always been limited by his impatience with the sheer technical business of making movies, the endless days spent getting a few minutes of usable stuff. He hates retakes, whereas upon any song he will lavish care in the recording studio if necessary. As he observed to Robin Douglas-Home, the first writer to produce a slim book which was more than a collection of articles about him: 'I adore making records. I'd rather do that than almost anything else. Once you're on that record singing, it's you and you alone.' Things were taken out of his hands in movies, he believed, and his lack of patience, almost indifference, has shown too often, bewailed by more than one film director and critic.

So, setting the films aside, there are two other important aspects of the Sinatra image which are crucial in the unparalleled impact he has had upon the western world as an entertainer. The first, which has already been touched on, is the paradoxes of his character, the remarkable mixture of niceness and meanness (in the American sense) that he offers to the world. The second is the switchback nature of his career: the highs and lows he has endured.

His whole history shows that Sinatra can at different times be caring and insensitive, classy and tasteless, charming and bad-tempered, tender and tough, family man and player of the field, appealing underdog and unattractive bully. He has certainly exhibited symptoms of insecurity for most of his life, these springing perhaps from his rather lonely early years as

18

an only child, and his ego has sometimes appeared monstrous large. In this respect I adore Sammy Cahn's remark, he who put the words to *All The Way, The Tender Trap, Come Fly With Me*, when asked to explain a very fierce and heavy snowstorm: 'That's God reminding Frank Sinatra He's still around.'

It is probably true of many people whose opinions of themselves are high that a little adversity does them good. Sinatra is no exception. 'When he was down and out, he was so sweet,' his second wife, Ava Gardner, once said. 'But now that he's got successful again, he's become his old arrogant self. We were happy when he was on the skids.' The arrogance has won Sinatra a horde of enemies just as surely as his magnetic artistry has won friends. Remember the hundreds of congratulatory telegrams received by the Las Vegas casino manager who knocked Sinatra down in a brawl in 1970? People don't like the bodyguards with whom he has increasingly surrounded himself, and again that attitude can be summed up in a single instance — the comedian who once told this story: 'Frank Sinatra saved my life one night. Five guys were beating me up in front of the Fontainebleau. After a while Frank said, "OK fellas, that's enough".'

Two specific downside elements of the paradoxes of Sinatra's personality have gained him particular notoriety. His bitter verbal fights with journalists and newspapers down the years are to a substantial degree understandable. The spectacle of the gutter Press in full cry, in America, Britain or anywhere else, has over the past 40 years or so grown increasingly unedifying and disgusting. Sinatra was hassled from the start by journalists, then disgracefully treated in his more liberal days by the Roosevelt-hating hacks of the extreme Republican papers in America, and in later years pursued relentlessly by friend and foe alike. I well remember Sinatra interrupting his singing at an Albert Hall concert in May 1975, bitterly to attack the German newspapers who

he claimed had run a concerted and scurrilous campaign against him – as they undoubtedly had. A large part of the 7,000-strong audience cheered him. I sympathised with him surely, while doubting if the Albert Hall stage, and a truly joyful concert, was the place for him to answer his critics. That's always been Sinatra's problem with writers and journalists. He has often been appallingly treated – equally often, however, he has tended to overreact in his own choice of language, and has never seemed able to distinguish between quality and rubbish, fair criticism and malicious gossip, friends and foes, in his blanket attacks on the Press. His wise old buddy of the 1950s, Humphrey Bogart, once made an interesting observation. 'Frank's idea of paradise is a place where there are plenty of women and no newspapermen. He doesn't realize it, but he'd be better off if it were the other way round.' Consider, too – which is what, doubtless, led to the misguided attacks in German newspapers – the stories which have virtually all his life alleged associations between Sinatra and the Mafia. You can say that he has been seen too much in odd company, even that he hasn't always chosen his friends wisely, but the hard fact is that pursuit by US Government agencies for 40 years has failed to make one charge stick, and that Sinatra's defence of himself in an article he wrote for *The New York Times* of 24 July 1972 was an almost classic statement of the rights of the individual.

I do not know the truth about every dubious nook and cranny of Sinatra's life. What I *do* know, however, is the effect which the many rumours (and known truths) about him have had on the world. One highly surprising spin-off from his turbulent life is that so many of the less savoury things reported about him have rebounded in his favour. The newspapers are far less popular than they imagine, as are journalists, and when Sinatra has a go at the press he carries a mass of hearts and minds with him. Women have detected in him – Deborah Kerr was one of the most outspoken of them

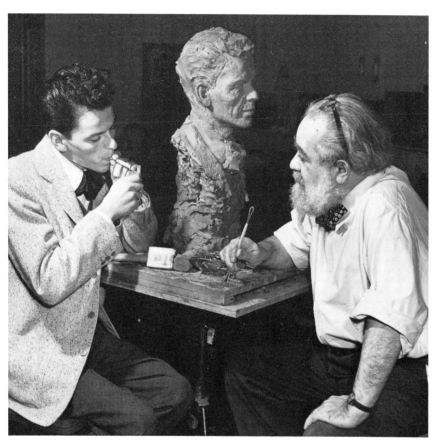

– not only a blend of toughness and tenderness which seems to appeal to them, but also an acute vulnerability that sets them firmly on his side. Faye Dunaway, the co-star of his final movie (1980), thought him incredibly courteous and charming. That he had a reputation in the old days as one of the world's great studs has, oddly, done him no harm with either sex. One part of feminine sensibility responds to rakes; and although men may envy the individual who has made marriages with childhood sweetheart (Nancy), sex symbol (Ava), gamine (Mia), smart and mature prop (his fourth wife, Barbara), and has made love to dozens more of the world's most desirable women, chief among them Marilyn Monroe, many don't dislike him for it. They wish they could do the same, just as they also wish in their heart of hearts they could take a swing at those who frustrate them. Even the Sinatra Clan, so often silly and juvenile in behaviour, appeals to the 'clubbability' of males who, *en masse*, are as prone to daft pranks as women are to gossip.

His substantial biographer of the 1960s, Arnold Shaw, shrewdly observed that for many years the harshest revelations about his affairs scarcely affected his public appeal. He demonstrated 'that one could be a bastard as long as one was totally talented and did not dissemble with the public' – or, to put it another way, in the Jekyll-and-Hyde battle which seems eternally to rage inside Sinatra, shaping his image to the world, the near-hoodlum, sexual-hyena, bullyboy half is so often overcome by the portrait of Sinatra as American hero, living like a fighter, staking out his territory and battling to keep it, being nice to (most) ladies, taking no bullshit from anyone, generous to a fault, supporter of the poor and the underdog, almost a swashbuckling throwback to the frontier days.

Men can wish they were in his shoes, women in his arms, and if anyone is in any doubt about his credentials and testimonials, did he not collect over a million dollars for children on one memorable world tour, entirely at his own expense? Did not the so-called show-business priest, Father Bob Perrella, say in his book of virtually that title: 'When tragedy struck the lives of the Judy Garlands, the Ethel Barrymores, the unlucky ones never knew the identity of the man who paid their rents and bought their food'? There is a long list of unlucky ones who *did* know, headed by actors like Bela Lugosi, George Raft and Lee J. Cobb, musicians and entertainers (Buddy Rich, Phil Silvers) and sportsmen (Joe Louis), who have spoken out warmly in praise of Sinatra's kindness and generosity. So did the late David Niven, whose books *The Moon's a Balloon* and *Bring On The Empty Horses*, contain some delightful reminiscences of Sinatra. 'He is one of the few people in the world I would instinctively think of if I needed help of any sort. I

thought of him once when I was in a very bad spot: help was provided instantly and in full measure without a question being asked. It was not, incidentally, money.' What is more, very few men, if any, can have had compliments paid so lavishly to them by Presidents of the United States *of opposite persuasions*. He went to tea with Roosevelt, was termed 'dear friend' by John F. Kennedy and Ronald Reagan, was greeted at the White House encomium-fashion by Richard Nixon and, as recently as April, 1985, was awarded the Presidential Medal of Freedom for his 'contributions in the field of the arts, entertainment and public service' by Reagan.

And what, too, of simple 'nice things,' which Sinatra has done down the years? David Niven, again, is the source for one of the most surprising. He recalled a cruise aboard Humphrey Bogart's boat *Santana* one July 4 evening. They dropped anchor in a cove – and then Sinatra, on another boat, moored alongside, accompanied by several beautiful girls and a piano. 'After dinner, with Jimmy van Heusen accompanying him, Sinatra began to sing,' wrote Niven. 'He sang all night. There were many yachts in Cherry Cove that weekend and by two in the morning, under a full moon, *Santana* was surrounded by an audience sitting in dozens of dinghies and rubber tenders of every shape and size. Frank sang as only he can, with his monumental talent and exquisite phrasing undimmed by a bottle of Jack Daniels on top of the piano. He sang till the dew came down heavily and the boys in the listening fleet fetched blankets for their girl's shoulders. He sang till the moon and the stars paled in the pre-dawn sky – only then did he stop and only then did the awed and grateful audience paddle silently away.'

All of these things, the beautiful and the ugly, are known to those who listen to him on record or who sit in the half-dark of concert halls and arenas and supper rooms to hear him sing. It is because they know so much about him, because he sings for them, because he pours so much of himself into his songs that there is always that magical extra frisson for his audiences, what the *New York Times* writer John Rockwell summed up as 'musical skill combined with image', which 'invested his music with its last degree of dangerous allure.' Robin Douglas-Home caught the flavour even more comprehensively almost 25 years ago, and nothing in the interim has changed the truth of his words.

'He has, by the peculiarly potent chemistry of his nature and image, become the living symbol of an ideal that millions subconsciously would like to emulate, but consciously realise would never work out in practice. He is everyman's dreamland *alter ego* and every woman's dreamland paramour. The paradoxes in his makeup are all part of it – the swashbuckling toughness together with the poignant tenderness, the idolised hero yet simultaneously the small-boy underdog, the family man yet the emancipated charmer of the world. This honesty, this passion, this vitality, forms the essential element of his singing.'

One of the few songs which Sinatra has recorded four times is the beautiful creation of Jerome Kern and Oscar Hammerstein II, *The Song Is You*. It can almost stand as an anthem for him, since the song is indeed he, and he the song. When you celebrate Sinatra, you celebrate the whole of him. It is his life which has created his artistic style, and our lives of which he is the symbol – either factually or in fantasy. It is the knowledge, however dimly perceived, of what Sinatra is as a person that is crucial in the effect his performances have on audiences. They *know* he is both luxuriating and tortured soul, and therein lies the magic. He is the prisoner of his success and his music, as his music is the hostage of his near-half century of rakehellery.

Only one more fascinating stroke is needed to complete a preliminary portrait of this man. It concerns the switchback rises and falls of his

And now, a side of Sinatra which is a blend of clubbability, of near-juvenile pranks and the Italian theme of the *padrone*, whose circle receive his gifts and blessings in return for absolute respect and loyalty. The Clan, at its peak in the late 1950s and early 1960s, was the name then usually given to Sinatra and his associates who appeared at parties, in movies and on stage together. This was one such occasion at The Sands, Las Vegas, and the quintet conveniently stand (left to right) in the same order as their billing – Sinatra, Martin, Davis, Lawford and Joey Bishop.

our society has come to call 'charisma', which simply means when it comes down to it that someone *is* well-known. And since, if people *are* well-known, they get all the headlines, and more is written, shown and spoken about them than those who are little known, the whole system is a self-perpetuating, vicious circle.

God knows if George Evans, all those years ago in the 1940s, at first paid little girls to faint, scream and pee whenever Frankie appeared, as has been widely alleged. It doesn't matter one way or the other. After a while it was obvious that bobbysoxers *would* do all these things anyway. The publicity machine had started spinning, and from then on its wheels needed only discreet greasing. It may seem exaggerated to view the rumbustious Sinatra as the victim of anything, but in one way he has been the victim of his own publicity, usually acting as if he believes it as much as he believes the lyrics he sings, always ready to come out smiling or bawling 'in character'. You might say he's been swallowed and thoroughly digested by the publicity generated around him.

The shape of Sinatra's life, so heavily delineated by publicity, which always lays on the colour too thick, is a critical element in his world conquests. How people love to see success stories acted out, the poor-boy-makes-good saga; how they love to see the super-confident and loud-mouthed overreach themselves and fail, pride coming before the fall; how they love to see the conventional wisdom which says 'They never come back' overthrown and scorned, although not too often. Sinatra has acted out all these dramas, more than once, the very stuff of soap operas, and has thereby been the most striking exemplar in my lifetime of those two commonest day-dreams: the rise-and-fall story, and the comeback against the odds. This it is which puts the final gloss of champion upon him. Anyone who can so consistently overcome adversities which would sink lesser mortals, and with equal persistence snatch defeat from the jaws of victory, must be very special.

life, and the publicity which has attended them, often generated by the people in his own camp, beginning with George Evans, who was Sinatra's faithful press agent from 1943 until he died in 1950. Such irony it was, too, that when Sinatra temporarily retired in 1971, his plan for a period of self-examination and reflection should be shouted from the rooftops way ahead of his 'last concert'! Publicity is the nostrum of our age. It makes people known, self-evidently. It creates the images of people that come to be widely accepted. It creates what

'He says he's the greatest'

2 ROUGH DIAMOND

NOTHING COULD HAVE BEEN MORE SPECIAL – idiosyncratic and frequently far from pleasant – than Sinatra's first few minutes of life and the childhood years which succeeded them. He was a huge baby, $13\frac{1}{2}$ pounds in weight, and he only survived at all on 12 December 1915 because his maternal grandmother, Rosa Garavanti, held him under a cold tap until he choked into life. Forceps tore one ear and cheek, leaving him scarred, marks which he has accepted fatalistically. He told Robin Douglas-Home: 'People have suggested to me I ought to hide those scars. But no. They're there, and that's that. Why bother?'

Home's opinion, after a couple of months in Sinatra's company, was that his childhood was far from happy. The evidence points clearly to that conclusion. Natalie Garavanti, his mother, usually called Dolly, came from Genoa in Northern Italy; his father, Antony Martin Sinatra, was Sicilian, from the town of Catania. Their son, who was to be their only child, was born after they had been married six years. Dolly had wanted a girl, and said with painful gaucheness some years later: 'I bought a lot of pink clothes when Frank was born. I didn't care. I dressed him in pink anyway. Later, I got my mother to make him Lord Fauntleroy suits'. That was not the only service Rosa Garavanti performed. Dolly was the dominant force in the household, a trained nurse and very swiftly an organiser of people in their neighbourhood, graduating inevitably from petitioning and protesting to local politics for the Democratic Party. Sinatra saw not too much of his mother as he grew up, but a great deal of his grandmother, who ran a small grocery store, and also an elderly Jewish woman, Mrs Goldberg. It taught him to like Jews, and for years he wore a Star of David symbol round his neck, a gift from Mrs Goldberg. Paradoxically (since we are dealing, as we know, with a paradoxical man) this pushing of Sinatra on to other people did not appear to turn him against his mother. Far from it. He idolised her in his adult years, respect tinged with awe, was forever seeking her approval, and was devastated when she was killed in an air crash at the age of 82 in 1977.

His hometown, and the place where he grew up, was Hoboken, New Jersey. It's a scruffy port close to Jersey City, with straggling railroad yards and docks on the banks of the River Hudson opposite lower Manhattan island; to say it's like Liverpool is probably to overpraise it – more like Liverpool's Merseyside neighbours, Birkenhead or Bootle. Hoboken is no place for weaklings. Although Sinatra was shielded from many of its worst aspects early on, lived in an unslumlike frame house – his birthplace is now a dirt parking lot – and was apparently regarded by his relatives as someone special for having survived the trauma of his birth, he had to go out on the streets and to school sooner or later. Racial jibes were common. 'Dirty guinea' or 'wop' would have been the norm for Italians. The ethnic groups – black, Jewish, Italian, Poles, Irish – fought among themselves, and the Italians were near the bottom of the heap. Sinatra recalls once seeing a group of his Italian Catholic neighbours breaking up a threatening gathering of the Klu Klux Klan with baseball bats. 'I was raised in a breeding-ground for juvenile delinquency,' he said. 'Gang fights were commonplace. I've been on the wrong end of a cycle chain and a broken beer bottle. All the guys used to carry long pieces of metal pipe. And they weren't studying to be plumbers.'

Sinatra will have known that his father spent some time in professional prizefighting as a bantamweight, using the name of Marty O'Brien, the Irish switch being more 'acceptable' in the area – imagine the feelings of a Sicilian, from the island of 'respect', *omerta*, patronage, loyalty and 'families', having to go along with a different kind of bigotry. The son, nevertheless, grew more interested in boxing later in his career, investing in several fighters, having them as part of his entourage and sometimes working out, with gloves, at gymnasiums or backstage. Linking this passion with

25

The parents who meant so much to Frank Sinatra, on their wedding day (right), and their dolled-up very young son. In some ways he seems to have spent a rather lonely boyhood, his energetic mother, Dolly, and father, Martin, too busy to spend many hours with their only child. Whether Sinatra appreciated his first top hat is not known. His mother wanted a girl. 'I dressed him in pink anyway,' she said. 'Later, I got my mother to make him Lord Fauntleroy suits.'

Sinatra's tendency to aggressiveness, Arnold Shaw called him 'a frustrated prize-fighter', with his early publicists not averse to him striking the occasional blow – properly provoked, of course – as an aid to his masculine image.

Later on it was Dolly who pushed Martin Sinatra on to a different road, using her political influence to get him into a busy wartime Hoboken shipyard as a boilermaker and later into the local fire department through which he rose to be captain. Martin also ran a bar for a time, bought after the shipyards laid off men with the end of the war, and his son will have very early on lived close to the half-world of speakeasies and their connection with both bigtime and petty crooks once Prohibition was introduced in the United States in 1920. It was, shall we say, a hard and mixed-up environment which might well produce quite a few tough yet hypersensitive mixed-up kids.

Francis Albert Sinatra duly went to school, but was no scholar. 'Very uninteresting,' he said later. 'Homework we never bothered with.' Music was, however, part of the curriculum from his tenderest years. He heard his maternal grandfather sing at family gatherings and sometimes his mother. His mother's brother, Domenico Garavanti, claims that Sinatra grew up with 'a lot of music around him, good music, real music.' He it was who bought the boy a ukulele for his fifteenth birthday on which Frank quickly learned enough chords to accompany Italian songs at parties – or his own voice. He was very sure by his early teens that he could sing well. Reminiscing in the 1970s he had to struggle to remember when he first sang in public. He *thought* it would have been when he was 12 years old, at an hotel in Elizabeth, New Jersey. 'I probably sang *Am I Blue?* and I probably got paid a couple of packs of cigarettes and maybe a sandwich.'

Music was not, however, on the agenda for Sinatra's parents as a fit career for their son. He was to say later, with a strangely bitter choice of words: 'In your teens there's always someone to spit on your dreams.' And that's exactly what both his parents seemed to do. His plump, outgoing, ambitious political climber of a mother – 'a kind of Catherine de Medici of Hoboken's third ward', in Gay Talese's neat phrase – wanted a more conventional, respectable path for her son. She fought her way into bigger, better-street apartments and houses; by the time he was 14 they had central heating and a bath tub. So she couldn't have him looking poor, since appearance was crucial for immigrants trying to better themselves, and she dressed him so well that he got the half-admiring, half-pejorative nickname of Slacksey O'Brien because he had so many pairs of trousers. Not that he needed much encouragement to look good. Along with the neat clothes went an obsession with cleanliness and good grooming. In his adult years Sinatra has always had beautifully fitting, well-creased suits, gleaming shoes, crisp linen, clean nails; when he was on the road with the Tommy Dorsey band in the early 1940s he earned another nickname, Lady Macbeth, because he was always washing his hands.

He had, of course, a lot of cleaning up to do in these subteen and early-teen years. For a start he was always getting into fights, having his nose bloodied and his eyes blackly puffed. He went around with street and school gangs without ever forming many deep friendships. He was already attractive to girls, a known big spender within the limits of his environment – as that rarity, an Italian family only child, he tended to be spoiled in money terms – and was beginning to develop his *padrone* image in a small way. Probably his loneliness as a child, with no brothers and sisters, was the key factor in his determination to surround himself with groups of people like the Clan in its 1950s–1960s heyday and with bodyguards too. And, like hundreds of thousands of other American youngsters in the 1930s, he was falling under the spell of motion pictures. If the girls wanted to be like Jean Harlow or Garbo or Hepburn, aping their dress styles and their lipstick and

hair, then what got to American working-class boys was the movies with gangster-heroes played by actors like Edward G. Robinson, Paul Muni and James Cagney. There were at least 50 of them going the rounds of movie-houses when Sinatra was 16. The kids identi-fied, if only in fantasy mostly, ran around in gangs and carried some of the memories and attitudes into later life.

Dolly Sinatra couldn't have been much encouraged about her son's career prospects as his teens unrolled. He did graduate from David E. Rue Junior High at 15, but left Demarest High School after only a year or so, having spent a lot of his time hiring musicians for school dances, which gave him the right to sing the odd number with the band. A contempor-ary observed of this habit that he was 'a bag of bones in a padded jacket' but already had the girls swinging round to watch as he sang. Another neighbour, Nick Sevano, later hired by the Sinatra organisation, graphically des-cribed how the teenager had to endure ridicule when he started going round singing. 'His goals were much, much higher than anyone had ever dreamt of . . . . He was a rough diamond and of course people were very slow to see his talent.' To please his mother he enrolled briefly at a business school; then as The Depression

rolled across America and the world, he took a job on newspaper delivery trucks at the *Jersey Observer*, glamourised by his publicity mach-ine later, with posed photographs, into being a junior sports writer. Nothing of these early jobs mattered to him, except as a means to an end or a way of filling in time. All he wanted to do was to sing, and the advent of coast-to-coast radio in 1927 (NBC) and 1928 (CBS) gave him even more chance than did phono-graph records to hear artists like Al Jolson, Gene Austin, Will Osborne, Rudy Vallee and, of course, Bing Crosby, all of them just begin-ning to emerge from the shadow of the big bands, like Paul Whiteman's, who were the standard 'pop' providers of the day and were to become even more so during the classic swing-band decade of the 1930s.

It was Crosby who finally set Sinatra's resolve in concrete. The Hoboken kid was just 18 when he took his girl-friend, Nancy Bar-bato, to hear Crosby in a Jersey City theatre. He emerged starstruck and resolute. He *could* do it; he *would* do it. He was going to be a singer. Nancy knew it and his family knew it. His mother, no fool, saw that he wouldn't be dissuaded and gave him $65 (a great deal of money then) to buy a secondhand portable amplifying system, microphone and loud-

A series of photographs (opposite page and left) illustrate the closeness of Sinatra's family ties and, especially, his relationship with his mother. The large family picture, filled with uncles, aunts, cousins and friends, was taken at the Sinatra family's favourite summer resort spot, Echo Farm House in the Catskill Mountains, upstate New York. Frank Sinatra, 8 years old, is the child seated on the far right; his mother holds a guitar – a symbol of the family's musical interests. The young Sinatra was taken travelling, with baggage, by his mother, too, and as he became famous, the closeness of the pair would be undimmed. She came to show after show to see him perform, and in late 1976 – the final picture in this sequence – he would take her to Israel to see him receive the Mount Scopus award for his charitable activities. Only a few months later, in January, 1977, she died in a plane crash flying from Palm Springs to Las Vegas to see him perform.

speaker in a rhinestone-studded case, which for much of the next five years or so of his life he lugged round clubs and dancehalls playing dates for a few dollars a time. She still kept hoping he might forget about being a singer. His father made his disapproval even more pointed. 'My old man thought that anyone who wanted to go into the music business must be a bum,' Sinatra told Robin Douglas Home in 1962. 'So I picked up and left home for New York.'

There were other reasons for expanding his horizons across the river to Manhattan. The club scene of New Jersey was alive and well but essentially a dead end. He had to make it into New York and beyond. He did, singing his first songs on a New York stage in an amateur contest where he avoided getting either catcalls or the dreaded 'hook' (revived on TV in recent years to drag acts which don't please audiences off the stage) and soon got to know what it felt like to pound the streets of Broadway and especially the 28th Street district, Tin Pan Alley as it was known, because of the battle sounds of a hundred pianos in a hundred publishers plugging out a hundred different songs. His visits there had a purpose. He tried, often successfully, to persuade the music publishers to give him free music sheets and orchestrations. He argued it was good for them – he would be plugging their product, and song-plugging, not to mention liberal doses of payola, was the name of the game then. It was, though, even better for Sinatra. His mike, his music sheets and, after 18 months, the gift of a car from his parents gave him a distinct edge in getting dates with local bands who could draw on his 'library'. He played with so many different outfits he learned fast how to project his voice against the drowning big band noise. He learned about light and shade, about attacking particular lines and words, about microphone technique, even about pulling attention to the singer rather than the bandleader, a trick which Tommy Dorsey later was not to appreciate. He was already living up to that tough-tender

image of his – as a radio station accompanist, Jimmy Rich, was later to say: 'He was a pusher, but polite.'

What seemed like a big chance for him, and the best-known milestone of his early career, was his appearance on one of the most successful stage talent shows, the Major Bowes Amateur Hour, with three local Italian truck-drivers. They had been called The Three Flashes; some pressure from Dolly Sinatra and local Democratic Party bosses persuaded them to expand into the close-harmony Hoboken Four. Perhaps it was the pressure that the truckdrivers didn't like. Perhaps it was the fact that soon after their first show at the Capitol Theatre in New York on 8 September 1935, heard on local radio and good enough to persuade Bowes to sign them up for his road show, Sinatra became lead singer and was obviously in a different league from his partners. As the show moved west towards California, with Sinatra passing his twentieth birthday and picking up $50 a week plus food, they resented his talent, resented how much other people seemed to fall for him, resented his success with girls. Two of them did what most frustrated and mediocre males from their background would have done – especially since Sinatra no doubt did not hide his feelings about lack of talent or idleness any more than later in life. They swore at him and from time to time engaged in violent arguments. Someone in the travelling circus recalled a particularly vicious fight which floored Sinatra in their dressing room after a show had been fouled up one night. Soon afterwards, with several months of travelling and a glimpse of Hollywood and California behind him, Sinatra quit and went to Hoboken.

The Bowes experience had not been either fruitful or happy, and his big chance it certainly was not. It wasn't only the hassle, the unpleasantness, the eternal travelling, the cheapskate nature of the production. The point was that Sinatra could see it was leading to no more desirable a destination than had the

limited New Jersey club circuit. Radio, and especially network radio, was the only way to the big-time. Sinatra came back east resolved to push open every radio station door he could get his hands on. He even gave up the first club job he got, at the Union in Hoboken, earning $40 a week – thanks to his mother's contacts in the Hoboken Sicilian Cultural League, whose members patronised the place – because the manager wouldn't install a 'wire', a telephone link so that radio stations could broadcast club acts.

He was then left just pushing open radio station doors, which got him lots of air-time at all hours of day and night, but no money. In his anxiety for exposure he offered stations and bandleaders his services free. Radio stations like WNEW in New York took him

Virtually every top big band in America sooner or later played the famous Steel Pier in the East Coast resort of Atlantic City. In the summer of 1939 it was the turn of the newly-formed, still struggling Harry James outfit – the band which gave Sinatra his first big chance (below). He sits in regulation band garb beside the pale-suited bandleader (notice how all the men seem to be wearing two-tone shoes) and on the other side of James is singer Connie Haines. Sinatra loved working with James so much, he wept when he quit to go with the bigger star, Tommy Dorsey. 'There was such spirit and enthusiasm in that band, I hated leaving it.'

at his word; only WAAT in Newark, New Jersey, gave him anything, and that was just the 70 cent bus fare to get to the studio gig. He needed the support – loving and moral and sometimes financial – of his sweetheart, Nancy, as well as the patronage (for that's what it often was – not much different from favours given for delivering the vote at elections) of his mother. Dolly didn't rate Nancy too highly; she had hoped for better things for her son than the quiet daughter of a Jersey City plasterer. Frank's view was much different. 'In Nancy I found beauty, warmth and understanding . . . . All I knew up to that time were tough kids on street corners, gang fights and parents who were always busy trying to make money.' That is the Jekyll side of Sinatra speaking. The Hyde reverse of the coin glinted dangerously when he also told her, 'I don't want anyone dragging on my neck.' Like the good old-fashioned Italian wife whom Sinatra, has always seemed to want, she is said to have answered, 'I won't get in your way.' She was to prove as good as her word.

Dolly, meantime, wasn't idle. She may not have wanted her son to be a singer, but she kept rooting for him in Democratic circles. It could have been this which yielded an offer of a regular night job as compere, singer and occasional waiter at the Rustic Cabin, a roadhouse near Alpine, New Jersey. The money was terrible: $15 a week, and only raised to $25 when he'd shown that with all the airtime he was getting – up to 20 spots on local radio a week – he was pulling in the customers. But he had a regular band to sing with, a radio 'wire' in the club and the never-ending hope that one day a top bandleader might hear him and like him enough to offer him a job. With the swing bands of Benny Goodman, Jimmy Dorsey, Tommy Dorsey and hundreds more in the ascendant, that was the dream of every young singer in the American boondocks. And it came to pass that the bandleader's name was Harry James.

James, who played trumpet in a clear, soar-

ing and rather flashy style, later came to make a huge name in the big band swing field; some of his records – *You Made Me Love You, Flight Of The Bumble Bee, Ciribiribin, Trumpet Blues and Cantabile, Two O'clock Jump* – were continually played on radio around the world in the 1940s and 1950s, and his bandleading career lasted until the 1980s. In the summer of 1939, however, he was one of many young musicians stepping out on his own into a field populated with literally hundreds of competitors. Benny Goodman, the so-called 'King of Swing' and probably the most prestigious leader of the day, had discovered James and employed him for two years. Now he lent the smooth-dressing 22-year-old, just three months younger than Sinatra, the money to form his own band, the Music Makers, but it was a hard road. The band had an engagement at the Paramount Theatre on Broadway, later to be the scene of Sinatra's earliest major breakthrough and an elegant pleasure dome in the finest New York tradition which could take almost 5,000 people at a squeeze. Yet the fight for survival was intense. James needed a singer to help the cause, and one night heard Sinatra performing at the Rustic Cabin on WNEW's 'Dance Parade' show.

'I liked Frank's way of talking a lyric', James explained later. He also thought the voice was good, warm and different at a time when, more and more, there was a public demand for band singers rather than outfits playing endless instrumentals, a change in taste which was to be the springboard for singers like Peggy Lee (with Benny Goodman), Perry Como (Ted Weems) and Ella Fitzgerald (Chick Webb) as well as Sinatra, who could not have timed his big-band opportunity better. Thanks to the intervention of a sympathetic song-plugger, Hank Sanicola (he called Sinatra a 'wild-eyed bag of bones', but liked him) who heard that James was asking around about the singer, the two men first met at the Paramount. They got on well. Soon afterwards James went to the Rustic Cabin to hear Sinatra in the flesh. That

clinched it. James signed the singer for a wage of $75 a week, three times what he was then earning.

The Rustic Cabin had, nevertheless, fully served its purpose for Sinatra. It was, in a sense, the first major vindication of his belief in himself and his way of going about it. He was correct in believing that radio would be his bridge to the wider world of entertainment, for that was how he had got through to James. It had taken a long time for the big break – he began in August 1937 at the Rustic Cabin and left in June 1939 – but in that period he gained immense experience of handling crowds, of handling music, of handling the microphone. It was at the roadhouse that he had put into practice all that he was learning from his frequent visits to New York clubs, especially the jazz-and-jam joints on Fifty-Second Street, where he could hear artists like Billie Holiday and Mabel Mercer, another of those who gave him insights into how to extract the maximum

a bronze plaque reads: 'It must truly be said that he did it his way and it all started right here.'

Sinatra's way with James in those early days was as true to his character as at any other time in his life. James wanted him to change his name to something more Anglo-Saxon – the bandleader had already turned into 'Connie Haines' a lady from Savannah, Georgia, called Yvonne Marie Jamais – but Sinatra scorned the idea. 'I'm gonna be famous!' That faith in himself came through as the band moved to the famous Roseland Ballroom on Broadway for a season and then, working its way west, to Chicago and onwards towards California. A critic for *Metronome* magazine, George T. Simon, who later became one of the most distinguished of all big band chroniclers, helped Sinatra's self-esteem with a mention. 'Easy phrasing' . . . 'pleasing vocals' . . . words which were doubtless sincerely meant, although Simon had been badgered by the band manager to write up the singer. Another music magazine, *Down Beat*, which unlike *Metronome* still exists, reported a conversation which went like this:

Journalist: 'Who's that skinny little singer? He sings a great song.'
Harry James: 'Not so loud. The kid's name is Sinatra. He considers himself the greatest vocalist in the business. Get that! No one ever heard of him. He's never had a hit record. He looks like a wet rag. But he says he is the greatest.'

Soon he was cutting his first record with James, in July, and others followed. Sinatra got no credit for them – he was just the 'vocal refrain'; nor did any of them cause much of a stir. The best was *All Or Nothing At All*, laid down on 31 August in New York City, and even that sold only 8,000 copies when first released. 'The band still has a long way to go', commented *Down Beat*. Four years later, with a musicians' strike in full swing and the record companies

impact from lyrics. There is no person in the world more at ease than Sinatra in dealing with an audience, and the Manhattan comedians helped him with that too, especially the increasingly fashionable 'audience-insult' techniques. A typical line, to a woman on her way to the ladies' room, might be: 'Just mention my name and get a good seat.'

It was also while he was at the Rustic Cabin that, on 4 February 1939, he married Nancy Barbato at Jersey City's Church of Our Lady of Sorrows. They moved into an apartment on Garfield Avenue, Jersey City, and Sinatra threw himself ever more frantically into his career. He and his bride saw his busy parents but seldom; he was determined, desperately pushing for that taste of success which Harry James was soon to give him. He played his first date with the band on 30 June in the Hippodrome Theatre at Baltimore and, in the course of time, the Rustic Cabin was to be torn down and replaced by a petrol station where desperate for anything by Sinatra from the vaults, it was put out again. This time it sold a million copies and has become a treasured piece for collectors everywhere.

The time on the road with James was largely happy for Sinatra and for Nancy, who went with him until pregnancy forced her to return to New Jersey, but the band wasn't making it. It reached Hollywood all right, but the fat cats who frequented the sophisticated club called Victor Hugo's (a hurried switch date in place of the Palomar Ballroom in Los Angeles, which had burned down) were driven out by the swing and blare of what was essentially a dance-hall outfit. Sinatra sensed that things could not go on like this, especially when *Down Beat*'s annual band poll in December placed the James boys a mere twelfth, and although he had no real national reputation he was becoming quite well known inside the business. People noticed the effect he had on audiences, including Connie Haines who told Earl Wilson, the New York showbiz writer with a deep knowledge of Sinatra's career covering four decades, about that first theatre date for the singer and the James band at Baltimore's Hippodrome. 'Already the kids were hanging around the stage door, screaming for Frank. People said those kids were 'plants'. Plants! That's ridiculous. Who could afford to pay plants?'

Another person, more important than Connie Haines in the employment stakes, had noticed Sinatra too – Tommy Dorsey, who had pushed himself right to the top as a bandleader. He was egged on by the faithful Hank Sanicola, later to be Sinatra's manager, who forwarded a copy of *All Or Nothing At All*, and by an important CBS executive, Jimmy Hilliard, who had been tremendously impressed with Sinatra at the Sherman Hotel in Chicago. 'My back was to the bandstand, but when the kid started talking a chorus, I had to turn around. I couldn't resist going back the next night.' The growing interest of Dorsey became very sharply focused once his very popular singer,

Jack Leonard, announced that he was to take a chance on going solo. Sinatra was aware of the opportunity to step into what was then virtually the top band vocalist spot, since Dorsey gave much more prominence to his singers than did his nearest swing-and-sweet rival, Glenn Miller. He called Dorsey, a canny businessman who kept Sinatra on the hook through two meetings before finally offering him the job, reckoning that this way the price might be less. It wasn't so expensive, just $100 a week, and one of Sinatra's earliest fans, Connie Haines, went to Dorsey as well.

Harry James was a gentlemen. He held a two-year contract for Sinatra, but with a cheerfulness which belied his near-bankrupt state said he wouldn't stand in the singer's way. The two men parted friends, a relationship which endured, and Sinatra looked back benignly on his days with that band, making one of his warmest and most emotional statements about the parting of the ways:

'When I told Harry about Tommy's offer and said I wanted to leave, he just tore up my contract there and then and wished me luck. That night the bus pulled out with the rest of the boys at about half-past midnight. I'd said goodbye to them all and it was snowing, I remember . . . I stood alone with my suitcase in the snow and watched the tail-lights disappear. Then the tears started and I tried to run after the bus. There was such spirit and enthusiasm in that band, I hated leaving it.'

It was January, 1940. The 'rough diamond', getting less rough by the month, was about to enter the crucial polishing phase of his career. While Europe pursued its 'phoney' war, with the fall of France, the Battle of Britain and the entry of Russia into the conflict still to come, America was still living through its phoney peace. By December 1941 when Pearl Harbor, jolted the USA into fullscale hostilities alongside the Allies, Sinatra would be halfway along the route which was to make him the most successful singer in history.

In the early years of marriage, almost all was sweetness
and light for Sinatra and Nancy . . . for a deal of the time,
except when pregnancy intervened, she travelled along,
helping him even in the studying of scripts and songs at
times.

*'The boy in every corner
drug store'*

3

TOP DOG

THE YEARS WITH TOMMY DORSEY WERE CRUCIAL in the making of Frank Sinatra, just as the unique magnetism of his rapidly emerging style and personality was of immeasurable help in keeping the velvet-toned trombonist's band at the top between January 1940 and September 1942 when Sinatra left. He hadn't quite the same warm feeling about those years as he had about his six months with Harry James, not least because there was a residual core of Jack Leonard's friends in the band who at first made him feel uncomfortable. But about his professional good fortune he was in no doubt. Dorsey was the best of the bandleaders on presentation and showmanship. His band was superb, plump with musicians who were kings in their specialities – trumpeters Bunny Berigan and Ziggy Elman, pianist Joe Bushkin, drummer Buddy Rich and the arranger Axel Stordahl, who within a few years was to be an ace in Sinatra's pack.

The reaction of most of the musicians to Sinatra was reflected when later he became their spokesman on complaints, as well as in the words of Jo Stafford, a member of the splendid Dorsey close-harmony group, The Pied Pipers, with which Sinatra sometimes sang. 'There was no upstaging when he sang with us. I have never seen anyone try so hard to blend in. He really worked at it.' And, even more glowingly, she has recalled his first appearance. 'By the end of eight bars I was thinking, "This is the greatest sound I've ever heard."' So, despite any initial problems, the proud and independent Sinatra soon fitted in as well as he could fit in anywhere. His first band room-mate was Lee Castle, who said: 'Even then you could see this boy was tough. If you crossed him, you were dead, but if you were friends, there wasn't anything he wouldn't do for you.' He ended up sharing a room with another outspoken iconoclast, Buddy Rich, a friendship which has survived the years despite various ructions on the road with Dorsey. Sinatra is supposed to have once hurled a heavy pitcher filled with water and ice cubes at Rich during a backstage argument; it missed, but it shattered against the wall with such force that pieces of glass were embedded in the plaster. Yet there was Rich with his band backing Sinatra at his London concerts in the autumn of 1984 and making the fiercest of defences of the singer in the British magazine *Crescendo International* in 1985 after the very mixed Press reception given to those concerts. 'The Press treated him as though he were a criminal,' he declared, and of one woman journalist (whose scrofulous story deserved every acid word Rich aimed at her) he said: 'There's some lady who wrote about him who started to talk about his hairpiece and his weight – it was degrading. If they'd written like that about me, I'd try to find you; I'd bust your face open. I took it as a personal affront to *me* – the man's my friend.' The constancy of most of Sinatra's friends is remarkable, as the affection shown for the man by his peers has always seemed something of an antidote to the more poisonous things written about him.

Even with Dorsey, Sinatra took time to gain national recognition. He first made an impression with The Pied Pipers, although uncredited, on a version of *I'll Never Smile Again*, a song written by a young woman in Toronto, Ruth Lowe, grieving at the premature death of her husband. Connie Haines, who also sang on the record, claims she got $10 for doing so and Sinatra $25. It's a fascinating performance, and every now and again Sinatra's voice comes clearly and unmistakably out of the ensemble. By July 1940 it was top of the *Billboard* record sales chart, held on at No. 1 in the USA for an unprecedented seven weeks, and stayed in the ten-disc-only chart (hence its short name of Top Ten) for four months. On the seventh day of the same month, his first child Nancy was born, Tommy Dorsey being chosen as godfather, but joys of this kind were balanced by the mixed nature of occasional reviews – 'Sock all the way' in *Variety* set against the 'nil on showmanship' from *Billboard* – and by the sheer hard grind

Sinatra joined Tommy Dorsey's Orchestra in January 1940. It was rivalled only by Glenn Miller's as the top swing-and-sweet band of the day, and as Miller would make movies like *Sun Valley Serenade* and *Orchestra Wives*, so the Dorsey crew had theirs, too – *Las Vegas Nights* (below) where the young crooner can be spotted third from the left. The year was 1941, and hits like *I'll Never Smile Again*, sung in the film, helped uplift him to top place in the polls for best male band singer. So did his work with Dorsey's superb vocal group, The Pied Pipers (right), where Sinatra is at the mike with girl lead Jo Stafford, and the lessons he was picking up from Dorsey's trombone playing method. The singer learned smoothness of phrasing and legato (stringing together phrases without appearing to breathe) from watching Dorsey surreptitiously inhale air through 'a sneak pinhole' in the corner of his mouth.

The theatres and the cities (and the supporting bands and movies) may have been different, but the scene was usually the same once Sinatramania gripped America in the 1940s: lines of teenage girls, many in that form of short hosiery known as bobbysox, waiting patiently to see their idol – and a lot of police to control them. Points to note in this assemblage . . . the girls (right) wearing various expressions of ecstasy were pictured inside the Paramount in New York, 1943 . . . the line of cops (below) were fitted out with bowties, perhaps in emulation of Sinatra's early trademark, as he left a train in Pasadena, California . . . while in the picture of queues (far bottom right) you will just see the name of the Paramount. That was the place where the crooner, with his characteristic kiss-lick of hair on his forehead, started a riot of 30,000 curfew-defying fans in 1944.

of the life he was living. The existence of the travelling bands at this period has been well documented, and nothing can really parallel it today since stars don't kill themselves rushing from gig to gig, and embryonic rock groups trying to make it at least have their own vans or trucks as they belt along the highways of the UK or USA. In 1940 and 1941, the very success of the Dorsey band made for severe discomfort to its members. Continual one-night stands, the venues often hundreds of miles apart, could involve overnight journeys of 12 to 18 hours on uncomfortable buses with snatched meals or sandwiches as the staple. Even in settled seasons of a week or two, especially as added attraction at movie-houses, the pressure of work was intense – eight or nine shows a day, each lasting threequarters of an hour, and Sinatra having to sing perhaps ten or a dozen songs per show. It was the kind of schedule which will either wreck or strengthen a voice. Sinatra was so good he didn't even bother to warm up before shows. 'I had real strong pipes in those days.'

He was learning about himself and his potential in other ways. The 'nil on showmanship' comment rankled. He watched the way Dorsey did it – the pacing, the contrasts, the careful use of spotlight on soloists and the rest. All of it he would pour into his own shows and records. Dorsey played his trombone, smooth and flowing, almost as if it were the human voice. Again, Sinatra picked up on Dorsey's 'singing' technique, learning the importance of phrasing and dynamics, and has also said that the violin playing of Jascha Heifetz taught him similar lessons. He became the master of the legato line, meaning the ability to sing tunefully and smoothly through six or eight bars without any awkward breaks to gulp in air. He noticed Dorsey taking in air through what he termed 'a sneak pinhole' in the corner of the mouth as the lips pressed against the trombone, and evolved his own version of this, as well as continually trying to strengthen his lungs and chest. It's ironic, in retrospect, that he was to

be thought of as weak and weedy when he first emerged as a soloist – 'a pipecleaner in suspenders' was an early gag – for beneath the thin, gaunt-faced figure was a tough and prematurely experienced artist, the kind who would say to E.J. Kahn of a rival 'I can sing that son of a bitch off the stage any time', and even more importantly the kind who could give the impression (as with his breathing trick) that he was doing what comes naturally when in fact his easy charm disguised years of hard work and swathes of artistic cleverness. As the perspicacious Pleasants observed: 'The absence of any impression of art was imperative to his style. His accomplishment in avoiding it was the most compelling evidence of his stature as an artist.'

So the young Sinatra grew and grew, even building a relationship with Dorsey, a remote and lonely figure, a strict disciplinarian, a 'god' in the business, insofar as this was possible. 'One night,' as Sinatra told Robin Douglas-Home, 'two of us decided to hell with it, we'd ask him out to dinner. He came along and really appreciated it. After that he became almost like a father towards me – and this in spite of the fact that, being a John Rebel, I was always the guy who had to pass on the beefs of the boys in the band.'

Any paternal feelings Dorsey had towards Sinatra must, however, have been somewhat ambivalent. The worldly-wise and hot-tempered bandleader – he'd had fist fights with brother Jimmy after they had broken up their one-time Dorsey Brothers outfit and gone their separate ways – would have realised very swiftly that he'd got a powerful competitor as well as ally in the singer. As 1940 and 1941 unrolled, Sinatra began to be named on radio shows, and Victor Records also put his name on discs as a second credit to Dorsey. In ballrooms, Sinatra could stop the dancing for a large proportion of the clients as they moved to the bandstand to listen whenever he came to the microphone. With the odd movie appearance – first *Las Vegas Nights* and then

Ship Ahoy – also enhancing his exposure, Sinatra began to challenge the more established band singers like Dick Haymes and the brothers Ray Eberle and Bob Eberly (the slight difference in spellings was deliberate), and even Bing Crosby who had been out on his own for a decade. The climax came in December 1941 when Sinatra knocked Crosby from the top of the most prestigious of all the polls, *Down Beat*'s, and Dorsey was relegated to second in both 'Sweet' and 'Swing' polls, behind Glenn Miller and Benny Goodman, and only reached fourth in the soloist stakes, where even Sinatra's old boss, Harry James, beat him.

By the mid-1940s, Sinatra was the star everyone wanted
to be seen with, for whose radio shows everyone wanted
to be chosen as guest star. The enormously popular
Andrews Sisters (below) were no exception, nor were the
less well known Slim Gaillard and his trio (right).

Dorsey may not have liked it, but he was
realistic enough to programme things to give
himself the best chance of holding on to
Sinatra. With America at war, and the band
business becoming even more difficult as travel
grew more tedious and more uncomfortable,
he began to shape band programmes increasingly to highlight Sinatra's singing, a process
which ended up with the voice *closing* the show
– unheard of in a band so renowned for high-
powered instrumentals as well as sweet vocal
harmonies, not least because the singer then
took all the final applause and, if lucky, would
have cries of 'encore, encore' ringing in his ears.
Sinatra was often so lucky, and Dorsey also
had to yield to pressure, from both his singer
and the people at Victor, to allow the emerging
star to record as a soloist. He made a sneaky
move by insisting that Sinatra's discs would
come out only on the cheap second-string Blue-
bird label, but that could not hold back the
singer's determination or his explosive enthusiasm once he put down four songs on 19 January 1942, almost inevitably using his talented
friend, Axel Stordahl, as arranger and
conductor.

Cole Porter's *Night and Day*, Jerome Kern's
The Song Is You, together with the less glitter-
ing *Lamplighter's Serenade* and *The Night We
Called It a Day* were the pieces for that first
historic solo outing in Los Angeles, with
Sinatra's name atop the label, and the circumstances were exactly what one would have
expected of the super-confident singer.
Stordahl, recalling Sinatra's excitement when
he heard the first finished playbacks, believes
it was the turning point in his career, the dawn-
ing realisation for the soloist of what he could
do artistically. For an A and R man in charge
of the session, the memory was different.
'Frank was not like a band vocalist at all. He
came in self-assured, slugging. He knew exactly
what he wanted. . . . Most singers tend to begin
with the humble bit. At first, they're licking
your hand. Then, the moment they catch a big
one, you can't get them on the phone.

46

Popularity didn't really change Sinatra. He started out by having a good opinion of himself. On that first date, he stood his ground and displayed no humility, phoney or real.' The words ring true. In a sense, recording sessions – especially those of the 1950s and 1960s – were *the* performances of Sinatra's life rather than any of the occasions when he stood upon theatre stages.

These first records in his own right brought him no particular success, however – it was his records with Dorsey which were the sellers, with twelve of them in the *Billboard* chart in 1941 – and it is even more illustrative of Sinatra's supreme self-confidence that he still decided during 1941 to go it alone. He was impatient to move ahead. He was looking closely at two of his rivals, Bob Eberly and Dick Haymes, who both looked set soon to join Bing Crosby as singers in their own right. Sinatra was fearful they would steal a march on him and it was this, according to him, which finally drove him to forsake the safe, steady and well-paid berth with Tommy Dorsey's band. He will undoubtedly have sensed, maybe before others did, that the balance of power was swinging towards the singers and away from the instrumentalists and bandleaders, but it was still a gamble. In the summer Sinatra told Dorsey he was leaving. Dorsey didn't like it at all and is believed at first to have refused to release Sinatra from his contract. When a deal was finally done, with or without the help of threats against Dorsey by a leading New Jersey gangster, a story given wide circulation but never proven, the bandleader certainly extracted his pound of flesh.

The terms gave Dorsey one third of Sinatra's earnings for the next ten years, and Dorsey's manager got another 10 per cent. *Down Beat* said that with extra fees and side-deals included, Sinatra was actually getting only about seven per cent of what he made. A deal so outrageous could not be expected to last, and it did not. With a characteristic touch of lordliness, the newly-emancipated singer told the newspapers: 'You can quote Sinatra as saying that he believes it is wrong for anybody to own a piece of him and and collect on it when that owner is doing nothing for Sinatra.' It nevertheless still took a year for the arrangement finally to be revoked, and the parting price was allegedly $60,000. This, however, was specifically denied by Sinatra in one of his many conversations with Robin Douglas-Home, to whom he appeared to give a straightforward and credible account in 1960. He described Dorsey's great fury even when he gave the bandleader a year's notice. Dorsey refused to speak to Sinatra for months, and grew even angrier when the singer poached Alex Stordahl to be his arranger, paying him $650 a week compared with Dorsey's bargain-basement $150. How remarkable, then, that Sinatra should still continue to speak so warmly of his former employer. 'I certainly learned everything I know about phrasing and breath control from listening to the way he played that trombone,' he told Douglas-Home. 'It was a wonderful life, they were great days.' In 1961, having founded his own record label, almost the first step by Sinatra was to put together an immensely sentimental tribute to the so-called 'sentimental gentleman of swing' with an album entitled *I Remember Tommy*. Even more surprisingly, the feisty Dorsey would say: 'I used to stand there on the bandstand so amazed I'd almost forget to take my own solos. . . . Remember, he was no matinee idol. He was a skinny kid with big ears. And yet what he did to women was something awful. And he did it every night, everywhere he went.'

Whatever it was he did, Sinatra was now going to do it on his own, and there were some in the Dorsey retinue who doubted he could make it. They pointed to his insecurities, to that side of him which Dorsey had once called 'brittle'. His temper flared easily. He was never one to forgive or forget, a trait evident all through his life. He particularly lost his cool and let his fists fly in situations where bigotry was flouted or ethnic insults were made.

Without band-buddies to support him, without a band organisation to look after the business side for him, said a goodly number of the dismal in 1942, he'll soon slip on his skinny backside. And for the first couple of months, it looked as if they must be right. After Sinatra sang his last show with Dorsey on 19 September 1942, he found nothing more to do than a three-minute spot singing *Night and Day* in a wartime movie called *Reveille with Beverly*, which was simply an excuse to string a lot of top musical talent together on celluloid; a kind of extended pop video of the day. Even worse, recording studios were silent because of a nationwide musicians' strike which had just begun – and, ironically, when Sinatra finally did get a No. 1 record hit again, in December, it was with *There Are Such Things* which he had cut with the Dorsey band back in July. Should have stayed where he was, said the doubters. But they were wrong, horrendously wrong, as the penultimate day of that fateful year of 1942 was to prove.

Luck . . . and being in the right place at the right time . . . played their part as so often they do, for a CBS radio series set up by Sinatra's early ally, Manie Sachs of Columbia Records, won him a booking at the Mosque Theatre in Newark, New Jersey. In attendance one night was Bob Weitman, manager of the fabled Paramount Theatre, the mecca for bands and singers in New York. In a half-empty, flat theatre he could scarcely believe what he saw. 'This skinny kid walks out on the stage. . . . As soon as they saw him, the kids went crazy. And when he started to sing, they stood up and yelled and moaned and carried on until I thought – you should excuse the expression – his pants had fallen down.' Weitman thought that, with Sinatra's home-patch so close, it would be a bright idea to book him as an 'extra added attraction' for the Benny Goodman show due to open on 30 December. The decision was not only an inspiration. It would herald a sea-change in the course of popular music – and no one can tell the story better than Sinatra himself, in what has become the famous version as given to Robin Douglas-Home. A Bing Crosby film was being shown at the Paramount, supported by the world's top band led by an inturned clarinet player who hadn't even heard of Sinatra. He just flatly announced the singer's name. . . .

Although his marriage of six years to hometown sweetheart, Nancy, was under constant strain by 1945, and continued to be so until his mad affair with Ava Gardner some years later, his publicity colleagues made sure that an image of happy home life came through as an antidote to rumours of affairs, fights and Mafia connections. He was often pictured with his wife (opposite page, and below) and with his family, which ultimately numbered three – eldest child Nancy, son Frank junior, and the youngest, Tina.

'I stuck my head and one foot out through the organdie curtains – and *froze!* The kids let out the loudest scream you ever heard. I couldn't move a muscle – I was as nervous as a son of a bitch. Benny had never heard the kids holler before and he froze too – with his arms raised on the up-beat. He looked round over one shoulder and said, 'What the hell was that?' That somehow broke the tension and I couldn't stop laughing for the first three numbers.'

It was a watershed, this Paramount appearance, for Sinatra and for music. Within a few months of it he would be called 'the hottest thing in showbiz' by the trade paper *Variety*. With even more magniloquence, *Life* magazine would term it 'the proclamation of a new era', as indeed it was, with the ascendancy of singers and the death of big bands to be confirmed within a couple of years. And hundreds of sparkling phrases about Sinatra's reign would flow from writers at the top end of the scale – E. J. Kahn's memorable words spring to mind, describing the singer's teenage followers as trapped in 'the desperate chemistry of adolescence'.

It was incontrovertibly those hordes of chemically desperate bobbysoxers (as they were then called, even though many painted their legs to simulate stockings) who first up-lifted Sinatra. Notice was given at once of the way things would go. The theatre was sold out from first show to last for the month Benny Goodman stayed. Sinatra was retained for another month after that, and newspapers and magazines were awash with stories attempting to explain the hysterical effect he had. It was put down to everything from religious fanaticism to the mothering instinct. He was frail; he also had a curl on his forehead. 'Not since the days of Rudolph Valentino has American womanhood made such unabashed public love to an entertainer,' said *Time* magazine, making a similar point to E. J. Kahn, who would however go back further to Liszt and Strauss for his parallels.

In the early days of his stardom, Sinatra was a well-known liberal, drawing the angry fire of Republican columnists, campaigning hard for the re-election of Franklin Delano Roosevelt (the first name was the one he gave his son) as President in 1944. It was no surprise to see him, as early as August 1940, in the company of the President's wife, Eleanor (below) together with bandleaders (left to right) Fred Norman, Bunny Berigan, Tommy Dorsey and Lionel Hampton, all getting together for a charity show for a black college at Daytona, Florida. In 1944 he appeared in an Oscar-winning short campaigning against racial prejudice, *The House I Live In*, at whose preview he is pictured (right) with Frank Ross, and in the same year was on the campaign trail for Roosevelt accompanied by composer Moss Hart and Broadway star, Ethel Merman

Within a day or so it seemed irrelevant whether or not George Evans, Sinatra's canny publicity man, had paid kids to scream or 'papered' the house with free tickets, both suggestions being freely bandied about. The fact is that once there was enough publicity around, it created more publicity; as we have pointed out, publicity is self-sustaining, feeding upon itself. The truth is probably that Evans and company did no more than oil an already-moving machine. Again, Connie Haines is among the most reliable of witnesses, recalling Sinatra with Harry James almost three years before the Paramount shows. 'It was something about him being so frail and skinny. Something about the way he'd hang on to that microphone. Something in his singing that reached out to the audience – like he was saying, "I'm giving this to you with everything I got; what have you got to give me?"'

They gave him, the young women and the relatively young and many of the young men too, a devotion which was overwhelming and extreme, a shattering affection whose intensity and sheer size had never been seen in showbusiness before. Sinatra, as cool an analyst of his own success as any outsider, probably got it nearest to right when he rejected the argument that females wanted to mother him (females of 12 or 13?) and said simply that in an age of war, with American manhood scattered to the corners of the globe, 'there was great loneliness. I was the boy in every corner drugstore, the boy who'd gone off, drafted to the war.'

That is simple, neat and tight, but it leaves out several other elements in Sinatra's success. Timing was one, for as his career expanded in the three years from 1943 to 1945 into the all-conquering period of success known generally as Sinatramania, precursor of Beatlemania, so was American influence around the world becoming ever more pervasive, the gospel of gum and nylons, music and mayhem carried everywhere by the conquering GIs to soldiers, sailors, airmen and civilians alike. Remember Alexander Shiwarg's memory of the first news

from those who freed him in Hong Kong in 1945; servicemen of all nations were Sinatra's great ambassadors. Then, Sinatra got his musicians right as well. Axel Stordahl could write swinging stuff, it's often forgotten, as well as syrupy string-laden echoes of Tchaikowsky – but it was the syrup which got to audiences then. That was right, too, for the times. This was the age of the runaway success of Richard Addinsell's *The Warsaw Concerto*, of songs based on Tchaikowsky themes (like *And When We Kiss*, using the No. 1 Piano Concerto music), of Vera Lynn in Britain making *We'll Meet Again* and *The White Cliffs of Dover* into national anthems. Romance, sentiment, tears were in demand, in movies and in songs. Sinatra provided them, and used excellent songwriters like Jule Styne, Sammy Cahn and Jimmy van Heusen to help him. What was more, just as I, an English teenager, had found him convincing, so, unknown to me, had an American writer called George Frazier in *Life*

Sox Have Wilted, But The Memory Remains Fresh, and she certainly wrote as if the ecstasy of being a Boston bobbysoxer in 1944 was still with her:

'"Frankie!", we screamed from the balcony, because you couldn't get an orchestra seat unless you were standing on line at dawn, and how could you explain to Mom leaving for school before dawn? "Frankie, *I love you!*" And that glorious shouldered spaghetti strand way down there in the spotlight would croon on serenely, giving us a quick little flick of a smile or, as a special bonus, a sidelong tremor of the lower lip. I used to bring binoculars just to watch that lower lip. And then, the other thing: The voice had that *trick*, you know, that funny little sliding, skimming slur that it would do coming off the end of a note. It drove us bonkers ... It was an invitation to hysteria. He'd give us that little slur – "All . . . or nothing at a-alll . . . and we'd start swooning all over the place, in the aisles, on each other's shoulders, in the arms of cops, poor bewildered men in blue. It was like pressing a button.

We *loved* to swoon. Back from the RKO-Boston, we would gather behind locked bedroom doors, in rooms where rosebud wallpaper was plastered over with pictures of The Voice, to practise swooning. We would take off our saddle shoes, put on his records and stand around groaning for a while. Then the song would end and we would fall down on the floor. We would do that for an hour or so, and then, before going home for supper, we would forge the notes from our parents: "Please excuse Martha's absence from school yesterday as she was sick . . .".

'We were sick, all right. Crazy. The sociologists were out there in force in those mid-forties, speculating about the dynamics of mass hysteria, blathering on about how his yearning vulnerability appealed to our mother instincts. What yo-yo's. Whatever he stirred beneath our barely budding breasts, it wasn't motherly ... Croon, swoon, moon, spoon, June, Nancy with the Smiling Face, all those sweeteners notwith-

magazine in 1943. 'Sinatra', he said, 'has the ability to believe implicitly the rhythmic goo he sings. He is utterly convinced that a kiss is still a kiss, a sigh is still a sigh.'

Sex, too, was a perfectly straightforward part of his appeal. *All Or Nothing At All* and *Saturday Night (Is The Loneliest Night In The Week)* were only two of the songs through which Sinatra funnelled sex and passion back into popular music. That his wife, Nancy, was thought of by some smalltown girl fans as an 'older sister', that some women may have wanted to mother him, even that lots of males liked him too – he caused a mini-boom for bowtie manufacturers with his penchant for floppy neckwear, a trend aided by Winston Churchill – should not hide the sexual magnetism which Sinatra had for women. A salutory reminder of this teenage love affair centred on Sinatra was given in a retrospective piece of the *New York Times* on 13 October 1974, by Martha Weinman Lear. It was called *The Bobby*

54

Girls, girls, girls . . . that was the Sinatra message in the mid-to-late 1940s, and he seemed to be photographed with them all the time – whether singly, as with Jane Powell (far left), then a 16-year-old movie singer who was appearing in 1947 on his *Songs By Sinatra* radio show, or with lines of movie people in very obviously posed pictures. But there was another, very important, side to his nature – a desire to help the underdogs of life. He was plainly a hit with two young girls (below) during a visit he made to an orphanage in Richmond, Virginia.

standing, the thing we had going with Frankie was sexy. It was exciting. It was terrific.'

Harold Hobson, longtime drama critic of *The Sunday Times* of London, picked up on Sinatra's smile too. 'The shy deprecating smile, with the quiver at the corner of the mouth, makes the young ladies in the gallery swoon in ecstasy and the maturer patrons in the dress circle gargle with delight,' he wrote of a Sinatra performance in London.

There was also the element of vulnerability about Sinatra, created by the slightness of his frame, but not that alone, since Robin Douglas-Home could say of the plumper, lived-in Sinatra 15 years later: 'The voice I heard was that of an insecure man, alone, calling for understanding from the depths of a cold, private wilderness . . . a vulnerable child, crying itself to sleep in the secrecy of his room.' The best contemporary writing witness of the phenomenon was, of course, E. J. Kahn who

noted as had others that Sinatra gave 'the impression he believes all the sentiments he is obliged to express, an accomplishment that is at times heroic' and who dug up a psychologist who would say that Sinatra performed 'a sort of melodic striptease in which he lays bare his soul. His voice haunts me because it is so reminiscent of the sound of the loon I hear in the summer at a New Hampshire lake, a loon who lost his mate several years ago and still is hopefully calling for her return.' The loon, presumably, told the psychologist all this. Writing in the *New Republic*, a most intellectual organ, a writer called Bruce Bliven dubbed Sinatramania a phenomenon of mass hysteria, occurring only two or three times in a century, 'comparable to the Children's Crusade in the Middle Ages, or the dance madness that overwhelmed the young in certain medieval German villages'.

A sense of humour was highly useful for Sinatramania-watchers, and Kahn had it. He painted a picture of an American nation which, by the mid-1940s, was divided into two armies: those who liked Sinatra and those who didn't – and especially the Sinatra fans versus the Crosby fans. His wonderful grandfather of 88, who loathed popular music and had never heard Sinatra sing, was quite positive that Crosby must be a better singer because Bing owned racehorses. He, E. J. Kahn Jr., was also bright enough, while observing how right-wing commentators were already gathering to accuse the liberal-minded Sinatra of depravity, to capture the extremism of many Sinatra fans. 'You should burn in oil, pegs should be driven through your body, and you should be hung by your thumbs,' wrote one to an unconverted newspaper critic. Then there was the dappy way in which Sinatra wheedled himself into the fabric of daily American life.

A tympanist with the Indianapolis Symphony Orchestra called Frank Sinatra ended up getting more publicity than the conductor. Kahn tracked down a salesman who could only boast the surname of Sinatra. Summoned to

Sinatra's recording career really got off the ground from the magic date of 13 November 1944, when a long dispute between musicians and record companies ended. On that day (top left picture on opposite page) he recorded *There's No You* and *White Christmas* with Axel Stordahl as conductor and arranger – the man who was to give a distinctive sweeping strings style to so many early Sinatra ballads. The best part of three years later, on 22 October 1947, Stordhal was still his man (top right) rehearsing the orchestra as Sinatra studied the score of *Laura*. During that three-year period, Sinatra was expanding his musical range and image all the time, including aiding symphony orchestras to balance their budgets by appearing with them at concerts, as he did (bottom two pictures) with the New York Philharmonic.

court to answer traffic offences, this Sinatra was let off with a miniscule fine by the judge, who proclaimed that the name was a cross heavy enough for the accused to bear. 'You have been punished by a cruel and merciless fate,' said this idiosyncratic dispenser of American justice.

To plumb the Sinatramania of the 1940s really adequately would fill the rest of this book, but I have spent so much time on it because it was the fuel of the singer's career. It was a bizarre phenomenon for the time – illustrative in one way of how, despite the nation's massive involvement in the world conflict, the USA in some respects was isolated from many of the horrors of war. Somehow, the Sinatra phenomenon couldn't have happened in London. Once it began in America, however, Sinatra's career took off like a rocket. Within a year of the Paramount launch he'd been signed up for the top weekly pop show, *Your Hit Parade*, had become an obligatory part of every impressionist's and comedian's act ('He's so skinny that both of us are trying to get together to do a record'), had whizzed to four major cities to appear with symphony orchestras, supposedly to raise money for them but equally usefully to raise publicity for himself, had charmed even the hard old hags of the Hollywood papers, and had managed, in perhaps his most significant move of all, to go upmarket and break into the adult night-club circuit with appearances at high-class places like the Wedgwood Room at the Waldorf Astoria and the Riobamba.

The latter venue was especially good to him. Just as he had swamped Benny Goodman when billed simply as a cautious 'extra added attraction' at the Paramount, so at the Riobamba he did the same to the comedian Walter O'Keefe. According to Sinatra, O'Keefe came on to do his act after the singer had performed – and been well received. 'Ladies and gentlemen, I *was* your star of the evening,' said O'Keefe. 'But tonight, in this club, we have all just seen a star born.' He then walked off.

No such drama attended his disc career, which was stalled by the musicians' union ban on recording during 1943. Sinatra was far from stopped completely, however. First, thanks to Manie Sachs, the old *All Or Nothing At All* master with Harry James was discovered and put out, climbing to the top of the hit parade. He followed that with a series of *a cappella* recordings accompanied by vocal groups, and as *You'll Never Know*, *People Will Say We're In Love* and *Sunday, Monday or Always* all became No. 1s, Americans could scarcely avoid hearing him. He even, very smartly, formed his own music publishing operation with Hank Sanicola.

As 1944 arrived, Sinatra's life-style was set – dates at theatres and clubs, mixed in with radio once a week and movies from time to time. Only records were a problem, and once singers decided they would respect the musicians' strike picket lines, Sinatra and the rest of the crooners didn't record commercially, a situation which persisted for a year until November 1944. This only, of course, put an extra premium on any Sinatra appearances on stage, a spur to the extremism of fans, who would tear at his clothes and even deep-freeze lumps of snow which bore his footprints. The shennanigans reached their apogee in the notorious 'Columbus Day Riot' of October 1944 when Sinatra returned to the Paramount. Generations which have grown up on rock-'n'roll extravagances, Woodstock and Beatlemania may find the record of that day relatively unsurprising now, but for juveniles in New York to ignore a curfew set by the revered Mayor La Guardia, for 30,000 hysterical fans to run amok in Times Square as they fought to get into the theatre, and for hundreds and hundreds of policemen to be called out to control them was unprecedented in wartime America.

He survived the explosion of worship, however, and once he could sing on record again he winged rapidly into the studios to cut 17 songs in the last few weeks of 1944, including

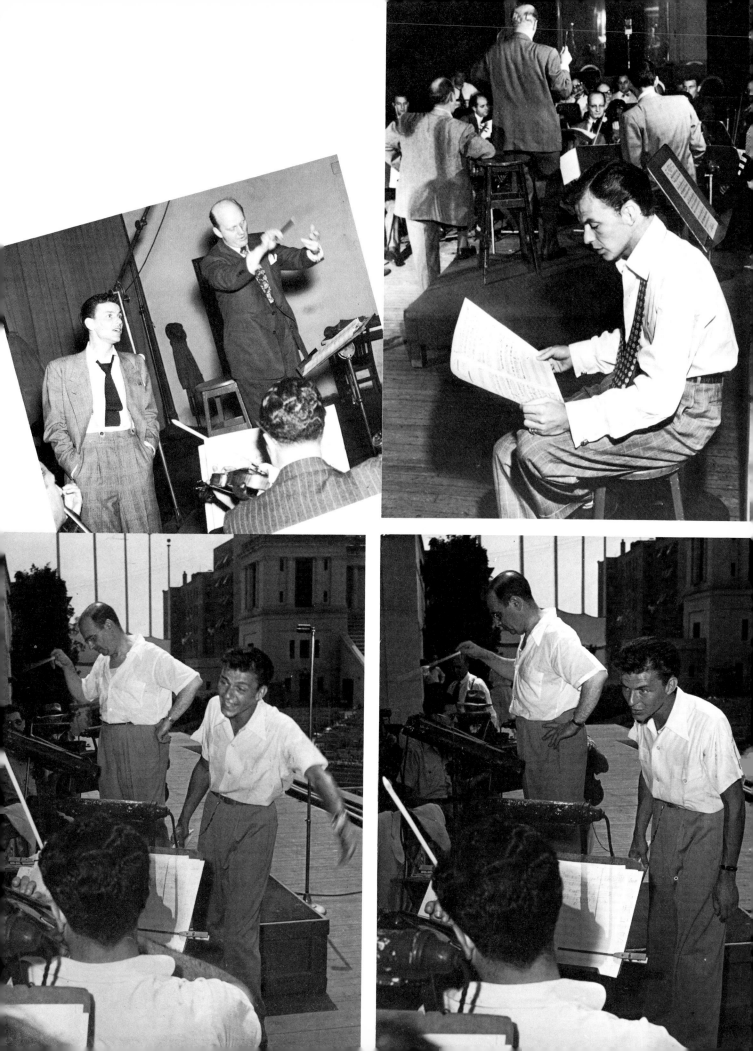

Still the Axel Stordahl years in Sinatra's recording career – and this time (right) he's also joined by the comedian Jimmy (Schnozzle) Durante. And in the picture immediately below he's with Judy Garland (left) and Lotte Lehmann at the famous Hollywood Canteen niterie for the armed services. In the scene at the bottom of this page, Bobe Hope and Dinah Shore join the line-up, whilst on the opposite page in the inevitable golfing pose it's Sinatra, Hope and Bing Crosby, who joined Sinatra's record label, Reprise, in 1963, as well as the old groaner with Buddy Morris and Sinatra.

a failed version – the famous one was redone in August 1945 – of the song dedicated to his daughter, for which Phil Silvers had provided the words, *Nancy*. He produced a surprise packet, in true Sinatra style, by interrupting a varied recording roster in 1945 with a session where he conducted an orchestra in a composition by Alec Wilder (he who wrote *I'll Be Around*) even though he didn't read music. 'Frank was smart', said Manie Sachs, describing how Sinatra dealt with the orchestra. '"I need your help", he said right off, "and I want to help this music". By the time he was through, they were applauding him and hugging him and patting him on the back' – an early example of Sinatra's extraordinary rapport with musicians.

Way back in 1943, his sudden fame had had one startling result for his film career. Although his *Reveille with Beverly* role was a one-song affair, he was swiftly promoted to star billing. Then followed fairly ordinary things like *Higher and Higher*, *Step Lively* and *Anchors Aweigh*; the sort of films you would expect a pop singer of that era to make, but which gained him by and large fairly friendly words from critics. Always, newspaper stories seemed to grow around him like weeds. His first screen kiss (with Gloria de Haven) brought him four pages in *Life* magazine; but his sensitivity about his lack of height rated less favourable comment when he stalked off the set because Miss de Haven wouldn't change her tall hat. In another plus-minus situation he was praised for his part in helping the Jimmy McHugh-Harold Adamson song *I Couldn't Sleep a Wink Last Night*, from *Higher and Higher*, to an Oscar nomination; then, he unwisely shot his mouth off when steamed up on a very hot studio floor, an early pointer to his well known impatience with the processes of film-making. 'Pictures stink. Most of the people in them do, too,' is what the papers had him saying. 'I don't want any more movie acting.'

He had to apologise publicly for that silli-

ness, and it was indicative that even when he was riding high, right at the top, already probably a millionaire, his volatile nature would always threaten to detonate explosions to bring him down. There were telltale signs of troubles aplenty to come in 1945. His marriage was far from secure. His wife, Nancy, was right in detecting that a very successful Sinatra was a far less comfortable spouse than one who had to cope with setbacks. Living still in New Jersey, however, she was not close enough to Sinatra's philandering and many affairs for the marriage to be mortally wounded – that would come later, when they moved to Hollywood.

Then there was the problem over Sinatra's absence from the armed services. In 1943 he was at first passed 1-A after a medical. Later, with thousands of his girl fans weeping and praying he wouldn't be called to arms, he went to a second examination in December 1943. This time a doctor found a hole in his left eardrum and made him 4-F, unfit for service. Still the issue wouldn't rest. Inevitably there were mutterings about the questionability of it all, and Sinatra got involved in several incidents – a fight with two Marines who shouted at him in a club, 'Hey, wop, why aren't you in uniform?' was just one. The issue dragged on for over a year until February 1945 when the war against both Japan and Germany was winding down but still not over. It looked as if Sinatra might actually be called up, but with fan hysteria at its peak he was yet again reclassified – 2A-F, signifying that his customary job was regarded as 'essential to the national health, safety and interest'. More furore. More newspaper stories. In the end he was dumped back into the 4-F medically unfit category.

He fell into more hot water, some of it self-induced, when he at last flew off to entertain US forces for seven weeks in Europe and North Africa *after* VE Day (8 May 1945). He was well-received, but once back in America blasted off about tour conditions, low-standard shows and the amateurishness of tour organisers. He may have been right, but as so often his timing was dubious, his language extreme ('shoemakers in uniform' was unnecessary) and, said many, who was he to talk? The sour comment of the services newspaper, *Stars and Stripes*, was: 'Mice make women faint too', while one of the syndicated columnists, Lee Mortimer, was even more cutting. He pointed out how Sinatra had waited until the Mediterranean war was over before taking his 'joy ride'. On the other hand 'fragile dolls like Carole Landis and aging, ailing men like Joe E. Brown and Al Jolson subjected themselves to enemy action, jungle disease and the dangers of travel through hostile skies from the beginning of the war.'

Sinatra was beginning, indeed, to become a marked man for certain sections of the powerful Republican Press, notably the wide-flung chains of Scripps-Howard and Hearst newspapers. His whole background made him a 'natural' Democrat; his whole life was punctuated by incidents reflecting his hatred of bigotry, racial or religious. He had been in a fight sparked by an anti-Jewish joke when touring with Dorsey. When his son, born on 10 January 1944 and named Franklin after President Franklin Delano Roosevelt, was christened, Sinatra had disputed loudly with the Roman Catholic priest who objected to the naming of Manie Sachs, a Jew, as godfather. Once Sinatra threw in his lot publicly with the Democrats in the Presidential election campaign of 1944, took tea with Roosevelt at a White House party, called him 'the greatest guy alive' and, later, having chipped in a $5,000 contribution, told a huge rally in Madison Square Garden, 'He is good for me and my kids and my country', the knives of practically every Republican columnist in the country were out for him.

Of course, Sinatra already had a reputation as a brawler and a philanderer. Of course, he seemed at times to attract trouble like a roof conductor attracts lightning. Of course, he went out of his way occasionally to be particu-

larly obnoxious to his opponents – as when he pranced around outside the Waldorf to distract crowds and media attention away from a reception being staged for FDR's Republican opponent, Thomas Dewey. But the reasons why he was poisonously attacked by columnists like Lee Mortimer and the ultra-right Westbrook Pegler were far more sinister and vicious. As Sinatra himself was later to write: 'My first real criticism from the Press came when I campaigned for President Roosevelt in 1944. . . . I feel it is the duty of every American citizen to help elect the candidates of his choice. Ginger Rogers, George Murphy and other stars supported Tom Dewey during this campaign, and I noted that none of my critics lambasted them.'

Ironically, Sinatra's first Oscar award – a special and highly unusual Oscar, awarded to him and director Mervyn LeRoy for *The House I Live In*, a propagandist short feature directed against racial prejudice – was further to annoy those who believed that entertainers should not meddle in politics, and those who had especial political reasons of their own for saying so.

Such attitudes may seem old-fashioned, even outlandish, today. But these were strange and strained times. The year of 1945 saw victory for the Allies over the Nazis and the Japanese and all the joy that went with it. Even as the war ended, however, the fragile unity which had bound the USA, the British Commonwealth and the USSR together was crumbling. Russia was making it quite clear that she wouldn't get out of her bit of Germany, nor out of Eastern Europe. The Red menace would replace the Nazi threat, and after the death of Roosevelt before victory was official, fear and loathing in America would soon usher in the age of Senator Joe McCarthy and his witch hunts. That would bring no good at all to the impetuous Sinatra. As America at large realised it had simply replaced one set of problems with another, so too would Sinatra face the penalties of his success in the entertainment war.

'Everything to lose'

FALLING IDOL

4

IN THE YEAR OF 1946, SINATRA WAS GETTING 5,000 fan letters a week. He had several thousand fan clubs around the United States. They rejoiced in innocently silly names like Subjects of the Sultan of Swoon and Society for Swooning Souls of the Sensational Sinatra. This latter body, based in Philadelphia, had a rule which said: 'We will never believe anything awful about Frank unless we hear him verify it.' Which suggests, perhaps, that some awful things were being written and, from time to time, so they were, especially by the politically-driven journalists who had begun to home in on him. Mostly, however, he was riding the rainbow. Jokes about him tended to be sharp but not cruel – like that 'pipe cleaner in suspenders' description of him – as did the sort of stories which circulated. One of his bodyguards who used to be in boxing said after an encounter with girl fans that heavyweights fought cleaner. His liberal views continued to gain him admirers as well as enemies. His reputation for generosity likewise grew steadily.

He was reported to have handed out more than 300 gold watches at $150 or more a time. One of the recipients was the comedian Rags Ragland, on whose timepiece Sinatra had inscribed, with rare wit: 'From Riches To Rags'. To the 15-man crew of a Navy patrol boat who named their number-only craft 'Oh Frankie', and its dinghy 'Oh Frankie Junior', he sent gold St Christopher medals. When that same Ragland died, in August 1946, Sinatra interrupted work in Hollywood on *It Happened In Brooklyn* to fly to New York as replacement for the comedian at a night club opening.

Such stories made excellent PR at the time, faithfully exploited by publicist George Evans, but there was nothing phoney about them. They were essentially true to the nature of Sinatra, and his emerging *padrone* image, just as was his gesture against racial bigotry when he insisted on changing the opening words of *Ol' Man River* which he sang as the closing piece to the so-called 'film biography' of Jerome Kern, *Till The Clouds Roll By*. Instead of 'Darkies all work on the Mississippi', Sinatra inserted 'Here we all work on the Mississippi''. Yet, to show that taste was not consistently his preserve, Sinatra still allowed himself to be pictured singing the song, and singing it quite brilliantly, wearing all-white while an all-in-white orchestra and chorus played on an all-white platform suspended in a studio heaven from which an all-white staircase twirled its way to earth. *Life* magazine voted it the year's worst moment on film.

There was, too, very little wrong with his standing in the entertainment world or his income. Ever since he'd broken out of the no-record period in late 1944 with the smash hit, *Saturday Night (Is The Loneliest Night In The Week)*, he had enjoyed nothing but success in the charts, becoming more and more prolific with a remarkable 51 songs cut in 1946 and 72 in 1947. His singing movies kept pulling the customers in too, so that by October 1946, in addition to his established routine of winning polls as a record artist (the *Down Beat* award for favourite singer of 1946 was his third consecutive success), he could be voted the most popular film star of the year by *Modern Screen* magazine. When they held the celebration dinner he received a present – his head, immortalised in a bronze bust fashioned by the sculptor Jo Davidson, who proclaimed: 'Those cheekbones! Those bulges around the cheeks! That heavy lower lip! He's like a young Lincoln. His radio series, *Tin Pan Alley*, continued to go great guns at a $12,000 per programme fee. Equally indicative of his earning power were Kahn's estimate that he made $4 million between 1944 and 1946, the five-year film contract he signed with MGM at a guaranteed $1½ million, plus lucrative residuals, and the $93,000 he was paid for a week of shows in Chicago.

How, it might well have been asked, could Sinatra possibly go wrong? Not least did this appear to be so because it was the young, the next generation of voters and workers, who uplifted him. They were the ones who, not

untypically, could scrawl in lipstick on one letter, 'I love you so bad it hurts. Do you think
I should see a doctor?' and in pen, on another,
'I wish Frank were twins, one for me, and one
for big Nancy.' He was, at the time, trying to
run a clean-cut as well as sexy image by being
photographed à la Crosby – with pipe, flowery
sports shirt and yachting cap. To small-town,
lonely, lower middle-class girls in particular, he
seemed like the man of their adolescent
dreams, but his appeal was still broader, to
males as well as females, summed up supremely
in the words of one teenager who said: 'We
were kids who never got much attention, but
he's made us feel like we're *something*.'

Indeed then, how could he, against all the
predictions, go wrong? Not only could he, but
he did, and in the four or five years after this
1946–47 peak, he descended slowly, inexor-
ably, downhill to a point where the odds were
massively stacked against any professional
recovery. The reasons are, in retrospect, not
difficult to discern. He declined because he
unwisely made some bad films and appeared
to make some bad friends; because the climate
created by important sections of the media
grew increasingly hostile to liberals in general
and Sinatra in particular; because he lost some
crucial people in his professional life at a time
when the particular nature of the 1945 peace
after war was aiding a change of popular taste
in singers; and, most of all perhaps, because
of his own complex character. He made himself
an easy target by his continued feistiness and
aggression, however much he was provoked,
and his reputation for womanising which
ended in the collapse of his marriage and his
undignified pursuit of Ava Gardner only
exacerbated the situation, as well as causing
such pain to Sinatra that it scarred him and his
work for life.

The row over his failure to serve in the war,
his tendency to win enemies in the media, his
high profile and low boiling point were all
established minus points as he hit his peak, and
in 1946 he did nothing to play down those

weaknesses. He was continually being riled by
the star columnists of the ultra-Right,
notoriously by Lee Mortimer, who had
claimed to see moral decline and decay in the
excesses of Sinatramania, especially if the
singer could swing the young vote into the
Democratic column, and then by the equally
poisonous Westbrook Pegler, whose political
motivation had been clear from the moment he
called Sinatra the 'New Dealing Crooner'.
Finally Sinatra's cork popped. The *Daily News*
in Los Angeles published a story which detailed
his 'beefs', from 'wife trouble' to 'a battle with
a recording company'. George Evans was sadly
not around to subedit the cable which
thereupon flew from Sinatra . . . . 'Just continue to print lies about me, and my temper not
my temperament will see that you get a belt in
your stupid and vicious mouth.' Newspapers

don't forget those who claw back at them; Lee Mortimer in particular was to extract the nastiest of revenges a few years later.

Ammunition for his newspaper enemies was first given by the heavier emphasis on gossip about his womanising which inevitably accompanied the move of Sinatra's family from New Jersey to Hollywood in mid-1944. The names laundered in the gossip columns in the next couple of years were many, but those that shone the grimiest were Lana Turner and Marilyn Maxwell. All the hard work of George Evans to play down the affairs only took a little of the dirt out of the atmosphere. Even then Evans would point to the scarifying results of emotional turmoil upon his client. 'It absolutely destroyed him. You could always tell when he was troubled. He came down with a bad throat. Germs were never the cause unless there are guilt germs.' This psychosomatic trait in Sinatra would reach its peak, with voice totally gone, during the traumas of the Ava Gardner affair.

Even with Turner and Maxwell it was bad enough. In October 1946, when a trial separation between Frank and Nancy Sinatra took place, it was Turner who got interviewed by one of the most assiduous and spiteful of the hag-columnists of Hollywood, Louella Parsons, and had to deny being a home-wrecker. Soon, in the first awful year of Joseph McCarthy's witch-hunts, 1947, the papers which dubbed him a pawn of 'fellow travellers' – as did one in Philadelphia – or printed unsubstantiated 'pinko' smears by the score, were to have something even meatier to chomp their chops into. For the first time, by agency of the now notorious 'Lucky' Luciano incident, Sinatra's name began openly to be linked with the Mafia.

It was not a difficult story to construct, were any journalist so minded, since Sinatra, despite the lack of any specific proof against him, proceeded as so often in his life to give hostages to fortune. Was he not, those who pursued him would argue, an Italian raised in the state of New Jersey where, in bars and clubs and businesses as well as sometimes in Democratic politics and labour unions, there were known 'Organisation' connections? Had not Sinatra worked in said clubs, his mother in Democratic politics, and his father been born in Sicily, even though on the east coast of the island where the *cosa nostra* was not in control? There had, too, been rumours of Sinatra being helped by a mobster when Tommy Dorsey wouldn't release him from his contract with the band. The fiction (since it has never been proven) was that a gun was thrust into Dorsey's mouth by one Quarico 'Willie Moore' Moretti – a *mafioso* who died a backstreet death, by bullet, himself. The episode was later reflected, and thus perpetuated, in Francis Coppola's movie *The Godfather*, with Sinatra being widely cast as the loose model for the fictional singer, Johnny Fontane. This is the way that rumours grow and harden in the public mind. It is known as circumstantial evidence, and the anti-Sinatra forces saw to it that every possible smear was rewritten into accepted gospel.

Only God and Sinatra know the whole truth of each twist and turn of his remarkable life, and all one can say now is that usually he has been shown by the media in the worst possible light, and that his own behaviour has often demonstrated a desperate lack of judgment for a public figure who has done so much good work for so many good causes. So it was in February 1947, when Sinatra flew out for a short holiday in Cuba.

He arrived at precisely the same time as a most important meeting of underworld figures was opening, headed by the top Mafia man, 'Lucky' Luciano, who had been in prison in America in the 1930s, then deported, and was hoping to be allowed to return to the USA, presumably to run the 'Organisation' of Italian, Jewish and Irish crime clans whose 'territories' he had moulded into an almost-going concern when Prohibition ended. The coincidence, if such it was, could scarcely have been more unfortunate, as was the fact that Sinatra flew in to Havana on the same plane as Al Capone's cousins, the Fischetti brothers, Joe and Rocco.

The story rumbled on for years, with the witnesses on one side a Scripps-Howard journalist, Robert Ruark, using information said to have been supplied by one Henry Anslinger, chief of the Federal Narcotics Bureau and a McCarthyite, and Sinatra's unrelenting adversary, Lee Mortimer. In essence the prosecution said that Sinatra had been partying and gambling with the Luciano mob, and although Ruark would one day retract in part, four years later Mortimer repeated the smears, adding that Sinatra had smuggled in $2 million in Mafia funds for Luciano – in dollar bills. Sinatra's defence was short and fairly convincing. To Ruark he said that he had had the company of the Fischettis forced on him, and that his encounters with Luciano had both been accidental. To the perseveringly waspish Mortimer he said: 'Picture me, skinny Frankie, lifting $2 million in small bills. For the record, $1,000 in dollar bills weighs three pounds, which makes the load I am supposed to have carried 6,000 pounds . . . . This is the most ridiculous charge that has ever been levelled at me.'

All this, however, still lay in the future. In 1947, the Luciano serial was followed by an incident between Mortimer and Sinatra. Reviewing *It Happened In Brooklyn*, Mortimer sniped at Sinatra, whose performance had been mostly well received. The two men met, without forewarning, while dining at Ciro's in Los Angeles. Words flew, including jibes from Mortimer about Luciano and Sinatra – these by Mortimer's own admission. A fight erupted and Sinatra felled him. The singer was then arrested at a radio show date, got bail, and the headlines in the Hearst papers crucified him for almost a week, at the end of which the film mogul, Louis Mayer, more or less commanded him to settle out of court.

Whatever one's feelings about the darker side of Sinatra's nature may be, and his lack of candour sometimes when questioned about it, it is difficult not to have the acutest sympathy for him in face of this kind of treatment. He was being hounded and hounded by the kind of journalists who are, sadly, always with us. The terrible Hollywood and metropolitan hags of that day, of both sexes, like Mortimer and Pegler, Ruark and Hedda Hopper, Louella Parsons and Dorothy Kilgallen, have been succeeded by a monstrous regiment of Glenda Slags today, in both Britain and the USA, allowed to inflict their malevolent prejudices upon the masses. The sheer malice of that 1947 campaign was aptly illustrated when Sinatra had, by his standards, a poor three-week season at the Capitol Theatre, New York, in the wake of a 'planted' bad review co-authored by Lee Mortimer, who later rubbed his quarry's nose in it. 'Broadway whispers this will be Sinatra's last appearance here, and that didn't kill my appetite for the family turkey dinner.' Any stick to beat him with would do, it seemed, and there was always another one handy as this compulsive fighter, gambler, womaniser and frontiersman kept stumbling through the worst few years of his life.

As always with Sinatra, his life powerfully affected his art. There was, frankly, not much wrong with his music at this time, although fashions were changing – a tough, brash peace taking over from sentimental war – but there seems an element of panic about some of his movie decisions, as though he was so desperate to do *something* to save himself that he never took the time to think out sensible judgements on what he should do with his artistic life. He made two terrible movies in 1948, playing an over-righteous priest in *The Miracle of the Bells* and falling into the pits with Kathryn Grayson in *The Kissing Bandit*, as he himself later jokily recognised. At the same time his grip on the pop music scene was slipping. He had been at the top through 1946 and early 1947 with *Five Minutes More*, *The Coffee Song (They've Got an Awful Lot of Coffee in Brazil)*, and *Full Moon and Empty Arms*. Soon it would be different – the brash mood of materialistic

Miller. This direly tasteless A-and-R man loved screamers like Frankie Laine, loved corny novelty numbers even more, and so wore down the nerves of the world's greatest singer – who virtually always refused to chase fashion and radically amend his way of singing, whether it was Ray or Presley who were the rage – that he persuaded Sinatra in 1951 to record the dreadful *Mama Will Bark* 'duet' with the girl singer Dagmar (dog imitations by Donald Bain), an indignity which was never forgiven or forgotten. 'Fuck you, keep walking,' Sinatra snarled at Miller years later in a well-attested encounter in Las Vegas as the record producer stuck out his hand and tried to patch up the relationship.

Television, the bright new medium which artists now had to learn to cope with, was to be no different. Sinatra got a five-year contract with CBS in 1950, but his show never took off. He appeared ill at ease, which almost certainly reflected the way he felt at the time but could not be put down to that alone. He has never been a TV natural, struggling a little in the medium even when performing at his best. Finally the sponsors were to cancel, as were CBS, and Sinatra was a loser again. There was not much joy for him in his movies either. When you're down, you're down, and Sinatra must have seemed to the showbiz world in 1950 and 1951 the very epitome of yesterday's man; a player with virtually no stage to stand upon. Looking just a little ahead, he was to lose his final stage as a singer in December 1952 when Columbia refused to renew his recording contract and there were no other takers. Had he anything left to lose? Indeed he had, and he had been losing it along with his career all through the late 1940s and early 1950s. He had a marriage to lose, a deal of dignity to forfeit, and all peace of mind to evaporate. The madness and the pain began to happen on 8 December 1949, when he met Ava Gardner, divorced from Mickey Rooney and Artie Shaw after one-year marriages, at the New York premiere of *Gentlemen Prefer Blondes*.

peacetime somehow demanding loud, brash voices as belters like Frankie Laine, Eddie Fisher and Johnnie Ray took over. New crooners in the Sinatra school (Nat Cole, Tony Bennett, Vic Damone and Perry Como) also came to compete with him, while bebop on the jazz front, country in Nashville, and the stirrings of rock 'n' roll in the rhythm-and-blues market all signalled the market changes.

Suddenly, Sinatra began to be a loser artistically on every possible front. First, in the spring of 1949, after months of criticism from commentators – 'dull, pompous and raucous', said *Metronome* – Sinatra gave up his main radio showcase, *Tin Pan Alley*, which was the chart centrepiece of the day. Then he lost his crown as *the* pop singer, which he'd held on to for six years. Billy Eckstine was No. 1 in 1949 with *Down Beat*, Frankie Laine second, then Bing and Mel Torme ahead of fifth-placed Sinatra. Next year it would be Johnnie Ray on top. In January 1950, he lost both his canny publicity man and good friend, George Evans, dead of a heart attack, *and* his long-time ally at Columbia Records, Manie Sachs, who quit the company to make way for the notorious Mitch

67

'I'm a fool to want you'

THE GARDNER AFFAIR

5

NOTHING IN LIFE WOUNDED SINATRA MORE –
and, in the clearest fashion, gave even more
surprising depth to his art – than his affair and
marriage with Ava Gardner, the occasional
elation and frequent misery which were compounded within it. For this reason the undignified business is a key passage artistically in
any celebration, not mere tittle-tattle. The
essence can be summed up in the comments of
Sinatra's longtime observer Earl Wilson, who
described it as 'a two-year soap opera with
screaming fights heard around the world', and
the less friendly words of Ava Gardner's biographer, the American journalist Charles
Higham, who is worth quoting more fully:

'In 1950, Frank Sinatra was a hollow-chested,
scrawny-limbed stringbean who looked as
though a breeze would blow him over . . . . His
appeal to women was due partly to his frankly
sexual approach to songs – he would fling his
thin legs wide, thrust his meagre pelvis up into
the spotlight glare – partly to his little-boy-lost
look – they wanted to take care of him – and
not least to his easy Latin charm. Ava had
always found Latins, especially if they were
thin, olive-skinned, hairy-chested, and volatile,
irresistible. Frank was no exception. The fact
that Ava, as a rising star, was taking a gamble
in having an affair with a man apparently on
the decline, did not worry her at all . . . .

'They were drawn to each other because they
were so much alike. Both were night people,
barely capable of sleeping at all, liking to sit
up into the small hours. Both loved Italian
food, liquor, boxing matches; both were
generous, warm, fiercely honest, violent-
tempered, afraid of being used, deeply insecure
and sceptical of their own talents, neurotic,
tension-ridden. Their energies fused, and their
relationship was from the outset passionate
and yet deeply frustrating, tormenting because,
similar as they were, they had a terrifying
ability to seek out each other's weaknesses.'

The main drift of Higham's assessment is probably right, even if the detail is, at times,
dubious; the 'meagre pelvis' bit is overdone,
sounding almost like envy, whilst to confuse
Sinatra's undoubted insecurity with scepticism
about his talents is ludicrous in view of the evidence. Rarely has any man been more certain
about his talent and how it should be directed,
except briefly during his tempestuous episode
with Gardner; it was only showbusiness and
the public who were sometimes sceptical. So,
in December 1949, the two people who were
meant to excoriate each other met and began
the ritual of quarrels and laughter, pursuits and
scandals, breakups and reunions, which
covered a 24-month period when Sinatra in
particular scarcely seemed in total control of
himself. Melodrama did, indeed, flavour the
affair from its start – an odd coming-together
since Gardner had reportedly disliked him on
sight and had not relented for the previous
three years. Like Nancy, she at first preferred
him when he was vulnerably down rather than
arrogantly and conceitedly up. Now, one of her
friends, Ruth (Rosenthal) Schechter said, 'she
felt an overpowering attraction' at the fateful
Gentlemen Prefer Blondes premiere. They dis-
appeared together for several days.

The passion had madness in it, a kind of
teenage fantasy. Within a fortnight he was
stopping his car under a palm tree in Palm
Springs to sing to her – like a scene from a
never-never Crosby-Lamour movie – and then
taking her out into small towns firing blanks
from his gun through the car window.

As 1950 came in – with Sinatra losing Manie
Sachs and George Evans, remember – the affair
grew hotter. He took her to Houston when he
appeared in cabaret, quarrelled vigorously
with a photographer who tried to take a picture
of them together, and had to endure a gathering storm in the papers, especially after his fragile marriage collapsed again in February,
Nancy this time demanding that they separated. Ironically, their third child, Christina
(Tina) had been born only 18 months earlier
on 20 June 1948.

Ava Gardner now, of course, succeeded Lana Turner in being cast as home-wrecker, the classic tart, and letters poured in vilifying her. This first phase of the infatuation which aroused much of the American nation reached its climax when Sinatra moved to New York in March for a season at the Copacabana, his most important club date in years. Gardner, by now dubbed Hurricane Ava in the papers, came too and both booked in at the same hotel, the Hampshire House. Sinatra seemed embattled, strung up with tension, bothered by a severely infected throat for which he had medical treatment. On his first night the audience was, to say the least, unreceptive, chattering and near-hostile; at one point he pleaded, 'This is my first night. Give me a break.' The braying crowd didn't, and when he made the dire mistake of singing *Nancy* they turned and laughed uproariously at his new woman, sitting up front to give him support. The critics crucified him, but Ava kept coming back to listen to him until one night, presumably fed up with his demands, she left after his first show supposedly to wait for him at their hotel.

When Sinatra finally got back to the Hampshire House he found she was not there. A few 'phone calls established that she had gone out on the town and was at a club called Bop City, where her ex-husband, Artie Shaw, was performing. He telephoned her, reportedly 'screaming with jealousy', and after a conversation in which Sinatra threatened to shoot himself, he pulled out a gun and fired two shots into the mattress. That, at least, is the story, even though police denied finding evidence of any shooting; they were probably persuaded to remove the evidence, said those more cynical.

Gardner was now due to go to Spain to work on her movie with James Mason, *Pandora and the Flying Dutchman*, which also featured a bullfighter, Mario Cabre. As shooting began, rumours of a Gardner-Cabre romance arose like steam from a stew and when, in a remarkable coincidence, Sinatra's ailing voice finally gave out on the same day, 26 April, that his wife sued for separate maintenance – the most graphic illustration of George Evans' 'guilt germs' theory – he flew to Spain too during the course of the two weeks' rest he was prescribed. That trip was in defiance of doctor's orders, for as Sinatra's conductor at the Copa, Skitch Henderson, said afterwards, the voice breakdown was 'tragic and terrifying'. True. You don't fool with a throat haemorrhage. 'Frank opened his mouth to sing and nothing came out . . . I guess the colour drained out of my face as I caught the panic in his. It became so quiet, so intensely quiet in the club. Like they were watching a man walk off a cliff.'

Sinatra's Spanish 'holiday' was no cure for his malaise, especially when one of the pursuing army of Press people got a quote from Cabre declaring that he and the lady were passionately in love, just marking time till Sinatra departed. This Cabre was full of ripe old fanzine corn. After Sinatra, troubled and uneasy, flew back to Los Angeles Cabre staged a gaudy and fully-reported over-the-top scene – part of it belonging to the movie, part not – in which Ava Gardner blew kisses to him while the matador bared his chest to show his wounds, allegedly declaring in Spanish, 'This is where a bull gored me yesterday. I was distracted by my feeling for Ava. I think of her day and night. She is sublime.'

Oddly, Sinatra did not explode, and he and Gardner even had a happy couple of months in London during July and August while she was filming and he, playing his first live concerts at the Palladium, was rapturously received. The interlude was only the calm before further storms in the autumn, however. Sinatra appeared consumed with jealousy when they weren't together, and she was increasingly frustrated when Nancy refused even to consider divorce after a suit for separate maintenance in September had made her relatively secure, with a good income, a house to live in and custody of the three children.

During the sorry winter of 1950–51 Ava

71

Again, the happiest pictures in the happiest place –
London. The top photograph shows Sinatra and Ava only
one month after their marriage, being greeted by the Duke
of Edinburgh on 10 December 1951, at a dinner before a
midnight matinee in aid of the Duke's especial cause, the
National Playing Fields Association. The crowds were out
in force (lower picture) to see the singer and his new bride
as they arrived at the London Coliseum for the show.

began threatening not to see him unless he got
a divorce. They quarrelled over everything;
politics, sport, music, art. And as they
wrangled, her career kept heading upwards
with her portrayal of Julie in a remake of the
Kern-Hammerstein classic, *Show Boat*, while
his subsided further with a drab TV series.
Nothing could show his desperation more than
the recording of *I'm a Fool To Want You* that
he made in March of the new year; unsparing
autobiography it was, which he co-wrote, and
one of several songs which illumined even the
final unhappy and relatively undistinguished
years of his recording contract with Columbia.

Divorce proceedings did at last begin in
May, but dragged on and on until in August,
having completed another film – *Lone Star*,
which she loathed – Ava demanded a vacation
in Mexico. She got it, but she could not really
have expected that the tracker-dogs of the
Press would give up. Not far short of a hundred
journalists sniffed out most of their moves.
Sinatra, who looked pale and strained
whenever he and Gardner appeared in public,
hit one of the tribe and almost ran another
down in the Los Angeles airport car park on
their return, allegedly shouting, 'Next time I'll
kill you, you son of a bitch!', and later even
apologised, saying he was 'upset' when it happened. The media continued their hunt, alleg-
ing a suicide attempt in September (Sinatra
said it was just his allergic reaction to a couple
of sleeping pills taken following the intake of
some brandies, cured once he vomited after a
doctor gave him a glass of warm salted water),
and in October making the most of speculation
about what was keeping Ava in hospital. The
newspapers were even to do their best to spoil
the wedding.

For marry at last the stormy couple did, after
further quarrels, on 7 November 1951, in
Philadelphia at the home of Lester Sachs,
Manie's cousin. Axel Stordahl was the best
man. The place was supposed to be secret, but
a crowd, including many journalists, was
camped outside in force. 'How did those creeps

know where we were?' Sinatra screamed. 'I'll
knock the first guy who tries to get inside on
his can!' But with a Cuban honeymoon behind
him, he was soon to have a rapid change of
heart about the media, an enforced attempt to
shore up his disintegrated career.

His new press agent, Mack Miller, was the
man who insisted that Sinatra *had* to eat some
humble pie, but the singer must himself have
clearly seen the writing on the wall. He was
tepidly received in London at a charity show
whereas a year earlier he had been feted. When
he flew in to New York early before a season
at the Paramount Theatre, untypically ready to
give interviews and pose for photographs, he
was virtually ignored.

He began almost pleading to be taken notice
of, sending a note to the Press Photographers'
Association which promised, 'I'll always be

made up and ready in case you want to shoot any pictures of me', telling a reporter that he bore at least *some* blame for his rows with the Press. 'I lost control of my temper and said things. They were said under great stress and pressure. I'm honestly sorry.' He even had two articles in the Hearst publication, *American Weekly*, trying to combat charges of being a political 'pinko' or a Mafia associate – all the dirt which had been re-raked by Lee Mortimer in an article described by the far-from-blameless *Hollywood Reporter* as 'the filthiest piece of gutter journalism ever composed'.

All of these moves, as the months of 1952 unfolded, proved pointless. He had a mediocre Paramount season. He no longer packed them in at nightclubs or shifted records. The day when Columbia would drop him was looming, as was the end of his network TV series, the end of any movie contracts and, in a sense, the biggest indignity of all: being told by his agency, MCA, that they no longer wished to represent him. Sinatra's sour words about that event – 'Can you imagine being fired by an agency that never had to sell you?' – were richly justified, but put no money in the bank or self-esteem in his soul.

No wonder that Sinatra was – it would seem for the first and probably last time in his career – afflicted by paralysing doubt, which in turn led to a desperate need for Ava to be with him continually, for her to mother, support, encourage and generally spoil him, just like a good Italian wife should. That, however, was not her style. So they quarrelled some more, feuding so much that (as one biographer, Tony Scaduto, pointed out) the fan magazine which had headlined their wedding *New Name For Happiness* came out four months later with *The Battling Sinatras*. Paradoxically, Ava objected to the time her husband spent with his ex-wife and children, a custom of his which translates easily as another attempt to find support and reassurance as well as fulfilling his Italian head-of-the-family image of himself. She seemed to fear she would lose him back to them.

Two incidents in the spring and fall of 1952 vividly show the panic which was overtaking the doomed marriage. Gardner had agreed to play in a movie version of Ernest Hemingway's *The Snows of Kilimanjaro*. The whole schedule was arranged so that she could be away from Sinatra for the shortest possible time. 'Frank kept calling her on the set and making her life pretty damn miserable,' script-writer Casey Robinson told Charles Higham. 'I like Frank now, but at the time I hated the little bastard because he was making my girl unhappy. Now I understand him, he was so beaten and insecure.' So insecure, indeed, that later in the year, after Sinatra had gained some encouragement from warmer receptions in clubs like the Cocoanut Grove in Hollywood and the Desert Inn in Las Vegas, a quarrel of the utmost violence erupted at their Palm Springs cottage, when he – according to the most bruited version of the tale – heard Ava Gardner and Lana Turner, now close friends, discussing him behind his back.

Police were summoned to the scene by neighbours as Sinatra raged at the women, ordering them from the house. When Ava refused, Sinatra himself quit and moved in with song-writer Jimmy van Heusen. Within a few days he was telling newspapers he wanted her back. Not long after that, having appeared in public at a rally for the Democratic Presidential candidate, Adlai Stevenson, to demonstrate their reconciliation, they flew in November to Africa where Gardner was to film with Clark Gable in a remake of Gable's *Red Dust*, this time called *Mogambo* (Swahili dialect for 'passion'), with the legendary John Ford directing.

Sinatra's journey was a sign of his utter dependence upon his wife, despite everything. He also, in terms of work, hadn't too much else to do. He was no longer especially flush with money. He truly did appear to be somewhere near the end of the line, a has-been destined for obscurity. There was only one faint hope that he might get something he was to crave for with increasing desperation and obsession.

A light of burning desire had entered Sinatra's life when, that fall, he had read James Jones' *From Here to Eternity*, a war novel set in Hawaii around the time of Pearl Harbor. There was one part in it he coveted with a desperate conviction that must have reflected his genius. He knew how well he could do it; it seems certain also that he knew it was probably his one chance of climbing out of the slough of despond. The role was that of Angelo Maggio, a spunky Italian boy from the slums of the American Depression, streetwise and fast-talking, a soldier consumed with beating the Army system before it broke him. As Sinatra observed: 'I knew Maggio, I went to high school with him in Hoboken. I was beaten up with him. I might have been Maggio.'

Before he left for Africa he hustled for the part like he hadn't needed to hustle since he was a kid singer in New Jersey. He tried without success to get the studio boss, Harry Cohn, to give him the part through Gardner and Cohn's wife and, reputedly, through the Organisation, who had power in the film unions – a suggestion which Sinatra successfully refuted in a later court case. Then, swallowing his pride in a way which showed just how desperate he was, he went to see Cohn, who treated him with mock horror, almost as if enjoying taking part in Sinatra's humiliation. 'But you're a singer. We need an actor,' Sinatra was told. Even when Sinatra offered to play the part for a paltry $1,000 a week (instead of his one-time going rate of $150,000) Cohn would only promise that he *might* get a screen test.

Out in Africa, the fallen star having to watch the rising star who also happened to be his wife at work, Sinatra fretted and brooded and picked fights with her. He was getting news from Hollywood and apprehensively watched more and more stars join the *Eternity* roster – Deborah Kerr and Donna Reed, Montgomery Clift and Burt Lancaster. The *Mogambo* company, meantime, were trekking through Kenya, Tanganyika and Uganda, accompanied by baboons, prowling lions, charging rhinos, African tribesmen and violent rainstorms and floods. The first anniversary of their marriage was celebrated before, at last, Sinatra got a cable inviting him to film-test. Cohn, however, was still playing his mean little game. Sinatra had to pay himself for a return trip of 27,000 miles, but within 36 hours he was at the Columbia studios. He did two scenes, in one of which he played Maggio being found drunk and absent without leave in a hotel garden. Director Fred Zinneman called producer Buddy Adler to come and see the tests. 'You'd better come down here,' he declared. 'You'll see something unbelievable.' Adler watched Sinatra doing another take, although Zinneman had no film in the camera. He was just as impressed as the director.

But still Sinatra was denied any knowledge of whether or not he might get the part of Maggio, for which Eli Wallach was hot favourite. He flew back to Africa in good spirits for Christmas since he at least knew he'd done his stuff superbly, but in the interim Ava had fallen victim to the heat and hardship of Africa and had flown to London for medical treatment. Charles Higham's biography quotes her as saying she in fact had a miscarriage. 'All of my life I had wanted a baby and the news that I lost him was the cruellest blow I had ever received. Even though my marriage to Frank was getting shakier every day I didn't care. I wanted a baby by him.'

Christmas in Africa was exuberant fun for the movie people, with parties and carols, led by Sinatra. Surtees again was the source of a memorable story – in this case, though, a funny episode, one of the best cameos known to Sinatraphiles. John Ford introduced Ava Gardner to the Governor of Kenya and his wife at a party thrown by British officials. He thought he would pull her leg. 'Ava, why don't you tell the Governor what you see in this 120 pound runt you're married to.' And Ava replied, 'Well, there's only ten pounds of Frank but there's 110 pounds of cock!' The British pair, according to Surtees, fell over laughing.

74

The holiday ended, filming resumed, and Sinatra and Ava were bickering again as he waited and waited. It was a cruel time for him, nearly impossible for her, until the cable he had been waiting for arrived one early January morning in 1953. He could play Maggio – for a measly $8,000 fee. By the evening, as the film-makers returned to base camp, he was both ecstatic and aggressive, telling everyone how he'd show 'those wise guys' who had watched him suffer.

A week after the cable came, Sinatra flew back to Hollywood. He was going to make a success of playing Maggio, he was resolved – a success, in a sense, of playing himself. He was going to make the comeback of comebacks, a resurrection so audacious it would never be allowed in fiction.

'Life beyond Eternity'

RESURRECTION

6

THE LAST SEVEN YEARS OF THE 1950S WERE, BY more or less common consent, the most fruitful and creative of Frank Sinatra's life. His has been the kind of existence which is shot through with wondrous irony, never more so than at this period. How ironic that his downturn should have been played out against a backcloth of his incredible passion for Ava Gardner, and that his renaissance should take place in the years when the relationship had soured and the marriage was ending. How ironic, too, that a man who was born to be a singer above all else should suddenly come to life again by agency of a film in which he did not sing. That was what *From Here to Eternity* did for him, however. The cause for celebration was not only the quality of his movie performance. *Eternity* seemed, much more importantly, to unlock the whole treasure house of his genius, to give him style and confidence and creativity again – as also, less welcomely, it revived some of the brasher and less-to-be-celebrated aspects of his character.

Our filmography goes more specifically into the artistic power of Sinatra's Maggio, which was the complementary emotionally-charged performance of Montgomery Clift, playing the former boxer whose only friend is Maggio. More to the point at this stage is to see how others viewed Sinatra's behaviour during the making of the movie in Hawaii. He was unconcerned as the weeks of March and April went by, displaying none of his customary impatience at the mechanics of film-making. 'He dreamed, slept and ate his part,' recalled producer Buddy Adler, to which director Fred Zinneman added: 'He played Maggio so spontaneously we almost never had to reshoot a scene.' Adler picked up on something else which was the key to Sinatra as artist, whether acting or singing. 'He has the most amazing sense of timing and occasionally he'll drop in a word or two that makes the line actually bounce. It's just right. He never made a fluff.' The comparison with his singing, which contributed to his acting, scarcely needs underlining.

Finally, and crucially, Sinatra expanded in confidence. 'It was like watching a man grow day by day,' said one of the production crew. 'When he first walked on that set he was like a school kid playing hookey with the adults. Then he kind of filled out and his head went back and he started looking you straight in the eye again. And when he walked off at the end of the picture, he walked out like he was King once more' – or, in the words of Joan Cohn Harvey, her name after husband Harry Cohn died, like 'a don't-give-a-damn guy'.

The Academy Award for Best Male Supporting Actor which set the seal on the brilliance of his comeback was still a year away, but Sinatra's demeanour clearly showed he knew he might be on the way to bringing off something quite spectacular. The next step was a new recording contract which he signed as *Eternity* was still in production. It wasn't exactly a flattering deal which his new agents, the William Morris organisation, did with Capitol. It was for only a year, with no advance, and it was down to Sinatra to pay for his arranger and orchestra and all the rest. Still, it was a beginning, and Sinatra did not waste the opportunity. Sadly, his old friend of the lush strings, Axel Stordahl, could not be part of the deal for long. The belters had weaned public taste away from the dreamy approach. Sinatra had to find some swing, and even heart-rending ballads had to be orchestrated with more muscle, more of a bitter-sweet flavour, if he was to succeed. He found exactly the man he needed in Nelson Riddle, with valuable alternates in Billy May and Gordon Jenkins, and in a period of seven years or so this team would between them create an impressive 16 'concept' albums of impeccable quality, a collection of outstanding popular music good enough to have been reissued in 1984 entire, improved marginally by digital remastering.

Many people have written about the Sinatra resurrection which *Eternity* and his new wave of recordings and movies manifested in the 1950s, but for sheer whizzbang enthusiasm and

One of the most renowned of all Sinatra pictures (left) and one which perfectly captures his 'saloon singer' swinging image of the 1950s – hat tipped back, cigarette smoke wreathing his head in the half-light. And the moment which allowed him again to become the swinger and the singer for all seasons is equally perfectly captured on the opposite page. He has just received, in March 1954, from actress Mercedes McCambridge, his Oscar as Best Supporting Actor for his role as Angelo Maggio in *From Here To Eternity*.

genuineness I enjoy most the words of Martha Weinman Lear—she who wrote in 1974 about the memories of her infatuation with The Voice in the 1940s – precisely because she was no Jenny-come-lately observer, because she had been through it all – grieving as she saw her idol fall into being the kind of schlep (ecstatic Americanism) who in the late Forties and early Fifties could sing *Mairzy Doats*, appear on a barking-dog disc and in movies play the kind of bumpkin who kept losing Kathryn Grayson to somebody else. 'I wept,' said Lear, 'for the glory of empire' but all that changed as he brought off what 'must still stand as the most fantastic comeback in showbusiness history, because he really *had* been reduced to total schlephood, not only professionally, which we can forgive, but in the personal image, which we usually cannot. And to come back from that kind of rockbottom takes – what? An extraordinary self-discipline I suppose. What clicked in that head, what kind of lights went on? All of a sudden the little loser was coming on like a bigger winner than we or he had ever dreamed, the voice sounding great and the man coming on cool, arrogant, exuberant, extravagant, *powerful* – the Swinger, *Il Padrone*, Chairman of the Board, all that business, with his pinkie rings flashing and his cuffs splendidly shot and his women and his starched $100 bills at the gambling tables in Las Vegas, with his own Rat Pack and his own Clan, his own court jesters, all those Dinos and Sammys and Joeys, his own myth in his own time. And even if only a fraction of it were true, what a myth!'

The key musical collaboration with Nelson Riddle began as *Eternity* was winding up, at the end of April, and even the titles will stimulate waves of nostalgia in Sinatraphiles: *My One and Only Love, I've Got The World on a String, Don't Worry 'Bout Me*. It was the particular confluence of brass, reeds and strings which gave the style and sound their unique flavour, each section reacting to the other so it seemed, the blare never too extreme, the softness never too cloying, and the whole sustained

by a bounding beat in the faster numbers, and a pulse which was inescapable even in the slower ones. I have never totally understood what Robin Douglas-Home meant when he said that these albums, embodying the spirit of the time, also epitomised 'the Age of Romantic Cynicism as exactly as Chopin epitomised the Age of Romantic Idealism'. We took Sinatra straight in the 1950s, happy when his songs were upbeat, sad when they were grieving.

What was cynical about *I'm a Fool To Want You* or *One For My Baby* or *In the Wee Small Hours*? And since Sinatra was often singing songs of the 1930s and 1940s at the time, it's difficult to make the idea of romantic cynicism stand up. That came, surely, in the 1960s and the nasty 1970s when the Pill and drugs and the Me-Generation had diluted the quality of life as well as of idealism.

Nevertheless, it is to Douglas-Home that the literature of music is indebted for a first attempt at a book on the maturing Sinatra and some stunning quotes from both the singer and his right hand, Nelson Riddle. Listen to this, from Riddle:

'Our best albums together were *Songs for Swingin' Lovers*, *A Swingin' Affair* and *Only the Lonely*.' (Not to be disputed, that, except that I would certainly add the early 10-inch LP, *Songs for Young Lovers*, together with *No One Cares* of the Gordon Jenkins albums and *Come Fly With Me* from the Billy May collection.) 'Most of our best numbers were in what I call the tempo of the heartbeat. That's the tempo that strikes people easiest because, without their knowing it, they are moving to that pace all their working hours. Music to me is sex – it's all tied up somehow, and the rhythm of sex is the heartbeat. I always have some woman in mind for each song I arrange; it could be a reminiscence of some past romantic experience, or just a dream-scene I build in my own imagination.'

The tempo of the heartbeat . . . what a splendid, illuminating phrase from a man supposed to be aloof, pensive. Sinatra confirmed that when he said: 'Nelson is the greatest arranger in the world. . . . He's like a tranquilliser – calm, slightly aloof. Nothing ever ruffles him. There's a great depth somehow to the music he creates. And he's got a sort of stenographer's brain. If I say to him at a planning meeting, 'Make the eighth bar sound like Brahms,' he'll make a cryptic little note on the side of some scrappy

80

music sheet and, sure enough, when we come to the session the eighth bar will be Brahms. If I say "Make it like Puccini," Nelson will make exactly the same little note and that eighth bar will be Puccini all right and the roof will lift off.' The Riddle experience for Sinatra was quite different from that with May ('like having a cold shower or a bucket of cold water thrown in your face . . . you sometimes don't get the copies of the next number until you've finished the one before') or Jenkins ('With Gordon it's all so beautifully simple that to me it's like being back in the womb'). For Riddle, the experience of working with Sinatra was unparalleled at any time in his career, although he has worked with Ella Fitzgerald and a dozen other greats.

'Frank undoubtedly brought out my best work. He's stimulating to work with. You have to be right on mettle all the time. The man himself somehow draws everything out of you. . . . I suspect he *poses* as a spur-of-the-moment man, but all the time he's been thinking about it pretty heavily. He'd never record before 8 p.m. and we'd knock off sometimes after 11. We'd get about four numbers finished at a session with an average of three takes a number.'

Those sessions became, like the care and planning which went into them, legendary in the 1950s and early 1960s. Sinatra would almost inevitably have his tie loosened, hat pushed back on his head, jacket slung on shoulder or chair, superficially relaxed, however much his mind and heart might be pounding away. The audience would be friends, often celebrities like Lauren Bacall or Sophia Loren, fairly close acquaintances, technicians. This was Sinatra's private stage, his own theatre more than any film set or concert hall he ever trod, and here he gave *the* performances of his career. Pacing and timing were vital, once the creative concept for an album had been decided and a final batch of a dozen songs taken from the short list of around 60 which would be prepared. So

was shape, the architecture of a song. 'I look for the peak of a song and build to it. We're telling a story. It has to have a beginning, a middle, a *climax* and an ending,' Riddle once said. Sinatra added his dollar's worth, explaining of the format of *No One Cares*, which began with that title song, '*Why* did no one care? Because there's a *Cottage For Sale*, that's why – so it had to be track two. That song's the saddest ever written – it depicts the complete breakup of a home.'

His chief producer from 1958 to 1961, Dave Cavanaugh, explained the perfection of *One For My Baby*, the classic which rounded off *Only the Lonely*. Sixty or seventy people were present, and Cavanaugh felt compelled to switch out the lights all except for a spot. The atmosphere was exactly like a club as Cavanaugh set the tapes rolling, and the song was done in one take. 'The only time I've known it happen like that,' said Cavanaugh, who explained on another occasion: 'Singing was like a lightning rod, particularly when he was in good voice, it discharged the hostile electricity.' The one-take nature of *One For My Baby* is all the more remarkable when you analyse its nature, for it stands as an archetypal great Sinatra performance – a man explaining his predicament to that most classic of all American father confessors, the after-midnight bartender. He does it naturally, vulnerably, universally, for the words are so cast that it's everyman's hard-luck story. He sings like a master – hear how he varies the metric beat, hangs on to notes, will even slip in an odd slur, ping or syllable that shouldn't, in a strict score sense, be there. He's one hell of an actor too, and what a production Cavanaugh gives him, from the far-off piano sound, just as if you were sitting on the barstool with some Hoagy Carmichael doing a Casablanca down the room, distantly, through to the spare alto sax solo in the last chorus, when Sinatra's singing of 'This torch must be drowned . . . or it might soon explode' has him at his most broken-heartedly expressive. A husky patina envelops the voice,

at times it threatens to break, increasing the feeling of pain, and then it slowly fades, leaving the piano to an empathetic coda. Riddle's orchestration is masterly for what it omits. The saxophone is memorable, just as the occasional emotional colouring of horns or reeds on other tracks is memorable, because the album is marked by understatement, mostly piano carrying the tune, with strings enriching it.

Listening over and over to this heartbreaker, inevitably I recall Douglas-Home's graphic description of a Sinatra session in September 1961 when he was watching, but at first not hearing, the singer record *September Song*. 'I saw complete and utter involvement with the song he was singing – involvement so close that one might feel he was in the throes of composing both tune and lyric as he went along. . . . He was putting so much into that song, giving off so much of himself that it drained my own energy just to watch him – *without hearing a note he was singing*; left me so limp at the end that I felt I had actually been living through some serious emotional crisis.' Then the writer listened to the playback, and he was even more devastated. 'The voice I heard was that of an insecure man, alone, calling for understanding from the depths of a cold private wilderness.' Another aspect of those Sinatra sessions was painted in by Dave Cavanaugh. 'The most dangerous thing was to "yes" him, or to be critical without being able to articulate what you needed. He'd come at you, and if you backed away he was like a barracuda. . . . He missed nothing that was going on around him. His eyes were constantly roving round the studio.'

Two other points are worth making about Sinatra's music in the momentous ten years from the mid-50s to mid-60s. First, the long-playing record might have been invented just for him, and for other ballad-singers. While the singles market developed almost exclusively for brassy upbeat tunes often intended for dancing, albums allowed Sinatra fully to explore themes happy or sad around which songs could be grouped, the prevailing tenor of each album proclaimed by its title – *No One Cares, Come Fly With Me, Only the Lonely, Songs for Swingin' Lovers* or whatever. He had space and time to get every emphasis and shading he might desire. Although he kicked off his run early in 1954 with a very successful single, *Young at Heart*, which rose to the top and stayed in the charts for over 20 weeks, much more typical of his future was *In the Wee Small Hours*, an album made a year later in February 1955. It is remarkable when one thinks this was only his third Capitol album, for it is another classic: personal grief distilled into superb music, the very opposite to the swaggering, explosive feeling of Sinatra's up-albums with their great drive and jazz feel. It proclaimed his ability to do *both* kinds of collections of songs which was, in the ten years 1957–66, to give him 27 albums in the *Billboard* Top Ten and not one Top Ten single.

Secondly, Sinatra now brought to the long-playing record an artistry which could exploit the medium to the full. The whole emotional range of his singing had broadened and deepened, and that of course had sprung from the life he was leading. *In the Wee Small Hours* is a crucial record here, a successor to that earlier single, *I'm a Fool To Want You*, and in ending the collection with *When Your Lover Has Gone* the message about his failed marriage with Ava Gardner could scarcely be clearer. Maybe the public, many of whom had been deeply upset by their relationship and the pain to the mother of his children, Nancy, first began to see in this hurting, poignant record that the affair was for real, not some showbiz fantasy, and that in some things neither men nor women can help themselves, however self-destructive the consequences.

The years of 1953 and 1954 certainly took their toll of both Sinatra and Gardner. He, far from flush after the comparative pittance he received for playing Maggio, set off on a European tour with her in May 1953. The next three months were scarred with continual quarrels, and Sinatra's ill-temper, springing from his

unhappiness, spilled over into a series of angry incidents with audiences, journalists, musicians and even airport officials. He was booed in Stockholm, he stalked off-stage in Naples because of 'Ava, Ava' chants, and only a longish spell in London while he sang and she filmed *Knights of the Round Table* gave them any time for escaping the hassle of constant travelling.

The writing was on the wall when he returned to America in August while she insisted on going to Spain for a three-week holiday. And even when she got back to the USA, and they attended the *Mogambo* premiere together, she let him go by himself to Las Vegas to play The Sands and took herself off to Palm Springs. The situation grew more and more intolerable. Both were proud, explosive, touchy people; neither would be the first to back down in an argument or to say 'Sorry'. As with Nancy, he wanted Ava not to fence him in, to give him a lot of rope – for, among other things, all-night parties with the boys, who were flocking back to the resurrected emperor. When he didn't get his way he simply brooded sulkily. Listen to *Little Girl Blue*, recorded on 6 November 1953, to get an idea of the darkness of his feelings at the time, art reflecting life. She in turn hated the intrusiveness of the hangers-on, as Mia Farrow was to do at a later date, and in common with her predecessor, Nancy, preferred a struggling Sinatra, 'on the skids', to the brash, assertive man now re-emerging on his way back up.

On 27 October, MGM announced that they were separating and would divorce. Within a month or so Sinatra was in hospital in New York suffering from 'complete physical exhaustion, severe loss of weight and a tremendous amount of emotional strain.' She would then get German measles in Europe while filming *The Barefoot Contessa* and, in Madrid, would meet a bullfighter, Luis Miguel Dominguin, who drove Sinatra from first place in her mind for a time at least. Her husband's visit to her in Rome and Madrid around

Christmas could not be counted a success.

It is astonishing, against this continuingly miserable background, that Sinatra managed to rebuild his career so swiftly in the next two years – but perhaps not so astonishing, remembering the close collusion of his life and his art. With *Young at Heart*, and its almost despairing edge of gaiety, riding high in the charts, he duly got his Oscar for Maggio in March 1954. Hollywood plunged into one of those brimming baths of soapy emotion which are features of its rituals as Sinatra won. His peers thought it was well deserved; and they *wanted* the old 'they-never-come-back' line to be disproved, if only for themselves and for some of their own futures. The emotional applause was reminiscent of what had happened when Humphrey Bogart won his *African Queen* award three years earlier, and in a sentimental gesture – which is, nevertheless, enormously revealing of their lifelong relationship – his ex-wife Nancy and the three children had presented him, the night before, with their own miniature Oscar at a family dinner in Nancy's house. The inscription on it read 'Dad, we'll love you – from here to eternity'.

Soon the honours to which Sinatra had been accustomed in the mid-1940s returned to him again: top of *Down Beat*'s best male vocalist poll in 1954 after seven years of exile; singer of the year with *Metronome*; No. 1 singer, best album-maker (*Swing Easy*) and best single (*Young at Heart*) with the critics who cast their votes in *Billboard*. These events were the precursor to six years of the most intense activity during which Sinatra would record his greatest albums, star in 17 films, including the best he ever made, roar around doing concerts and club dates, and with girl friends and his gang of male associates continually make headlines as the carefree, exuberant adult swinger – as well as getting into more scrapes and rows, and offending as well as pleasing a large number of people. The key to his existence now was that he became essentially his own boss. Remembering the way people and corporations treated him when he was down, he resolved that he would be his own man in the future; he achieved that through a complex agglomeration of private companies which controlled him as he controlled them.

Film-making inevitably dominated much of his life. After *From Here to Eternity* he played the would-be assassin of a President in *Suddenly* – 'Sinatra will astonish viewers who flatly resent bobbysoxer idols', said *Newsweek* – and the run of movies which followed in the next four years or so, no fewer than five of them made in 1955, showed Sinatra in a wide range of roles, so different from the relatively lightweight 'Clan' movies of the 1960s and Sinatra's persistence then and in the 1970s and even 1980s in typecasting himself regularly as a tough, cynical, hardbitten cop, gangster or private detective. Sinatra in the 1950s played a goodly proportion of serious roles, as the junkie in *The Man with the Golden Arm* (1955), for which he received an Oscar nomination, and as Joe E. Lewis, the singer turned comic after his vocal cords were slashed by gangsters, in *The Joker Is Wild* (1956), as well as the kind of light-comedy or singing roles which one would have expected to come naturally to him.

Sinatra meets Queen Elizabeth II (opposite page) when he was in London in October 1958, for the premiere of Danny Kaye's movie, *Me And The Colonel*. At around this time, in the wake of his failed marriage with Ava Gardner, Sinatra was playing the field at a whirlwind rate. Among the belles, in descending order (left) were Lauren Bacall (1957), Lady Beatty (1958), Barbara Rush (1959) – no guesses for the other male figure, who just happens to be Ronald Reagan – and Juliet Prowse, one of the independent 'new women' who might have married him, but refused to give up her career.

Stories emerging from his film-making all build up that picture of his character and nature with which we have become increasingly familiar. On the set of *High Society* (1956), Sinatra and his co-star Bing Crosby were nicknamed Dexedrine and Nembutal, as their respective personalities resembled the pep-up and go-to-sleep drugs. While filming *Guys and Dolls* (1955), in which he played another made-for-Sinatra part as the gambler, Nathan Detroit, his impatience with the slowness of film-making and his contempt for the dragged-out processes of Method acting and its chief protagonist, Marlon Brando, emerged as he said to director Joe Mankiewicz: 'Don't put me in the game, coach, until Mumbles is through rehearsing.' The title role of the smooth, fast-talking singer in *Pal Joey* (1957), based on John O'Hara's novel and the Rodgers and Hart stage musical, was equally a natural for Sinatra, so much so that when O'Hara was asked if he'd seen the movie, he replied: 'No. I didn't have to see Sinatra. I invented him.'

Of all the good reviews of his films from those years, one is especially revealing. In *The Saturday Review*, Arthur Knight wrote of Sinatra's performance in *The Man with the Golden Arm*: 'The thin, unhandsome one-time crooner has an incredible instinct for the look, the gesture, the shading of the voice that suggests tenderness, uncertainty, weakness, fatigue, despair. Indeed he brings to the character much that has not been written into the script, a shade of sweetness, a sense of edgy indestructibility that actually creates the appeal and intrinsic interest of the role.' Nothing more vividly illustrates the overlap, even identical nature, of Sinatra's artistry in both acting and singing. Very similar comments might have been written about his performance of songs, even about his character. The colouring of the voice, the mixture of emotions, the ability to improvise and re-create, the combined sense of brashness, vulnerability, elation and despair which surrounds Sinatra – all are stated or implied in Knight's words. Like actor, like

It's 1955 (right) and Sinatra appears with a star-studded group (Stewart Granger, Deborah Kerr and Jean Simmons) for the premiere of the movie *Guys and Dolls*. In it, Sinatra played gambler Nathan Detroit, and showed his well-known scorn for Method acting and the general slowness of film-making when he quipped to the director, of Marlon Brando's performance: 'Don't put me in the game, coach, until Mumbles is through rehearsing.' Later in the decade the Soviet leader, Nikita Khrushchev (lower picture) came to visit the set where *Can Can* was being made by Sinatra, Louis Jourdan (left of Khrushchev) and Shirley MacLaine. He was plainly disgusted when a chorus line, all suspenders and frilly knickers, did the dance which gave the movie its name.

singer, and even in the busiest years of his most successful film-making, the primacy of music for Sinatra continued to be asserted.

In 1955 he was No. 1 with *Down Beat* and *Metronome* as he had been the previous year, and with the dark bestseller, *In the Wee Small Hours*, behind him, his LPs made a huge impact in 1956, with *Songs for Swingin' Lovers* the album of the year for *Metronome*. The young had Elvis Presley and emerging rock-'n'rollers, but the not-so-young had Frankie, swinger supreme, to help them forget the noises they didn't want to hear, the ideal antidote against the poison of passing your 30th birthday. They could see him, too, in pricey supper-rooms like The Sands in Las Vegas and the Copacabana in New York, which the scruffy, jeans-clad young would not penetrate, and Sinatra accordingly became King of Clubs as once he had been King of Ballrooms. And he would always aim a shrewd kick at the pretensions of the new noise-makers, which gave further comfort to his followers. In October 1957, for example, he violently attacked rock'n'roll, claiming in a French magazine, *Western World*, that it 'fosters almost totally negative and destructive reactions in young people. . . . My only deep sorrow is the unrelenting insistence of recording and motion picture companies upon purveying this most brutal, ugly, degenerate, vicious form of expression.' He did not stick to that view in later years, however. By the 1960s and 1970s he himself would flirt with soft rock and the work of artists who, by implication, he had earlier lashed – he even turned a TV spectacular into a 'Welcome Home Elvis' show in 1960, when the rockers' idol got out of the army.

The virulence of that Sinatra attack probably reflected many things: his own distaste for the sloppy unprofessionalism of much rock, his feeling of distance from the emerging youth culture and its looseness of dress and behaviour, perhaps some envy that he couldn't appeal to the young as once he had. Tellingly, the writer Gay Talese reported in an *Esquire*

article of 1966 how Sinatra once almost got into a fight in a California club with a young man whose clothes didn't appeal to the singer. By extension he was objecting to the whole youth culture. More positively, Sinatra's attack on rock reflected his feeling of outrage that the great Tin Pan Alley tradition of fine songs which had stretched from 1920 into the 1950s might be overwhelmed. He seemed in his Capitol years to be engaged on a one-man crusade (aided especially by artists like Ella Fitzgerald) to preserve the masterworks of George Gershwin, Richard Rodgers, Jerome Kern, Irving Berlin, Cole Porter, Duke Ellington *et al* on record for ever, casting sidelong glances at his old friends Sammy Cahn, Jule Styne and Jimmy van Heusen, who were still working in that same idiom.

Not only did he preserve that music; he enlivened and re-created it, turning almost everything he sang into an interpretation which others would aspire to match, although Sinatra's versions were so unique, with him virtually in the role of singer *and* songwriter (in a sense foreshadowing the singer-songwriter boom of the late 1960s and 1970s) that they were unmatchable. It was his ability in one melange to sing as tunefully and resonantly as Bing Crosby, with something of the jazz flair of Ella Fitzgerald and Mel Torme and with just as much dramatic power as Tony Bennett which sets him apart even from these towering artists – he was, interestingly, given more votes than all other nominees put together from 109 jazzmen asked by *Metronome* in December 1956 to name 'The Musicians' Musician Of The Year'.

As well as Riddle, May and Jenkins, Sinatra had other inseparable associates during the years of musical supremacy: instrumentalists like the one-time Count Basie trumpeter, Harry 'Sweets' Edison and his pianist for a quarter of a century, Bill Miller, and the two record producers, Voyle Gilmore from 1953 to 1958, whose masterpiece was probably the driving, kicking, confident *Swingin' Lovers*

album, even though he gets no credit on the reissued sleeve or any other sleeves for that matter, and Dave Cavanaugh, the creator of *Fever* with Peggy Lee, from 1958 until the Capitol association ended in 1961. Cavanaugh *does* get credited, although neither man had the power of modern producers, nor were they expected to achieve the wizardry by which these modern gentlemen, using electronics and myriads of overdubs, can often turn the mouldy ears of grunting sows into artificial silk purses. Their task was so to organise the ambience and timing of studio sessions that, in a club-like atmosphere, the setting would be right for Sinatra uniquely to create his stories in song. How well Cavanaugh could do that, carefully staging *One For My Baby*, we have already mentioned in our discussion of *Only the Lonely*, whose sleeve won an award for its clever depiction of Sinatra's clown-painted face with teardrop, and that moody lamp-post which harks back to the use of the same evocative symbol in the *Young Lovers* sleeve of 1954.

So in a sense Sinatra did it his way, alone and resilient, but there were many others with him adding essential touches to his masterworks. So strong was he in the late 1950s that despite severe damage to his image from fights, some movie and TV failures, political clashes and continuing Mafia rumours he seemed unassailable in popularity. The December of 1957 was typical – top male vocalist for *Playboy*, All-Round Entertainer Of The Year with *American Weekly*, Mr Personality in *Metronome*. 'Sinatra literally devoured this one,' said that magazine of their readers' poll. 'There was no chance for anyone else.'

As all that voting was going on, however, there were some warning signs again on the horizon for Sinatra, just as there had been a decade earlier before his big slump. He had been building up towards a possible fresh fall for two or three years. At first, still deeply upset by the Gardner affair, he'd been caught up in yet another brawl at a Los Angeles night club during which he was alleged to have snarled:

The face is familiar, so is the cocky grin and stride. This is Sinatra in the up-years, but whatever is he doing coming out of a 55-cent (reduced to 37-cent) bargain breakfast place? Maybe is was accidental, or just another attempt by Sinatra to stake his claim as a regular guy.

'I hate cops and newspapermen.' Then he was embroiled in numerous law suits, including suing Les Ambassadeurs, the London club, apparently over a membership dispute, and in the spring of 1955 got into the bitterest of battles with TV personality, Ed Sullivan, who had taken Sinatra's side so often in the past. Sinatra wanted a fee to appear on Sullivan's show to promote *Guys and Dolls*; Sullivan said that since it was a plug, there'd be no payment. In a full page *Variety* advertisement, Sullivan reminded Sinatra of his attitude in 1947, when Sullivan was backing him against his attackers. 'Ed, you can have my last drop of blood.' Sinatra answered in kind. 'Dear Ed, you are sick – Frankie. PS – Sick, sick, sick', trumpeted the pages of the showbiz weekly.

This was on several counts sad and silly, of course, but Sinatra's extreme reactions and constant tetchiness had obvious roots. Partly he was still suffering over Ava Gardner. Songwriter Jule Styne, who shared a maisonette with him during 1955, said: 'I enter the living room and it's like a funeral parlour. The lights are dim and they just about light up several pictures of Ava. Frank sits in front of them with a bottle of brandy. After I get into bed I can hear him pacing back and forth. It goes on for hours. At 4 a.m. I hear him dialling someone on the phone. It's his first wife, Nancy. I hear him say, "You're the only one who understands me." After he hangs up, he starts pacing again. He seldom falls asleep until the sun's high in the sky.' Vivid enough, with the ring of truth. Then, although he often deserved attention, the newspapers always went straight for the jugular, and kept the pot boiling to excess, whenever he erred. It is terrifying sometimes to see the gutter Press at work, and perhaps we do not fully understand the pressures exerted upon superstars. 'The little man with broken dreams . . . he stands on a corner and scratches everything that passes by,' said the *Daily Telegraph*, not untypically, in 1955.

One recalls Robin Douglas-Home's assessment of 1961, describing how Sinatra was mauled even by the English in a night club. He was, said Douglas-Home, not at all like the vandal depicted in the Press. 'The provocation and the cantankerousness came from everybody but him, and I was surprised at the even-keeled manner in which he gently ignored it.' Of the American Press, he would add: 'On at least three occasions while I was with Sinatra, items appeared in the columns referring to something he was meant to have said or done the previous evening – annoying items that certainly did not show him up in a favourable light. Yet I knew that these items were not based on any fact whatsoever, as I had been with him during the evenings in question.'

The English writer, Benny Green, said in 1970: 'What constantly amazes me is not that he has slugged a few reporters, but that he has not slugged all of them.' When Green met him in 1962 he was kind and considerate, but then 'he is probably kind and considerate to anyone who doesn't behave like a pig ... I found a Sinatra totally unrelated to the loudmouth I had read about ... I also found him an acutely understanding man with a marvellous sense of professionalism.' A similar message was being relayed as late as 1983 by Steve Wynn, owner of an Atlantic City casino and in 1985 a pioneer in the process of upgrading the tacky downtown area of Las Vegas, commenting on people trying to get at Sinatra all the time, so-called 'fans' copying the aggressive style of the tabloid Press. 'People go beserk. Nice, well-dressed people. They come up, push you out of the way and then grab at him. I'm talking about irrational behaviour. Sinatra needs security. It's the sickest thing I ever saw.'

Similarly telling on the plus side of Sinatra's balance is his well-attested kindness to all kinds of people in the 1950s – Bela Lugosi and Lee J. Cobb, for instance – his care and concern for Sammy Davis when he lost an eye in an auto accident, and the effect he had upon Sophia Loren. During the filming of *The Pride and the Passion*, she found him no problem. 'Before he came to Spain, I hear all sorts of things. He is moody, he is difficult, he is a tiger, he fights. Here he is kindly, friendly. He has even helped me with my English ... He is a regular gasser. I dig him.'

The misery over Gardner began, coincidentally, to wind down in 1956 while Sinatra was filming *The Pride and the Passion*, but not without more petty side-play between them. In April, his separated wife had prepared a guest suite for him at her Spanish home. He arrived with a girl-friend, and husband and wife ignored each other in public. She, apparently tit-for-tatting, announced from Rome on 31 July, the day of Sinatra's return to America, that divorce papers had been signed, although it was another 12 months before the divorce was technically filed for in Mexico City. The

swinging bachelor life-style was now rapidly sprouting around Sinatra.

He had his hilltop house at Coldwater Canyon in Los Angeles where he lived from 1956 to 1964. By the bell-button at the gate was a notice. 'If you haven't been invited, you better have a damn good reason for ringing this bell!' The fact that 'haven't' was actually rendered as 'have'nt' did little for Sinatra's pretensions to class, but the mess was exactly the kind of goad to make the *Los Angeles Mirror News* call him 'nasty, rude, inconsiderate, uncooperative and ungrateful', which they did. The Clan was also forming, its first model the so-called Holmby Hills Rat Pack, a loose group formed 'for the relief of boredom and the perpetuation of independence' around Humphrey Bogart and Lauren Bacall, with Sinatra, Judy Garland and even David Niven in membership. Niven claimed (in *The Moon's A Balloon*) that the Rat Pack got its name from a binge, with Sinatra footing the bill, to Las Vegas in 1955 to attend Noel Coward's opening night at the Desert Inn. Coward and Sinatra had a warm relationship for years and a few years later, during a gigantic midnight gala in Monaco, the British performer and writer would lavishly praise the American for his good taste ... 'Putting it musically, Mr Sinatra has never sounded a wrong note.' Among those present in Las Vegas, 1955, were Bogart and Bacall, Garland and her husband Sid Luft and Angie Dickinson. 'After four days and nights of concentrated self-indulgence, the only one in the party who seemed physically untouched was Sinatra himself. The rest were wrecks and it was then that Betty Bacall, surveying the bedraggled survivors, pronounced the fatal words – "You look like a goddam Rat Pack!"' After their return to Los Angeles a private dinner was given by the gang for Sinatra at Romanoff's restaurant, and each guest had a package, tied with pink ribbon, which contained ... a white rat! Mayhem ensued in the chic watering-hole when several escaped during the unpacking.

There was even a coat of arms designed by Nat Benchley, for use on letterheads and membership pins: a rat gnawing on a human hand with the legend *Never Rat On A Rat*. Bogart's death from throat cancer in January 1956, which affected Sinatra deeply, left the 'swinger' in command of the loose Pack, and a new group evolved with Dean Martin, Sammy Davis Junior, Joey Bishop and, for a long time, Peter Lawford, who died on Christmas Eve, 1984, as key members.

The behaviour of the Clan, which was at least in part a grouping of business associates with common interests, did nothing to help Sinatra's reputation as they whooped it up at parties and intruded gratuitous and self-indulgent passages into each other's stage acts. As Mia Farrow, complaining of 'Frank's nasty little chums', was to say after her brief marriage to Sinatra in 1966: 'All they know is how to tell dirty stories, break furniture, pinch waitresses' asses and bet on the horses.' A temporary Clan member, the British actor Richard Johnson, was quoted by Norman Giller in the British newspaper *The Sun* of 9 December 1975 thus: 'At heart Frank is basically a schoolboy. One night we flooded an entire hotel floor playing water games. Because it was the great untouchable Sinatra, the whole incident was laughed off by the hotel manager as a prank.'

Once the Clan started making movies, Sinatra's image as a serious film actor was further eroded. At least he had the grace and good sense once to shrug and say in his own defence that people took the Clan films too seriously; they were only meant to be entertainment, romping fun. Perhaps so, but to the young of the late 1950s and early 1960s, very aware that something revolutionary was happening in *their* generation, the spectacle of these aging heroes trying to behave in public like conventioneers or (to use an English parallel) a touring Rugby club, indulging in jolly japes to extend the illusion of youth, while using an ugly outdated cool slang and producing records with

outmoded ouch-titles like *Ring-a-Ding-Ding* must have been both bizarre and deterring.

With the bachelor style came also the endless affairs or gossip about affairs. God knows how many women Sinatra is supposed to have escorted or in many cases slept with, but they run into many scores, even hundreds, although one sometimes feels that if all the stories were true (as also of the Mafia allegations) there must have been a reporter in every closet in every house or hotel Sinatra has ever visited. He himself once observed that if he had had affairs with all the women there'd been stories about, he would long ago have wound up as a specimen in a jar at Harvard Medical School: 'I'm supposed to have a Ph.D. on the subject of women, but the truth is I've flunked more often than not. I'm very fond of women. I like women. But like all men, I don't understand them.'

In 1957 and early 1958, Lauren Bacall was the target of Press attention – so much so that she claimed it was this which killed any possibility of marriage, especially a Louella Parsons headline: 'Sinatra and Bacall To Marry'. Another report of imminent marriage, in the London *Daily Mail* later in 1958, is similarly said to have ended his British affair with Lady Adele Beatty, American-born and a society beauty divorced from Earl Beatty. In 1959 came his (at the time secret) affair with Marilyn Monroe, described graphically in Norman Mailer's biography of the tragically doomed actress. According to him, Marilyn complained to an intimate about the inefficient way twin beds at the Waldorf Astoria, where Sinatra was staying, had been put together, so that one or other kept sliding down the space between them, and when asked if he was good replied: 'He was no DiMaggio', a reference to her ex-husband, Joe DiMaggio, the baseball superstar with the New York Yankees. Sinatra

Sinatra was an enthusiastic supporter of John F Kennedy when he ran for the Presidency in 1960. With victory achieved, Kennedy asked Sinatra to organise his Inaugural celebration concert. Sinatra produced one of the most star-studded lineups ever seen – and in the photograph on the opposite page he was rehearsing (left to right) Nat King Cole, Harry Belafonte, Kay Thompson, Jimmy Durante, Helen Traubel, Sammy Cahn, Allan King, Gene Kelly, Janet Leigh, Peter Lawford and Milton Berle. Even in the hurlyburly of his life then, he still found time (below) for reflective moments.

biographer, Tony Scaduto, quotes Monroe as telling friends not too long before her death on 5 August 1962; 'Frank has always been so kind and understanding. When I'm with him I don't feel I have to take pills or see a psychiatrist or anything else. He makes me feel secure and happy. He makes me laugh, I think he is the only man who has taught me how to live life. And he's really a gentleman.'

On into the early 1960s, and Sinatra was briefly engaged to actress Juliet Prowse, besides having affairs with, among others, Dorothy Provine and Princess Soraya. The rationale for all these affairs was, according to many close observers, Sinatra's unabating feelings of loneliness – the same drive behind his all-night partying with Clan members and his general air of wild obsession with filling each moment of night and day with activity. Sid Skolsky put it graphically: 'On any night when the laughs get sleepy and there's no more booze and there are no more hours, Dean goes home to his wife, Lawford goes home to his, Sammy to his. But Frank just goes home.'

He had more and more problems as the new decade came closer. Although *Come Fly With Me* and *Only the Lonely* were the top two albums of 1958, his relations with Capitol were turning sour. He wanted independence, but he was contracted to the record company until 1962 and they didn't want to release him. 'They let me go on condition I cut four more albums for them to wind up the deal,' he said. But he stopped recording in May 1959, and that wasn't good for a star whose run of fortune in the movies had turned, with only modest or downright bad reviews for *Some Came Running* (in the making of which he'd shown great insensitivity to the inhabitants of Madison, Indiana), *A Hole in the Head, Never So Few* and *Can-Can*, which was the movie denounced as 'immoral' by the Russian leader, Nikita Kruschev, when he saw it while making an official visit to the 20th Century Fox Studios. It was during this same visit that Sinatra (according to David Niven) offered to take Madame

The late 1950s and early 1960s were the heyday of the Clan – parties were thrown, drinks were downed, movies were made. Very often in each other's company were Sinatra and Dean Martin (top right), Martin, Sammy Davis Jr and Sinatra (right) and, more occasionally, Sinatra and Judy Garland (opposite), a member originally of the Rat Pack spawned by the Bogarts, Humphrey and Lauren.

Kruschev and her daughter to Disneyland after the police had disappointed her expectations by saying they could not guarantee her safety. 'Screw the cops', he said, according to Niven. 'Tell the old broad you and I'll take 'em down there, this afternoon – we'll look after them.' Typical Sinatra, it sounds, but Kruschev vetoed the idea, coldly observing that the city of Los Angeles must be in a sad state if his wife would not be safe in a children's playground. It is also worth adding, as another detail in the portrait of Sinatra at this time, that *Never So Few* originally had Sammy Davis in the cast, but after his famous *faux pas* in making a modest criticism of Sinatra on TV, he was written out of the film and the part given to a then-unknown, Steve McQueen.

This kind of nonsense, followed by the circus of filming the first Clan movie, *Ocean's Eleven*, in Las Vegas, cast a fierce spotlight on Sinatra's activities, with *Playboy* writing a long account of the movie saga in lurid detail. Sinatra was also very very rich now, and the boss of a large corporate empire, with stakes in hotels and gambling, movies, music publishing, real estate and much more; his income was put at between $10 million and $20 million a year. He was an irresistible target for the Press, and not untypical of the stuff written in the early 1960s was Al Aronowitz's charge in the *New York Post* that Sinatra had vast influence or control through the corporations and the Clan of night clubs and studios. 'Sinatra is King and Dictator of Hollywood.' Paradoxically, and wickedly ironically, half of the attacks upon him as a kind of Citizen Kane came from the Hearst and other right-wing Republican papers. The political nature of the papers is relevant, for as John Fitzgerald Kennedy limbered up to fight the Presidential campaign of 1960 he had as an ally – and a very high-profile one – the liberal of old, Frank Sinatra. What happened in the next three years or so was to have a fundamental effect upon Sinatra, his way of thinking, and the man he would turn into in the 1970s.

'Trumpets sound, exit the warrior'

SEPTEMBER YEARS

THERE IS NOTHING OF THE QUITTER ABOUT FRANK Sinatra. Throughout his life, indeed, he has fought people and causes hard and long, often beyond the call of duty or good sense, and has sometimes seemed to seek confrontations with 'the trigger-happy paranoia of a gunslinger always waiting for a challenge and sometimes anticipating the threat when it is not even there', as John Howlett put it in his *Frank Sinatra*, or in the words of Robert Mitchum: 'The only man in town I'd be afraid to fight is Sinatra. I might knock him down, but he'd keep getting up until one of us was dead.' Imagine then Sinatra's feelings when he apparently made a huge sacrifice of principle in the cause of the Kennedy clan, gave them his best shots thereafter, only to end up being, as he surely must have seen it, grossly betrayed. For on one interpretation that is what happened between 1960 and 1963. He must have felt the situation all the more keenly because of his whole nature and philosophy. Even in the cavortings of the Clan, Sinatra was living out a version of the *padrone* fantasy with which he had tried to enlarge his life. Loyalty and respect are the cornerstones of that faith. The Kennedys gave him neither. Their betrayal of Sinatra is crucial to the later development of his character and behaviour – the growth in the defiant, cynical, ever more ornery side of him, as well as his move to the political right. The Kennedy episode is the key to the next decade and more of his life, and that is why – even in a celebration – we must begin this chapter with it.

It was plain from the late 1950s that Jack Kennedy would be Sinatra's man in the next Presidential election. He was a natural Democrat anyway; the brave new world which Kennedy promised must have appealed to him; and Kennedy's brother-in-law, Peter Lawford, was in the Clan too. The Republican Press loathed Sinatra enough already and now, seeing a man whose money, glamour and influence on the Italian vote could prove very important in the election, they waited to pounce. As so often, Sinatra duly produced his hostage to fortune when it was revealed in March 1960, after he had tried to keep it quiet, that he was hiring the novelist, Albert Maltz, to write the screenplay of William Bradford Huie's book, *The Execution of Private Slovik*. Maltz had been the scriptwriter on *The House I Live In*, the plea for racial tolerance which had won Sinatra his first Oscar.

The mixture was potential political dynamite. Maltz was one of the notorious 'Hollywood Ten', the left-wing screenwriters who had refused to testify before the House UnAmerican Activities Committee in 1950 at the height of the evil mania of McCarthyism. He had been imprisoned for a year, and blacklisted in Hollywood ever since, although working at cut rates under a pseudonym. Slovik was the only American soldier to have been executed by the Army since the Civil War. The witch-hunt began as soon as the news was known, and whatever the rights and wrongs of the matter, the renewed sight of the papers in full cry was not edifying. Hedda Hopper sounded tallyho in the *Los Angeles Times* with 'If Sinatra loves his country he won't do this', and the singer's attempt to reply in print, which revealed that Maltz agreed with Sinatra that the Army was right and appealed to the principles of the American Bill of Rights, cut no ice at all.

John Wayne had demanded to know what Kennedy's attitude might be to the hiring of this blacklisted 'pinko' writer. All kinds of other threats, financial and political, were made against Sinatra and his friends, and the crescendo was reached with a campaign run day after day in the *Hollywood Reporter* by one Mike Connolly. Samples from his writing – Sinatra as 'Commie apologist' and Maltz as 'a sneaky, switchhitting, strikebreaking FINK' – scarcely indicate the strength of his poison, which was squirted at Picasso, Charles Chaplin and Paul Robeson as well as Maltz and Sinatra. The uproar was too potentially damaging for a Presidential hopeful. According to Sinatra biographer Tony Scaduto, using the words of a Kennedy aide: 'Joe Kennedy' (JFK's father) 'called Sinatra and told him he'd either have to drop Maltz or dissociate himself from Jack Kennedy's campaign. Sinatra dropped Maltz.'

The public statement he made had a certain logic to it, but it must have hidden a deep well of bitterness and disappointment. 'Due to the reactions of my family, my friends and the American public, I have instructed my attorneys to make a settlement with Albert Maltz and to inform him that he will not write the screenplay of *The Execution of Private Slovik*. I had thought the major consideration was whether or not the resulting script would be in the best interests of the United States. Since my conversation with Mr Maltz had indicated that he had an affirmative, pro-American approach to the story, and since I felt fully capable as producer of enforcing such standards, I have defended my hiring of Mr Maltz. But the American public has indicated that it feels the morality of hiring Mr Maltz is the more crucial matter and I will accept the majority opinion.'

That problem out of the way, Sinatra and the Clan (he even tamely had to deny its existence when it, too, was used as a stick to beat Kennedy) moved into action to raise funds for the Democratic candidate. Sinatra and Lawford, Tony Curtis and Shirley MacLaine were in the forefront of the drive. Sammy Davis kept comparatively low, and even postponed his marriage to May Britt for a time, when a racial smear was tried. But nothing could stop the Kennedy bandwagon. It was no surprise when, after his victory at the polls, the new President asked Sinatra to organise his inaugural gala. It was among the greatest of all star-studded events of its kind ever seen. In alphabetical order, Harry Belafonte, Leonard Bernstein, Nat King Cole, Tony Curtis, Bette Davis, Jimmy Durante, Ella Fitzgerald, Gene Kelly, Frederic March, Ethel Merman (and she was a Republican!), Laurence Olivier, Sidney Poitier and Eleanor Roosevelt (widow of the late Franklin Delano Roosevelt) were only part of the line-up. Not even the worst-ever blizzard in Washington's history, on 19 January 1961, which trimmed the audience, could mar its success or Sinatra's triumph, with advance ticket sales at $1½ million. He built on it a week later with another all-star bill at Carnegie Hall to celebrate the new President's release of Martin Luther King from a Georgia jail. So positively did Sinatra bask in the glow of White House approval that, despite a *Time* magazine jibe (Sinatra was supposed to become Ambassador to Italy, Sammy Davis to Kenya or Israel, and Dean Martin Secretary of Liquor), it really seemed possible he might go seriously into politics. 'We are all indebted to a great friend, Frank Sinatra. Tonight we have seen excellence,' trumpeted JFK at the inaugural gala. Visiting Sinatra's office in Los Angeles not long afterwards, Robin Douglas-Home noticed on the piano a framed portrait of President Kennedy bearing the handwritten inscription: 'For Frank, with the warm regards and best wishes of his friend.' Ironically, a decade or two later, Republican presidents Nixon and Reagan would be using terminology very similar.

What went wrong with Sinatra's relationship with the Kennedys appears, in retrospect, all too predictable. He had never been accepted into the inner circles of the Kennedy camp. Several of the closest Presidential aides didn't like him; even more distrusted him, looking askance at the Clan, worried about their apparently growing influence in the White House, and so concerned about persisting Mafia rumours that JFK's brother, Bobby, due to become Attorney General in the new Administration, began a secret investigation into Sinatra's alleged links with *mafiosi*. Very soon after his brother's election, Bobby Kennedy advised Jack to stop being friends with Sinatra. Nothing had been proven, nothing was certain, but to the younger Kennedy, Sinatra had just too many friends and contacts with question marks against them, and had already implicated JFK in compromising situations. One such situation, at a Clan gathering in Las Vegas in

January 1960, had been John F. Kennedy's meeting with an ex-girl friend of Sinatra's, Judith Campbell Exner, who then filled the same role with Kennedy for a period. Later still Sinatra introduced her to Sam Giancana, once the number one *mafioso* in Chicago, with whom he had a long-standing acquaintance, and she became his and another Mafia suspect, John Roselli's, playmate. Giancana, under pressure from the FBI, was also reported to have asked Bobby Kennedy to 'get in touch with Frank to set up a meeting' if a discussion of the problem would be useful. Few knew anything of these stories until the 1970s when FBI and CIA files were opened during the post-Watergate investigations, but Bobby Kennedy was suspicious enough in 1962 to lay a report written by his own department before Jack.

The bluntest biographer of Sinatra, Tony Scaduto, was among the first to put extracts from this on the line. It is full of 'mays' and 'appears' . . . 'Sinatra has had a long associa-

tion with hoodlums and racketeers which seems to be continuing. The nature of Sinatra's work may, on occasion, bring him into contact with underworld figures, but this cannot account for his friendship and/or financial involvement with people such as Joe and Rocco Rischetti, cousins of Al Capone, Paul Emilio D'Amato, John Formosa and Sam Giancana, all of whom are on our list of racketeers. No other entertainer appears to be mentioned nearly so frequently with racketeers.' And so on. It was damning enough for John F. Kennedy – and there were other murky areas concerning girl-friends and affairs which writers have struggled to explain ever since, areas in which the name of Marilyn Monroe figured especially prominently.

Scaduto, has a Kennedy aide saying: 'The thing few people seem to understand is that Kennedy was a star-fucker, would you believe it? . . . the President of the United States, young, rich and handsome, a superstar in his

own right, and he was enamoured of Hollywood glamour. And glamorous Hollywood
women . . . Sinatra supplied a need for Jack
Kennedy. He could have gotten a lot from the
White House if it hadn't been for that Mafia
stuff.'

In his biography of Marilyn Monroe of
1973, Norman Mailer tossed a handful of different theories into the air, beginning with her
first introduction to the Kennedys brought
about through Sinatra and Peter Lawford. In
May 1962 she was invited to sing 'Happy Birthday' to the President at a huge Madison Square
Garden party. 'The twenty thousand guests
listened to a sexual electric of magnets and
velvets,' says Mailer, graphically, 'Her voice is
every mischief. Every dead ear in the house will
stir. "She sounds like she knows him awful
well!" Kennedy, with a fine grin, disengages
himself from so supreme a throb of secret
history by remarking in his speech, "I can now
retire from politics after having Happy Birthday sung to me by Miss Monroe."'

Later, Mailer discusses the possibility of
Bobby Kennedy having had an affair with
Monroe. 'If the thousand days of Jack Kennedy might yet be equally famous for its nights,
the same cannot be said of Bobby. He was
devout, well married, and prudent . . . His
brother had managed miracles of indiscretions,
but Bobby had a hard enough attorney's head
to recognise that he was vulnerable to scandal
. . . Still, what a flirtation! He would call her
when he came to stay at Peter Lawford's house.
She would come to see him. Given the species
of house arrest in which she lived, how superb
to see him, how absolutely indispensable to her
need for a fantasy in which she could begin to
believe?'

This assessment of the situation did not
prevent Mailer from airing other theories,
ranging from a real affair between the pair,
then to Monroe, on the night of her death in
August 1962, trying (successfully or unsuccess-
fully) to reach Bobby Kennedy by telephone,
and all the way through to possibilities of

murder. Was the mystery over Monroe's death a cover-up to protect the Kennedys or, much more sinisterly, a ploy to amass ammunition against them? Mailer speaks again: 'For who is the first to be certain it was of no interest to the CIA, or to the FBI, or to the Mafia, and half the secret police of the world, that the brother of the President was reputed to be having an affair with a movie star who had once been married to a playwright,' (Arthur Miller) 'denied a passport for "supporting Communist movements" . . . Is there some fear in the summits of the CIA that the President himself – it is not long after the Bay of Pigs – is the willing or unwitting leader of a movement from the left that will wash at the roots of America? If such a suspicion is much too grand, one can still suppose that the head of the FBI was interested in obtaining a few more pieces of information to trade against the time he might be asked to reduce his power . . . By the end, political stakes were riding on her life, and even more on her death. If she could be murdered in such a way as to appear a suicide in despair at the turn of her love, what a point of pressure could be maintained afterwards against the Kennedys. So one may be entitled to speak of a motive for murder. Of course, it is another matter to find that evidence exists.'

So, too, one may point to the way in which the Sinatra – Kennedy – Monroe link placed Sinatra more and more at risk in his relationship with the first family. In his book on Sinatra (1976) the showbiz columnist, Earl Wilson, was far more explicit than Mailer about everything, including detailing the star's reaction to Bobby Kennedy's attempts to cut him out of the Washington scene. 'Frank seethed at Bobby's suddenly becoming so moralistic. He knew Bobby to be as much a swinger as Jack, and both got it from their father, whose sexual proclivities, extramaritally, had been celebrated his whole lifetime. Kennedy, Senior, had been a whiskey baron. Historically, the whiskey business is as sinful and corruptible as the gambling business. So what was Bobby yelling about?'

This, though, was only the half of it. At another point, Wilson described how in December 1975, pictures of the recently murdered mobster, Sam Giancana, the notorious Judith Campbell Exner, and Sinatra with the late John F Kennedy were all put adjacently in newspapers. He reported Sinatra's famous 'Hell hath no fury like a hustler with a literary agent' quip after Exner had talked of Sinatra's kinky sex tastes – and then he added a devastating footnote . . .' Early in 1974, I first exposed John F Kennedy's "swinging White House" and Kennedy himself as "the sexiest, swingingest President of the century", saying he kept his many dalliances secret from his wife Jacqueline with the help of friendly co-conspirators who served as "beards." Now I can add that Jack and Bobby Kennedy's brother-to-brother sharing of Marilyn Monroe (and other girls), passing between them, caused a big White House "inside" scandal. JFK, Sinatra, and Sam Giancana seemed to have had similar sharing arrangements.' Whatever the truth of this miasma of claims and speculation, it all added up to death for the Sinatra-Kennedy relationship.

The cooling-off had begun when a Clan outing to Joseph Kennedy's French Riviera villa was cancelled in the summer of 1961. Sinatra had built a special wing at his Palm Springs home to receive Jack Kennedy in March 1962. Kennedy cancelled at the last moment and went, instead, to stay with Bing Crosby. Finally, Sinatra and Peter Lawford quarrelled. Nothing was ever the same again between Sinatra and the Democrats. 'Vicious lies', he would say of the Mafia allegations against him. 'I don't investigate everyone I meet before I shake hands with him.' But the most special year or so of his life was over. Humiliated, disappointed and extremely bitter about Bobby Kennedy's part in the end of a beautiful friendship and of his political dreams, Sinatra would in 1967 and 1968 try to get on Hubert Humphrey's team in his battle against Bobby

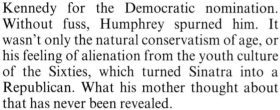

Kennedy for the Democratic nomination. Without fuss, Humphrey spurned him. It wasn't only the natural conservatism of age, or his feeling of alienation from the youth culture of the Sixties, which turned Sinatra into a Republican. What his mother thought about that has never been revealed.

If he could swallow his pride, however, there was more than enough for Sinatra to do. He did better than that. Rather in the fashion of 'showing them' which had been his motivation as he made his *From Here to Eternity* comeback, Sinatra plunged into the business of music and movies, the affairs of business and the job of helping himself while also helping those less fortunate than himself. He showed few signs of relaxing until the 1970s arrived.

Music first. Before the Kennedy break he had wound up his relationship with Capitol and, in typically drive-ahead style, founded his own record label, Reprise. He was deeply involved in everything to do with the new company, both musically and businesswise, especially after he realised that Capitol were going to mount a major campaign to kill off the new small label. They did so with even more gusto when he announced that the public would be hearing a 'new, happier, emancipated Sinatra, untrammelled, unfettered, unconfined', implying that at Capitol he had been trammelled, fettered and confined. In 1961 and 1962 there were writs flying between the two companies and a marketing battle over Sinatra titles in which the giant Capitol was almost bound to have the edge. But the massive publicity simply served to help the sales of *all* Sinatra albums. Sinatra on Capitol sold brilliantly (a dozen albums in the charts in summer 1962) and so did Sinatra on Reprise, with six best-sellers. Outselling even Elvis and the rockers, Sinatra

got so much money with his Capitol royalties he was able to get Reprise out of debt and make it a highly saleable proposition. In 1963 he got $10 million plus continuing one-third ownership plus all kinds of tasty residuals from Jack Warner of Warner Brothers in a merger deal. The roster of artists had become impressive: not only Clansmen like Sammy Davis Junior and Dean Martin, but also Count Basie, Duke Ellington and even Bing Crosby. There was an enthusiastic exclusive in the *Melody Maker* of 27 July 1963, when the old groaner signed at 59. 'Let's face it – Sinatra is a king,' said Crosby. 'He is a very sharp operator, a keen record chief, and has a keen appreciation of what the public wants.'

It was plain from a long interview which he gave to his unacknowledged press spokesman, Joe Hyams—who used to perform the same task for Humphrey Bogart—in the July 1962 issue of *Cosmopolitan* magazine that the affairs of business were increasingly important to him. 'Eventually, I want to be less and less before the public and more and more in the background,' said Sinatra. 'I figure that as an actor and as a singer I have only a few more years to go. I'll be 47 years old in December. I won't really have had it, but you know, when I get around that age there's not much I'll want to play or could play. Frankly, I'm fascinated with finances. I've been performing 30 years now and I'm getting a little lazy about this kind of work.' A piece in *Show Business Illustrated*, also by Hyams and entitled *Sinatra Inc*, had him looking forward to a future as 'a high-level executive', earning much more from business than from being a singer and actor – a pleasant prospect for someone reputed to have earned around eleven million dollars between 1941 and 1946, thirty million in the years 1953–60,

After his rejection by the Kennedys, Sinatra seemed to put more and more effort into his work for charities – work which inevitably brought him into contact with royalty in various countries. Princess Margaret would greet him at a charity show in London's Festival Hall in 1962, Prince Rainier and Princess Grace at the Monte Carlo Sporting Club. This year of 1962 was when he journeyed round the world, at his own expense, raising a million or more dollars for children – and, en route, visiting youngsters at the Sunshine Home for Blind Children in Northwood, England, and uplifting another child in his arms at a Paris nursing home for the treatment of crippled boys.

Sinatra's music in the 1960s became much more adventurous – and specifically, much more jazz-oriented. He worked with, among others, Sy Oliver, Duke Ellington and particularly (left) the great Count Basie. After they appeared together at the Newport Jazz Festival of 1965, one of Sinatra's biographers, Arnold Shaw, wrote: 'No one individual so electrified and literally possessed the festival as did Sinatra.'

and twenty million annually in the 1960s.

Sinatra the performer failed to fade away as decisively as he suggested he might, and his own musical output during the decade was, in general, of the highest quality. It is fashionable to knock some of his rock-tinged or modern-pop-influenced albums, and he made his mistakes – although I have the softest of spots for some of the experiments, like the song sequence, *Watertown*, by Bob Gaudio and Jake Holmes, which were very brave failures – but he grew all the time, broadening his range, for ever seeking a new way to do things. Typical of the early Reprise titles were gems like his salute to Tommy Dorsey, *I Remember Tommy*, and a collaboration with Nelson Riddle, *Sinatra's Sinatra*, a series of beautiful performances even if they did not have the passionate involvement of his 1950s work with Riddle. Then, and much more adventurously, he soared into jazz collaborations on record with Count Basie (three albums, 1961–66) using Neal Hefti as arranger, Duke Ellington (*Francis A. and Edward K.*, in 1968) and with the Brazil bossa nova composer, Antonio Carlos Jobim (1967 and again on part of the 1971 'retirement' album, *Sinatra and Company*).

His movement towards jazz climaxed perhaps in his historic appearance with Basie at the Newport Jazz Festival in 1965. Arnold Shaw's description in his book, *Sinatra*, is eminently quotable: 'I have attended these annual 4 July leviathan presentations since their inception in 1955. These have been many memorable moments, like the "discovery" of trumpeter Miles Davis in 1955 and the first appearance of Dave Brubeck in 1958. No one individual so electrified and literally possessed the Festival as did Sinatra in 1965.' There were those who sniffed, of course – like Whitney Balliett, who attacked Sinatra for turning Basie into a 'pop sideman' – but let's not worry with arguments about whether Sinatra's *really* a 'jazz singer' or not. Consistently he isn't, but sometimes he goes very close, and the liberal spicing of his work with jazz feeling, his

championing of the music, and the recognition of his talent by so many jazz musicians is good enough for me and, I think, most people. A poll of jazz musicians conducted by the English-born critic, Leonard Feather, in 1965 gave Sinatra the 'greatest ever' male vocalist title; closest to his 56 votes was Nat King Cole's 13.

That 1965 was one hell of a year all round. At 50, Sinatra could now aptly become sober, autumnal and reminiscent in mood, and the public took all that sentiment to its heart. Sinatra's faithful fans were middle-aged, as nostalgic as he. There was a brilliant single, arranged by Gordon Jenkins, *It Was a Very Good Year*, which won two Grammys, one more than did the similar kind of album, *September of my Years*, and yet again a touch of the autobiographical backward looks with the double album, *A Man and his Music*. Sinatra had never made the Top Ten in the 1960s. *Very Good Year* did, and amazingly three later singles – *Strangers in the Night*, *That's Life* and *Somethin' Stupid* (with daughter Nancy) – all made No. 1 in America, despite The Beatles, The Stones, The Beach Boys and all in a period when it was almost impossible for good balladeers to make the charts at all. And still to come in 1968 and 1969 were the Don Costa albums – *Cycles*, the Sinatra flag-waver, *My Way*, and *A Man Alone*, all of them vibrant at least in parts with that feeling of autobiographical truth which had made his first recordings of the 1950s so moving. His attempts to cope with rock-pop couldn't always work, for sometimes the sentiments were alien to him, often the language was too, and even the melodic and rhythmic patterns seemed apart from his world. Sinatra's roots were in the 1940s and 1950s and he has always seemed at his best extending that style, the tough little crooner from the tough hard streets of Hoboken and Broadway singing to make it in the world of Berlin, Gershwin and Cole Porter. Fey Rod McKuen words aren't really for him (*A Man Alone*), nor the wide-eyed naivety of Joni Mitchell's *Both Sides Now*

The 1960s unrolls, and soon it is time for more new ventures. In the picture below, Sinatra gets to work with Count Basie for one of his jazzier outings.
And on the opposite page, the romance between Sinatra and a Mia Farrow with long locks is blossoming. This picture was taken on the set of *Von Ryan's Express* at 20th Century Fox in Hollywood. Later they would marry, and in a gesture of the utmost mystery – but probably symbolic in some way – she would hack back her hair to a little-boy look.

(on *Cycles*), but there are composers who suit. Paul McCartney, Jimmy Webb and Paul Simon spring to mind among the moderns he has attempted. 'Attempted' is the point; Sinatra kept on trying, and while you keep on trying you keep on living.

He was still game to try it again even in the marriage stakes. He had had a run in 1961 with dancer Juliet Prowse, one of the 'new women' – meaning that she wasn't about to give up her career and be the good little subservient Italian wife that Sinatra in some moods seemed to want. After proposing marriage to her, they were engaged, but for six weeks only. Romance, romance with love, broke out again in unlikely fashion in the *annus mirabilis* of 1965. Perhaps Sinatra was riding on such a cresting wave that he felt he couldn't go wrong – records and concerts apart, there was a ratings-topping CBS documentary, *Sinatra*, an NBC special, *Sinatra, A Man and his Music*, in which he had for once been a knockout on TV, and his face had been cover material on three major news magazines, *Look*, *Newsweek* and *Life*, with the last-named having its first sellout issue since Kennedy's assassination. Whatever the reasons, and whatever the chemistry which happened between them, he and Mia Farrow, a woman almost 30 years younger, actress daughter of actress Maureen O'Sullivan, suddenly seemed to be in love. She was a 'new woman' too; independent of mind, brainy, and in the slightness of her frame rather different from most Sinatra belles. He met her while filming *Von Ryan's Express* in October 1964. In summer 1965 she and Sinatra went on a cruise to the Kennedy place at Hyannis Port. The media wrote reams on what *Time* described as 'the most closely observed cruise since Cleopatra floated down the Nile to meet Mark Antony.' Then ensued more waiting, with uncertainties and the occasional huff. Most newspaper writers assumed that when Mia chopped off her hair to its little-boy look it was a protest at not having been invited to Sinatra's 50th birthday party at Big Nancy's place.

Salvador Dali was pleased to call it 'mythical suicide'. No matter – on 19 July 1966, they were unexpectedly married, with no members of either family present, at the Sands Hotel, Las Vegas.

Talking of their first meeting, Mia Farrow said: 'I liked him instantly. He rings true. He is what he is.' Very true. The problem was, however, that either she didn't totally appreciate what Sinatra could be like, or that Sinatra the wooer was very different from Sinatra the husband who expected his wife to be compliant and obedient, or a mixture of both. In truth the odds against the marriage lasting must have been considerable, since Mia didn't care for Sinatra's entourage much and when he made that notorious Clan-type crack in public about 'a broad I can cheat on' (which was obviously not intended to be taken seriously) his young bride sat almost paralysed with shocked humiliation, in tears. She withdrew swiftly from him, and the needs of work often separ-

his father to sing with the official 'Tommy Dorsey Orchestra'. As he made his major debut at the Americana Hotel, New York, in September 1963, *Life* magazine put both Frank senior and junior on its cover. It was not only as a singer that he was to make the headlines. On 8 December, just over a fortnight after John F. Kennedy had been assassinated in Dallas, and with Sinatra senior having just come through a crisis over his holdings in two Nevada casinos, Frank junior was kidnapped from his motel room close by Harrah's Casino in the gambling resort of Lake Tahoe, Nevada. Sinatra senior, in Palm Springs at the time, flew through a snowstorm to work with FBI officers on the case and personally made delivery of the $240,000 demanded, via the usual telephone point-to-point routine, at a disused gas station in Los Angeles.

Following the release of Sinatra junior, the three kidnappers were soon caught. It was a fairly amateurish affair, so much so that at the trial in February 1964 the defence suggested the kidnapping had been arranged as a publicity stunt. This was not believed, and later Sinatra senior successfully sued ITV in Britain for a similar suggestion on a panel show, giving the substantial damages to the Sunshine Home for Blind Babies in the UK, just as he sued the BBC and won over the suggestion that Mafia influence had gained him the role of Maggio back in 1953. The publicity stunt idea seems ridiculous in retrospect. More to the point may be both the problem he had over his gambling interests in the summer of 1963 and his deep sense of shock at Kennedy's death, despite the rejection of Sinatra by the President. Without going deeply into the casino situation, the whole issue had blown up because of Bobby Kennedy's intensive drive against racketeers, during the course of which the name (yet again) of Sam Giancana was involved. He had been seen visiting the casino at the Cal-Neva Lodge in Lake Tahoe, in which Sinatra had a large holding, in defiance of a ban placed on him by the Nevada State Gaming Authority. Sinatra,

ated them in 1967. They quarrelled on the 'phone, he hectored her when she flew to see him in Miami and his public announcement on 22 November 1967 that they had 'mutually agreed to a trial separation' came as no surprise. Nor did the completion of divorce proceedings by Mia in Mexico the following August. The grounds cited were scarcely news either. Incompatability.

Sinatra's children were, of course, all around the same age as Mia Farrow and were making their way in showbiz just like her. He would help them and would perform with them whenever it seemed appropriate – he had hits, like *Somethin' Stupid* in 1967, with daughter Nancy – just as they would unite with him later to prepare the approved text of his life and the approved TV programmes to signal his 70th birthday in 1985. Perhaps the most fascinating of these familial connections was the emergence in 1963 of his son, Frank Sinatra Junior as he was called, almost as a clone of

with extreme vehemence, reacted against the demand that he should bar Giancana from the lodge and the threat to withdraw his gaming licence. The authority would not let go, and just as everyone was preparing for a real punch-up, Sinatra sidestepped it.

'Since I have decided that I belong in the entertainment industry and not in the gaming industry, no useful purpose would be served by devoting my time and energies convincing the Nevada gaming officials that I should be part of their gaming industry,' said his statement as he sold off his stake in the casinos of the Cal-Neva and The Sands in Las Vegas while keeping his investment in the hotels. Many reasons have been suggested for this. Perhaps he was threatened, maybe even by Giancana, himself shot in the head and killed mysteriously in 1975. Perhaps the later kidnapping was some kind of warning. Perhaps Sinatra had decided he would cooperate more fully in Bobby Kennedy's investigations. Perhaps he was still hoping to get back into the good books of the White House and decided to try removing some of the less publicly acceptable facets of his image. Perhaps none of these things – the exit from gambling a genuine response to his many other commitments, the kidnap just one of those dangers which the famous and their offspring have faced for years.

As for Sinatra junior's career, the Lake Tahoe episode was just an interruption. Little more than a month after his release he was in the UK, with the Tommy Dorsey band and a 260-pound ex-Washington Redskin 'minder', refusing to answer questions about his ordeal, the case being *sub judice*, but also telling me: 'It's my own judgement. Personally I choose to forget about it.' At 20, his voice was a fair sub-Sinatra senior model – although he claimed this was coincidental – but what struck me most forcibly was his similarity to his father in other ways. He had the same sallow complexion and prominent cheekbones, a bow-tie of course, and even shared his parent's then downbeat view of rock 'n' roll, although he

didn't put it as racily.

Possessed of a quaint formalism of speech – he kept calling me 'sir' – and impeccable politeness, he said: 'In my humble opinion, I find myself concerned about the third rate entertainment that comes out of my country. It sets up a bad image. American music has degenerated with rock 'n' roll. It's a disease that's spread across the world. We hope we can give Europe a better idea of our country's music.' Well, it didn't quite work out. The 1960s were too early for a 1940s and 1950s nostalgia kick. Frank junior has never made it really big as a singer and neither, despite her *These Boots Are Made For Walking* in 1967, has Nancy junior. Perhaps with a father so wealthy they have lacked the motivation for the long, hard showbiz slog. Maybe they had better things to do.

They have always been incredibly loyal to him, whatever the twists and turns of his life – as, again unusually, have been all three of his

ex-wives, with Nancy the first as a model mother for his children and Ava and Mia seemingly very supportive at his public appearances. The magnetic aura of the man in these situations does seem a truly remarkable phenomenon. During the 1960s they will have had many reasons to be proud of him other than his musical achievements. His movies may have been variable in quality, but there were still some good ones. Nothing in the decade exceeded his performance as an ex-POW in *The Manchurian Candidate* (1962). 'A thriller guaranteed to raise all but the limpest hair', said *The New Yorker* ... to which *Variety* added 'Sinatra is again a wide-awake pro creating a straight, quietly humorous character of some sensitivity.' He didn't reach such heights again until *The Detective* in 1968 in which he played a tough, honest career cop, bedazed by the failure of his marriage and appalled by the corruption around him. 'Sinatra has honed his laconic, hep veneer to

the point of maximum credibility,' commented *The Hollywood Reporter* of his painful, emotional and committed performance. For the rest there were the four Clan movies – *Ocean's Eleven* (1960), *Sergeants Three* (1962), *4 for Texas* (1963) and *Robin and the Seven Hoods* (1964), all following a formula, all full of self-indulgence, all mildly entertaining, and all profitable – plus other 'tough' roles like the cold-war spy in *The Naked Runner* (1967) and the quasi-Raymond Chandler-style private eye Tony Rome, both in the movie of that name (1967) and in *Lady in Cement* (1968). His sole try at being a director, the old-fashioned *None but the Brave* in 1965 – significantly the astonishingly successful year in which he celebrated his 50th birthday – was as technically faultless, if uninspired, as his temporary farewell to movies in 1970, the tacky and unfunny western spoof *Dirty Dingus Magee*, was dreadful.

One-time admirers, like *The New York Times*'s Bosley Crowther, couldn't stand it. 'It is provoking – nay, disturbing and depressing beyond belief – to see this acute and awesome figure turning up time and time again in strangely tacky and trashy motion pictures,' fumed Crowther. 'His *Von Ryan's Express* was an outrageous and totally disgusting display of romantic exhibitionism .... *Marriage on the Rocks* was a tawdry and witless trifle .... Now comes the latest selection, *Tony Rome* ....The clue to Sinatra's sad shortcoming is that he wilfully or carelessly allows his film – and his film it is, beyond question – to be sprinkled with many globs of sheer bad taste that manifest a calculated pandering to those who are easily and crudely amused. What grieves a longtime moviegoer is to remember how bright and promising he used to be, beginning with his charming performance in *Anchors Aweigh* and moving on into his poignant performance in *From Here to Eternity*.' Without wanting to praise many of Sinatra's Sixties films, that blast is perhaps a touch overdone, a touch unfair – but then there's none so savage as a critic on the rebound if, for whatever reason, his one-time protege lets down the side. That kind of reaction is a well-known phenomenon of the arts pages, not to be taken over-seriously, and it has been Sinatra's lot often to have praise mixed with criticism and snideness, as if people can't believe that there are times when he acts without cynical premeditation or boorish excess.

Such was the case with one of his most magnificent charitable gestures (as I see it) in the spring of 1962 when, on 15 April, he set out on a two-month world tour to raise money for children's charities, having declared himself 'an over-privileged adult'. He went from Los Angeles to Los Angeles, via Tokyo, Hong Kong, Tel Aviv, Athens, Rome, Milan, Paris, Monte Carlo, London (which he regarded as 'the climax of the whole tour', appearing at the Royal Festival Hall before Princess Margaret) and New York which, even if you do your best to wrap yourself in cottonwool, is quite a schedule. He paid all expenses, over $½ million, himself and he raised more than $1 million. This was still not enough for some of his long-established critics, including *Time* which produced a curiously ambivalent piece.

'Who is this prince of charity, this prophet of peace, this generous, sober, chaste diplomat, this new Frank Sinatra?' the magazine demanded, with high sarcasm, at first. Then, after suggesting that the tour was a stunt to 'camouflage his unappealing Rat Pack image' and to impress President Kennedy, the piece concluded, 'His friends insist that there is no new Sinatra, that the new innocent abroad is only the old Sinatra with the old resentments stripped away... And overseas the tour's inspiration matters less than the good it does.'

Of course, of course. Who cares about the motivation so long as things that help and uplift and give hope get done? This comment is equally applicable to the Band Aid and Live Aid extravaganzas to assist Ethiopian sufferers in 1985. Sinatra has been so clobbered to excess

for some of his less admirable characteristics that it seems, by the same token, excessively churlish to praise him with faint damns when he acts with splendid generosity. He has been generous all his life, and long may he continue to be so.

'Ruthless, yet sentimental ... a defier of convention who seemingly delights in flouting the rules and customs of accepted social behaviour,' Robin Douglas-Home had written of him in 1962: 'He emits a curious sort of electricity, a peculiar galvanism probably generated by the kinetic war that must continually rage between the paradoxes of his inner self.' By the end of the decade, the generator and the current were beginning to run low – and no wonder. It had been an action-packed decade, with more crammed into it than most superstars get through in a lifetime. Sinatra must have felt a trifle bruised as well, perhaps, as finding the pace rather hot for a man of 55.

He was immensely saddened by the death of his father, Martin, in January 1969 ... 'tight-lipped, tearful and grief-stricken' was Earl Wilson's description of Sinatra, whose red-rose wreath said simply 'Beloved Father'. He kept saying he couldn't find any good film scripts, when an equal part of his frustration seemed to be simple boredom with movies. As one film director said, watching him do a recording retake because just one consonant had been marginally overemphasised: 'Just try and get him to re-do scenes before the camera. He's a genius at thinking up ways of making cuts and insertions – anything to avoid a re-take.' The other side of that coin lay in Sinatra's observation to Arnold Shaw: 'The key to good acting on the screen is spontaneity, and that's something you lose a little with each take.' In the late 1960s, Sinatra was saying he couldn't find good songs, either – and that was probably more true. 'There's a lot of garbage out there. Nobody's writing any songs for me and I don't know what to do about it.'

Hearing that kind of comment made me think of one of his most memorable quotes, given during the course of a long and revealing piece in *Playboy* magazine in 1963 — memorable and typical too in the essential truth of its sentiments and gaucheness of its language. 'Being an 18-carat manic-depressive and having lived a life of violent emotional contradictions, I have an over-acute capacity for sadness as well as elation. . . . Whatever else has been said about me personally is unimportant. When I sing, I believe, I'm honest. . . . You can be the most artistically perfect performer in the world, but the audience is like a broad—if you're indifferent, endsville.'

With rock in the ascendent, perhaps he believed the audience was becoming as indifferent to him as he was, at least temporarily, to it. He even had a physical problem, a painful affliction in his right hand – the one in which he held the microphone, his instrument – called Dupuyten's Contracture, which distorts palm and fingers. An operation in 1970 alleviated the condition without totally curing it. A gun had been pulled on him, too, at Caesar's Palace in Las Vegas during a row there over gambling credit. No one could have been totally surprised when, on 21 March 1971, he announced his retirement. The man who never was a quitter was, it seemed, about to quit. The phraseology was revealing. . . .

'I wish to announce, effective immediately, my retirement from the entertainment world and public life,' it began, and went on to elaborate on his 'great and good fortune' in enjoying three decades which had been 'fruitful, busy, uptight, loose, sometimes boisterous, occasionally sad, but always exciting.' But, he continued, there had been 'little room or opportunity for reflection, reading, self-examination and that need which every thinking man has for a fallow period, a long pause in which to seek a better understanding of changes occurring in the world. This seems a proper time to take that breather.'

Some of the papers, like a correspondent in *The Guardian* in London, had a whale of a time with the style and context of that announcement, affectedly puzzled that anyone could enter into 'reflection and self-examination' by publicly announcing the phenomenon three months ahead of the event. Again, the media habit of getting the knife in. The whole way of handling the retirement was, take it or leave it, pure and quintessential Sinatra. So was his quip to Thomas Thompson, a writer who'd observed him for some time: 'Hell, I just quit, that's all. I don't want to put on any more makeup. I don't want to perform any more.' And so too, very very Sinatra, was the manner of his exit.

On 14 June 1971, at the Los Angeles Music Center, Sinatra made his farewell appearance. It was for charity, the Motion Picture and Television Relief Fund, and tickets were $250 apiece. 'It's time to put back the Kleenex and stifle the sob,' said actress Rosalind Russsell, introducing him, 'for we still have the man, we still have the blue eyes, those wonderful blue eyes, that smile, for one last time we have the man, the greatest entertainer of the twentieth century.' The famous and very neat description of the climax of Sinatra's performance is that of the writer who called the affair 'an epic evening of epic evenings', Earl Wilson . . . . 'He asked for the stage to be darkened, just a pinpoint spot on him. Midway through the song, he lit a cigarette. The smoke wrapped him within it. He was in silhouette. He came to the last line of the song, *Excuse me while I disappear*. And he did.''

Not quite as pat as that, however. The last line of *Angel Eyes*, apt as it seemed, was not the precise end, as Patrick Doncaster faithfully reported in London. Sinatra reappeared as Nelson Riddle reprised *My Way*. Next, Sammy Davis Junior clambered on-stage and dragged Sinatra back before the audience again, embracing and kissing him. Then it finally was over, and maybe it was a pity that the disappearing act hadn't been left *tout court* in its perfection – but then, where would showbusiness be without encores?

'Getting the keynote right'

TWO BARS REST

LIFE FOR SINATRA IN THE 1960S HAD BECOME increasingly centred on Palm Springs, California, that sandy bolthole to which most Hollywood stars run sooner or later, a place of incredibly green, manicured lawns and swish palaces, an inland suburb for the well-heeled which likes to call itself the golfing capital of the world. It became even more his stamping-ground after his retirement – a routine of endless golf, drinks at six and polite chat with the social crowd for the number one saloon singer, stud and hellraiser of the twentieth century, who predictably proceeded to go crazy with the sheer bland boredom of it all. It drove him back to work.

He was limbering up in stages for that return over a long period during the spring, summer and fall of 1973. In the words of one Joe Masters, resident pianist that year at the Hotel Trinidad in Palm Springs: 'Every night Frank's cooking up a storm,' he was reported as saying. 'Last night, after we closed here, I was up at his house playing till six this morning. I didn't get to bed till eight. I'll be going up there again later tonight, soon as we close, and God knows when I'll get to bed. . . . If this is retirement, then give me three weeks' workout with a chain gang to catch up with my sleep.'

The two-year charade of retirement had to be played out before the renewed action implied in Masters' words was taken. However, this period was not a wasted one for Sinatra. He needed the break at first, of that there could be little doubt, and he lived relatively quietly for around a year. Although it was perhaps not planned, he was also preparing himself for the next decade or so. At the most personal level, he would take what looked like his final and successful shot at building a lasting relationship with a woman, although even that was queried by the sensationalist *New York Post* in the summer of 1985, on the very day of the ninth anniversary of Sinatra's marriage to Barbara Marx. Rumours of a split between the two were vehemently denied by the Sinatra camp, however, and press reports called 'irresponsible'.

Sinatra had known Barbara Marx, wife of the onetime straight man of the Marx brothers, Zeppo, since the 1960s. The singer had even introduced her to Spiro Agnew, the politician who would become vice-president to Richard Nixon in 1973. A tennis party or two was arranged with Agnew and Mrs Marx, and for a time the newspaper columnists scented romance, until in 1970 she left her husband to live permanently with Sinatra. Their marriage in 1976, combined with the death of Sinatra's mother the following year, will doubtless have contributed to the softening of his personality.

One incident during his official 29 months of retirement was to rebound to Sinatra's credit, win him influential friends, and restrain considerably that tide of negative public opinion which had been fed liberally on stories linking him with the Mafia. This issue had been dormant for some years until, in 1972, the House Select Committee on Crime again began to pursue Sinatra. Incredibly, the noble Congresspeople did so on the basis of 'evidence' from a mobster called Joseph 'The Baron' Barboza, a hit-man for the Mafia with a score of twenty-seven admitted killings. Normal people may well blink at the credulity of the politicians and the morality of the whole business.

Amongst many allegations, Barboza maintained that Sinatra was 'vice-president' of the Berkshire Downs racecourse at Hancock, Massachusetts (a track long since closed, after a fire destroyed its main stands) when 'ringers' were run at long odds and Mafia money was invested in big winning bets. When Sinatra sidestepped the controversy by slipping off to England – ostensibly to have talks about a movie musical of the well-known fairy story, *The Little Prince* – and was sighted at the Epsom Derby, England's premier horseracing classic, always held in early June, the newspapers which disliked him had a field day with allegations that he was trying to avoid appearing before the House Committee. Even the Committee seemed to be having second thoughts about their tawdry witness and the propriety of the subpoenas they had issued against Sinatra. He foxed them all by accepting the invitation to appear before the Congress *after* his would-be inquisitors had nervously torn up their subpoenas.

He appeared, in open Committee session, on 18 July 1972, with around 500 people packed into the hearing room and with the TV cameras rolling. He then proceeded to tear the Committee to pieces. Growing in confidence, he answered every question thrown at him with considerable ease and some contempt, and no scriptwriter could have improved on the way he went on the attack from the start. Of Barboza he declared: 'This bum went running off at the mouth. I resent it. I won't have it. I'm not a second-class citizen and let's get that clear right now.' Next he waved about a newspaper containing a headline: WITNESS LINKS SINATRA TO REPUTED MAFIA FIGURE. 'That's charming, isn't it? Isn't that charming? That's all hearsay evidence, isn't it?'

The Committee cringed (except for those of its members who later shook him by the hand), conceded his point and was powerless under Sinatra's relentless and sometimes heated logic. He said that he had never been to Berkshire Downs and that, in his position, he was constantly open to exploitation by people he scarcely knew. The applause rang out as Sinatra walked triumphantly from the inquisition, and one of two Congressmen who shook his hand, Representative Charles Rangel, was reported by Earl Wilson to have said: 'You're still Chairman of the Board.' Sinatra underlined his victory with (such irony!) his now-famous piece of journalism which appeared in *The New York Times* of 24 July 1972, a week after the Committee hearing. It was headlined in customary sober *Times* fashion, *We Might Call This The Politics Of Fantasy*, with Sinatra's name in very small type and a discreet footnote which said, 'Frank Sinatra, singer and actor, is now retired.' These ringing paragraphs illustrate the tone:

'The most important (question) is the rights of a private citizen in this country when faced with the huge machine of the central Government. In theory, Congressional investigating committees are fact-finding devices which are supposed to lead to legislation. In practice, as we learned during the ugly era of Joe McCarthy, they can become star chambers in which 'facts' are confused with rumor, gossip and innuendo, and where reputations and character can be demolished in front of the largest possible audience.

'In my case, a convicted murderer was allowed to throw my name around with abandon, while the TV cameras rolled on. His vicious little fantasy was sent into millions of American homes, including my own. Sure, I was given a chance to refute it, but as we have all come to know, the accusation often remains longer in the public mind than the defense. In any case, an American citizen, no matter how famous or obscure, should not be placed in the position of defending himself before baseless charges, and no Congressional committee should become a forum for gutter hearsay that would not be admissable in a court of law.'

Whatever the previously held opinions about Sinatra of those who read those words or heard about them, there could be little dispute about the justice and good sense of his case. There was wide agreement with him, and there were many who said that enough was enough. Sinatra had been sufficiently hounded about alleged associations with crime and criminals, across three decades. Not one charge had stuck. It was, yet again, Presidential election year, and those whom he was going to support now had rather less cause to worry. There was little doubt that his side would no longer be the Democrats.

His change of allegiance to the Republicans had, as we have seen, been heavily foreshadowed in the 1960s because of his disillusion with the Democrats who had effectively rejected him where once he had been warmly embraced. It is, however, inadequate to ascribe the switch simply to pique at the treatment handed out to him by the Kennedys and Hubert Humphrey. Sinatra's case is far deeper than that. Throughout his life he had been an old-style American Democrat – a fighter, a soldier against racism and bigotry, a firm believer in the right of ordinary people to choose what they do and how they order their lives. When he was growing up, in the 1930s and 1940s, government and unions (and the Democratic party, especially in the shape of Franklin D. Roosevelt) were vitally needed to protect the little man against the robber barons of industry and business, and to rebuild Depression-mauled America. Approaching the 1970s, Sinatra undoubtedly felt – as his *New York Times* piece suggested – that America, and Britain and many other countries too, had too much government and too much union power. Bureaucracies of the state and of state-blessed agencies were the enemies of freedom now.

He was, too, growing older, and the aging tend to be more conservative; he didn't much care for the rock'n'roll generation, as so many of his contemporaries didn't, or for the exaggerated contempt its young people often showed for him and his generation, including their parents; and for a self-made, self-educated battler the sight of all that college protest from well-fed kids who had never had to struggle for anything very much must have been sickening. Apart even from all that, there were pretty positive pre-Watergate reasons for voting Republican after the many dishonesties of the Democratic 1960s and the hash both Kennedy and Johnson had made of Vietnam, of Cuba, of relations with China and the rest. Sinatra's move to the right seems, in many ways, totally true to the more sensible and more thoughtful side of the man.

He would be attacked soon by the radical wing, of course, just as he had been by the hard right in his early days. The comments of critic Ralph Gleason – once a supporter of Sinatra's early view of rock as music for 'cretinous goons', but then a rocker himself – were typical of the bitterness felt at Sinatra's change of allegiance. 'He behaves, even if only half the print is true, like an arrogant despot with a court of sycophants Uncle Tomming their asses off,' wrote Gleason in the 6 June 1974 issue of *Rolling Stone* magazine. 'The voice is good today, but I don't believe, anymore, that he is one of us. He's one of *them* now, singing from the other side of the street, and I guess he doesn't have a whiff of how power-mad and totalitarian it all seems, those bodyguards and the Rat Pack and all that egocentric trivia that has nothing to do with music.'

The change in Sinatra came gradually, both before and after his retirement, as he began to become aligned with specific Republicans. Spiro Agnew, Governor of Maryland when he and Sinatra grew close in 1969, was the first, and his language about Sinatra could not have been warmer. 'A legend in his own time, not only in the world of entertainment, but in the world of philanthropy,' he could declare in 1972 as Sinatra was presented with a Medallion of Valor at a State of Israel Bonds dinner in Los Angeles. Next, Sinatra sided with Ronald Reagan during the gubernatorial campaign of 1970 in California, allied politically with his onetime sworn enemy, John Wayne, and saw his man elected. In particular he backed Reagan's hard line with demonstrating students at the University of California, Berkeley, and other colleges. The final stage, inevitable it now seems, was his support of Richard Nixon in the 1972 Presidential campaign, a task into which he threw himself as whole-heartedly as once he had done for the election of John F. Kennedy, even though the Republicans may not have needed his fund-raising talents as much as the Democrats had. He did all the usual American election duties at dinners and rallies, including singing, even in his 'retirement', at a Young Voters For Nixon demonstration in Chicago, and once again had the satisfaction of seeing his man make the White House. The new

It became almost a cliché in the 1960s and 1970s for Sinatra to cast himself as tough detective, either as cop or private eye. On the set of *Tony Rome* (below) he looked the part of private eye, but a decade later (bottom picture) in the company of his fourth wife, Barbara, he looks much more the relaxed, solid senior citizen. The 1973 picture opposite is historic. Sinatra stands next to Signora Andreotti, wife of the President of Italy, and Pat and Richard Nixon, then President. Sinatra had just sung at the White House . . . Nixon had praised him fulsomely and urged him to make a comeback . . . Sinatra did!

President's role in Sinatra's comeback year of 1973, doubtless encouraged by his Vice-President, Spiro Agnew, should not be underestimated.

First, he was reported to have called Sinatra privately after the Select Committee on Crime imbroglio in 1972 to congratulate him. Second, he reacted in somewhat unexpected fashion after Sinatra was involved in one of his most spectacular confrontations with a newspaper writer. While attending a private party Sinatra encountered Maxine Cheshire, a correspondent of the liberal *Washington Post*, who had been rehashing the Mafia story yet again while being continually provocative about Sinatra's alliance with Agnew, Nixon and the Republicans generally. The party, ironically, was a private pre-inaugural Republican celebration in early 1973 at a Washington club. When Cheshire approached Barbara Marx, who was with Sinatra, he exploded uncontrollably. His words, in the widely reported and accepted version, were: 'Get away from me, you scum. Go home and take a bath. I'm getting out of here, to get rid of the stench of Mrs Cheshire. . . . You're nothing but a two-dollar broad. . . . You've been laying down for two dollars all your life. Here's two dollars, baby, that's what you're used to.' Thereupon he stuffed the requisite dollar bills into her drink and stormed off, Sinatra again in his Mr Hyde role. Cheshire, hammily, made the most of the situation as maligned innocent and the newspapers erupted into self-righteous sentences. Surprisingly, within a few months Nixon reacted by rewarding Sinatra with an invitation to perform at the White House. Nixon loathed the *Washington Post* (and this was before Watergate!) even more than Sinatra loathed Maxine Cheshire.

So, on 17 April 1973, Sinatra turned up at the White House to sing for the visiting Italian Prime Minister, Giulio Andreotti, and Nixon indulged in rhetoric on the subject of the entertainer. He said: 'Once in a while, there is

a moment when there is magic in the room, when a singer is able to move us and capture us all, and Frank Sinatra has done that and we thank him ... this house is honoured to have a man whose parents were born in Italy, but yet from humble beginnings went to the very top in entertainment.'

It was, one might say, so warm a tribute as to be almost Sicilian. Sinatra cried. The same evening, it is believed, Nixon suggested he should sing once more for a wider public than the diplomatic audience at the White House. Sinatra will scarcely have needed any such urging to cease his retirement, and only 12 days later he was cutting three titles (the masters all destroyed, however) in a Hollywood recording studio. Later, during a two-week period in June, he recorded enough songs for a comeback album. He was said to have received more than 30,000 letters imploring him to make such an album.

By that stage, however, Sinatra may not have wanted to let it be known so widely that Nixon was on his cheer-team, for the Watergate affair erupted with such force after the investigations of the *Washington Post* writers, Carl Bernstein and Bob Woodward, that the very foundations of American political life seemed threatened. Ethel Kennedy, widow of Bobby, made her famed wounding quip: 'Did you ever think you would see a time when Frank Sinatra would be ashamed to be seen with a President of the United States?' And Sinatra's name was dragged further into the scandal when the implicated John Dean alleged that the singer was among a group of friends for whom Nixon had attempted to obtain tax favours. That was the extent of it, though.

Mostly Sinatra escaped any serious implications and he demonstrated yet again his particular code of loyalty by supporting the disgraced Agnew, who finally resigned his office following revelations about financial scandals during his Governorship of Maryland. At first Sinatra sought reinstatement and funds for Agnew. At the same time Agnew was a frequent visitor to Sinatra's Palm Springs home, and later as the decade continued would become a part of Sinatra's entourage in many cities, including London. Whatever the brave face he puts on it, however, 1973 wasn't the greatest year for Sinatra; and his boredom with retirement was peaking.

In September he made an unscheduled appearance to sing four songs at a benefit concert for the Los Angeles Music and Art School. Soon afterwards, the Songwriters of America named him 'Entertainer of the Century'. Out came the album he had recorded in June under the title *Ol' Blue Eyes Is Back*, with stunning versions of the so-apt *Let Me Try Again* and *Send In The Clowns*. At last, on 18 November, the new resurrection was completed, using the same title as the album, in the form of a one-hour TV special on NBC. In front of an invited black-tie audience, Sinatra formally announced his 'retirement from retirement'. Even though the show came third to a Dinah Shore special and a movie, *The Hospital*, with George C. Scott, on CBS and ABC, the critics were pretty unanimous in their approval. 'We thought we were through writing love letters to Frank Sinatra,' said Kay Gardella of the *New York Daily News*, not untypically. 'Here we go again!' Ol' Blue Eyes was indeed back, back with a vengeance.

A great resurrection is in train . . . Sinatra has come out of retirement in 1973, reportedly after tens of thousands of letters from fans, but equally and probably because of his own boredom. Here he is getting back into action for records and concerts with his long time associate and arranger, Gordon Jenkins.

'In the open, behind the wall'

THREE SCORE AND TEN

THE PATTERN OF SINATRA'S NEXT TEN YEARS OR so, up to the brink of his 70th birthday, was both distinct and distinctive. It fell into three phases. In the first, he embarked upon a couple of years of frenetic activity, during which he also had public battles with the Press, especially in Australia and Germany, as bitter in tone as had been the Cheshire escapade. It was as if he was determined to make up for the quieter years of 1971 to 1973. The typical Sinatra full-page trade press ads at the end of 1975, his 60th year, boasted that in 105 days he had given 140 performances to audiences of more than half a million, several of them for charity. During this period the media mostly applauded his shows, often in glowing terms, while criticising him unmercifully whenever he transgressed in other ways.

In the second phase, from 1976 to the early 1980s, Sinatra continued to perform but at a slower pace. He even made a return to film-making. He also shouted a lot less, in public at least, and the general view was that, after his marriage and his mother's death, he was becoming more the acceptable senior citizen. The period was also marked by a withdrawal from the media, from his fans, and from contact with 'ordinary' life. A wall of bodyguards and sealed-off hotel floors separated him from the real world. Many people did not like this at all. Finally, as he moved closer to 70, Sinatra entered a phase during which no one was quite certain what he would do in personal or professional terms, when his voice was less convincing, when several writers savaged his shows as well as him, when it began to seem, to paraphrase the words of *My Way*, as if the end might indeed be near. This uncertainty persisted up to the time of writing in 1985.

The crucial question about Sinatra's 1973 comeback is, of course, this: artistically, was it worth it? And the answer must be powerfully in the affirmative. On record he had his ups and downs, no doubt about that, and the output was comparatively thin. After *Ol' Blue Eyes Is Back* came the albums *Some Nice Things I've Missed* (1974), with Don Costa joining Gordon Jenkins as the important renewed arranging force, *The Main Event* (a live recording, with Woody Herman's band, at Madison Square Garden on 13 October 1974), *Trilogy* (1980, a significant three-album set), *She Shot Me Down* (1981) and *LA Is My Lady* (1984), which witnessed the re-entry into Sinatra's world of the fabled Quincy Jones, whose reputation in the rock and pop field was sky-high. Of these records, the two I like best are *Some Nice Things* and *Trilogy*. On the former, Michel Legrand's *What Are You Doing the Rest of Your Life?* as well as Stevie Wonder's *You Are The Sunshine of My Life* might have been made for him alone, especially in Don Costa's arrangements. On the three-record latter, a kind of survey of his singing career, 'Past', 'Present', 'Future', he goes from the gentle, lush ballad end of the scale to the uptempo swingers, with one arranger for each record and period – in chronological order Billy May, Don Costa and Gordon Jenkins. Some songs seem prophetic, like *Before the Music Ends*, the finale, done in a big, big version with chorus and the Los Angeles Philharmonic Orchestra; others were revamped versions of old Sinatra favourites, notably the very first song, his fourth recording of *The Song Is You*, a swinger done with Billy May. This, recorded on 18 September 1979, is one of several remarkably energetic performances for a man of nearly 64. What is more, the uncertainties in Sinatra's voice, the tension as one wondered if he would *quite* make a note or a leap, gave an extra edge of poignancy to his ballads, like *More Than You Know*, a classic example of art overcoming age and ability.

Sinatra has never lost his dedication, his care, his absolute belief in his art – and that's why he has remained at the top, despite errors of judgement like his attempt at a disco version of Cole Porter's *Night and Day* (1977) and the tacky title song of his 1984 album, a palpable attempt to cash in on Los Angeles as the venue for the Olympic Games of that year. In the main, however, the remarkable aspect of Sinatra in the past ten years has been his survival as an artist. If his records since 1973 have been relatively few and, although often very good, not of the supreme quality of the 1950s and 1960s, then his concerts of the 1970s were usually quite marvellous. I saw many of them, in London and America, and thought that the kind of criticism typified by a writer in the *Globe and Mail*, Toronto, who called him 'a vocal hasbeen, ripping off those who care about his music rather than his personality' was not merely inaccurate in judgement but *factually* wrong. It was simply not true that the voice had gone, and all the rest of his trickery and art was intact. Quoting from my own reviews in *The Sunday Times* of London, the intention is simply to indicate how, in the past ten years my views, at least, have not much changed (except in 1984, which I shall come to). Here, then, are two extracts. . . .

'His traits have been listed too often. Notice just two things, though. First, how perfectly he enunciates every end consonant. Second – the heart of it all – see how he *enjoys* his work. Sinatra responds to, loves, gets a kick from every nuance of beat and colour in the music. He's just knocked out by a good orchestration, is transformed by it. No wonder he performs popular songs so well. No wonder he couldn't stay retired. He lives, I conclude, for music. And the music lives for him.'

(Frank Sinatra at the London Palladium, 16 November 1975)

'He happens, in my view, to be singing presently with virtually all the mastery of a decade ago. The fear in his fifties that the vibrato was getting too heavy, the breath a touch short and the sound uncertain was dispelled on the first night. But ultimately Sinatra never did lean on all that; it was more in the phrasing, the diction, and the weaving of the accompaniment around him.'

(Frank Sinatra at the Royal Albert Hall, 6 March 1977)

And finally, there is a review of 17 September 1978, around eighteen months later, see page 148, when a marginal change in the voice could be detected, but didn't matter two hoots. It didn't matter two hoots to his lifelong fans either. Here, again, is Martha Weinman Lear talking in 1974 about both the voice and the effect of the man: 'The punch was still there. I can't explain it, but it was still there. It was just two years ago that the prominent portrait painter Aaron Shickler got a business call from Sinatra's office. His wife, Pete, answered the phone. Wait a minute, a voice at the other end said, we have Mr Sinatra on the line. And, as Mrs Shickler tells it, she damn near died. Her hand was unsteady, her breath came heavy. And then he said "Hello", and here was this woman, mature, posed, veteran of a thousand cocktail-party ripostes . . . and what she said, her lips fluttering around the mouthpiece, was this: "Oh my goodness", she said, "It sounds *just like you*" . . . It's Ol' Blue Eyes, now, at 59, with the paunch and the jowl and the wig, and the hell with them. The blue eyes still burn, the cuffs are still incomparably shot, the style, the *style*, is still all there, and what's left of the voice still gets to me like no other voice, and it always will.' Two other points are worth mentioning. Sinatra had mellowed enough by 1975 actually to write and thank me for my good review. Second, he was already in 1977 using a quip he would employ over and over during the next few years – including, incredibly, when a Hoboken college gave him, amid some controversy, an honorary degree in *engineering* in May 1985. 'May you live forever, and I hope the last voice you'll hear is mine.'

That kind of surface confidence marked every one of the three phrases of his existence since 1977 which we have identified, and we should begin with the turbulent first phase. At all too many times in his life, trouble and aggravation have never been far from Sinatra and his circle. And before the decade which was to see him gradually quieten down got to its point of relative calmness, there would be erup-

In her latter years, Sinatra's mother still played a crucial role in his life. Here (near right) he introduces her to Spiro Agnew, the disgraced Vice-President who became a regular member of the Sinatra entourage in the 1970s, and Ronald and Nancy Reagan, not too many years afterwards to make their way into the White House. The other picture was one of the last major family reunions before her death. Together (left to right) are: daughter Nancy, Frank jr, his wife Barbara, Sinatra himself, his mother and his youngest child, Tina.

tions galore. The enigma of Sinatra's twin-sided nature can never be totally solved. As journalist Patrick Doncaster observed in 1975: 'Still the furtive Francis, hiding round corners, slipping into hotels, cocooned by cronies, flinching from the camera and humanity ... still pursuing his personal wars and taking on whole nations single-handed.... How, I am left wondering, can Sinatra stride the world with a kingsize chip on his well-tailored shoulder, when there is so much love going for him?'

The personal wars had been waged unabated through the 1960s and on into the 1970s. There was a fight, involving Sinatra and his group, but no charges following it, at the Beverly Hills Hotel, Los Angeles, in 1966 when a businessman, Frederick Weisman, was injured. In 1967 came a scrap between Sinatra and the vice-president of the Sands casino, Las Vegas – the very hotel in which the singer had a stake – supposedly because he was refused further gambling credit after losing $200,000. According to the *Review-Journal* in the gambling city, Sinatra tipped a table over on the vice-president, having left and then returned to the Sands some hours later on the same night. Sinatra got a bloody nose and broken front teeth as hostilities erupted, and caused other mayhem – tossing a chair, pulling telephone lines out of the hotel switchboard, driving a baggage cart through a window. In September 1970 came the famed incident at Caesar's Palace, similarly in Las Vegas. The versions of this range from another refusal of credit, ordered by casino manager Sandford Waterman, to a punch-up between Sinatra's escorts and the manager's men. Sinatra said afterwards that Waterman ordered the dealer not to include him in a blackjack game, and that he simply walked away. Waterman pulled a pearl-handled revolver after Sinatra struck him, said yet another version. What was for sure is that Sinatra didn't return to the Circus Maximus supper room of Caesar's Palace for further engagements, as he was supposed to,

before announcing his retirement in 1971, and that Sandford Waterman, like some High Noon character, received an awful lot of congratulatory messages. But Sinatra's anger with the place cooled enough for him to choose it as the arena for his return to real live performance after the bounce-back of Ol' Blue Eyes at the end of 1973. He had one shot in January 1974, but got 'Vegas throat' (a result of icy air conditioning versus 100-plus desert heat) after three shows. He made it in full in March, and Christopher Buckley, writing for *New York Magazine*, was one of those who came to observe the phenomenon. His words were graphic and revealing:

'When Sinatra descends from the third floor – where he is lodged in one of Caesar's most magnificent chambers – there is no problem with crowds. People do not get close to the man who causes the whole world to fall in love. When he arrived for the engagement, Caesar's Palace supplemented its regular security force of 100 armed-to-the-teeth Wyatt Earps by 25 per cent. So, should Sinatra desire to have a drink with friends after one of the shows, the 25-man security force, the DA's guards, and Sinatra's own muscle guarantee that no one is going to keep the drinks from flowing steadily from bar to table. No one in fact is going to get within 30 feet of the man . . . When Sinatra sits down,

a full complement of security people moves in, one for every person at the table. They stand behind their charges, arms crossed like so many Colossi of Rhodes, giving everyone within range The Beady Stare. No one is going to mess with Frank Sinatra.

'Cisco, one of the supplementary Sinatra guards, stands by the elevator in the lobby eight hours a day to keep "kids and rip-off artists" from prowling the upstairs corridors. Cisco looks something like an extra on the set of *Gunsmoke*. Sunburned face, a wisp of a white moustache, and wire-rimmed glasses. Cisco uses a Ruger .44 calibre single action revolver with a 4½ inch barrel. He prefers this gun to the standard hotel security .38 Special handgun because his bullets, while larger than others, are made of soft lead. The bullet will mushroom instantly on contact, keeping it from passing through three or four people. "Hell," he says . . . "when you're shootin' in a crowd, you don't want the damn thing whippin' through a coupla people."'

Nice of Cisco, that, as Buckley was implying as sardonically as humanly possible. His tone, and the acute distaste he felt at observing the Sinatra muscle, have been reflected scores of times in stories about the singer's progress since 1973, probably even more so than in any writing done during the previous thirty years.

A reporter for the London *Evening News*, who found himself in a rehearsal for the Las Vegas shows, was told, 'If they find out who you are they'll sail you out – through the wall,' and went on to comment: 'Sinatra's chums – big, ageing men with large-knuckled hands who talk like B-movie extras and look like refugees from *The Godfather*. They have names like Vigo, Joey, Lou and Julie. Their lifeline is Francis Albert Sinatra, and they aren't going to risk breaking it at any price.' Yet that writer, like Christopher Buckley, could do no other when it came to description of the actual performance (part of a two-week engagement for which Sinatra was reported to be getting around $300,000) than confirm Sinatra's special qualities, as so many had done before him. Buckley wrote:

'When the lone spotlight frames his face, 1,200 hearts beat together, and he sings: *If a face could launch a thousand ships, then where am I to go*? The question answers itself. This is the Moment, the same Moment Bob Dylan accomplishes with *Blowin' in the Wind*, the Moment the younger Paul McCartney reached in *Yesterday*, the Moment of worship Faustus felt when he gazed on the metempsychosis of Helen of Troy. Apotheosis. A few seconds spent in the company of the Sublime . . .'

In the 1970s, Frank Sinatra's charitable activities continued apace. The Waldorf Astoria in New York was so glad to throw a party for him during April 1977 after he had performed at Carnegie Hall in aid of the city's Lenox Hill Hospital, that they named an entrance after him! Both he and his wife are obviously appreciative.

It was a jamboree or, as Dermot Purgavie said in the London *Daily Mail*: 'Not since the end of the Depression can a return to work have been greeted with such jubilation, tumult and unabashed emotion.' Ex-wife Nancy, daughters Nancy and Tina (the latter to get married during father's run), mother Dolly were all in the celebrity audience. 'I persuaded him to retire,' observed Dolly. 'I wish I hadn't. He had too much time on his hands.' And Sinatra showed again his customary shaky taste by making a violent attack from the stage on Maxine Cheshire and another journalist, Rhona Barrett. He told a 'leprosy' joke about Barrett; declared, 'Not all the Press are garbage dealers. Only 99 and 9/10 per cent of them'; and in another crack said, 'Your applause didn't fool me. You'd have done the same thing if Pope Paul walked out here.' There were, however, no unfortunate episodes or scraps in Las Vegas in that March of 1974, but Sinatra was limbering up to take his act abroad again. What happened in Australia in July, and the explosions in Germany the following year, seemed to indicate that at close on 60, Sinatra was, if anything, getting feistier still. The Australian eruption happened almost the moment he and his party reached the country. He got into an argument with a persistent woman reporter and with other journalists who he thought were hounding him. Sinatra's bodyguards became embroiled in a fight with journalists – pictures of a photographer up against the heavies were widely published – and he exploded childishly when asked later for a comment. He described Australian journalists as 'bums, parasites, hookers and pimps', and the women as 'the hookers of the Press . . . I might offer them a buck and a half. I once paid a broad in Washington two dollars' (those he stuffed into Maxine Cheshire's drink). 'I overpaid her, I found out. She didn't even bathe. Most of them don't.'

The balloon went up. The Australian trade unions put up a united front in sympathy with the Australian Journalists' Association. No one would bring him food and drink in the hotel or move his baggage. The transport workers boycotted him, and he was effectively marooned in Australia, since no one would service his private plane or sell him a ticket for public transport. The whole tawdry mess was sorted out by Bob Hawke, chief of the Australian TUC, and Sinatra's American attorney, Milton Rudin, during four hours of negotiations. Hawke showed a diplomacy and humour which would serve him well in his successful drive towards the Australian Premiership. 'If you do not express regrets,' he told Sinatra, 'your stay in Australia might be indefinite, unless you can walk across water.' The final statements on both sides were fudged apologies, neither sounding as if they really meant what they said. The journalists agreed that their 'pursuit of Sinatra over five days had been a little provocative.' He, among other things, said he did not intend any general reflection upon the 'moral character of working members of the Australian media', apologised for any injuries caused to people 'as a result of attempts to ensure his personal safety', and reserved his right to attack journalists he thought were 'subject to criticism on professional grounds'. It was quite something, though, for Sinatra to say sorry to newspaper people, even less for him to promise to show a little more understanding for them.

The ruffian element of Sinatra's image was heavily in the ascendant after Australia, and a court case he faced upon his return didn't help either. This hinged around a squalid little incident at a Palm Springs hotel where a young businessman called Frank Weinstock alleged that he had been beaten up in the men's room by Sinatra's people after a silly dispute over who was eyeing whose woman. The sinister-looking figure of Jilly Rizzo – the heavily-built, tinted-spectacled restaurateur who during the 1960s had gradually taken over the role of confidant and chief of staff for Sinatra, with the gradual demise of the Clan – was found guilty

of assault and battery and heavily fined. As journalists Stephen Claypole and Kevin Childs had reported of Jilly Rizzo at the time of the Australian fracas: 'Even his admirers would not claim that sophistication ranks high among the many attributes which have endeared him to Sinatra.'

The German eruption was still to come, but many of those who had applauded his comeback were having second thoughts. Before long, you could take your pick of any number of critical opinions from areas of the media where they might not be expected. Ralph Gleason was delivering his 'arrogant despot' attack in *Rolling Stone*. 'Pricing himself out of the market', trumpeted *Variety* as his fall tour with Woody Herman's band failed to fill every seat, and the televised 13 October concert at Madison Square Garden did not win over the critics in the way the *Ol' Blue Eyes Is Back* show had done in 1973. The new concert was called *The Main Event*, and it came out on record, which drew barbed commentary from Dermot Purgavie in the London *Daily Mail* on 3 December, 1974:

'There is a new record out called with a simplicity born of boundless self-esteem: SINATRA – THE MAIN EVENT . . . "Let me try again", he sings . . . "Think of all we had before. Let me try again once more." There are a growing number of people who believe that in the interests of the Trade Descriptions Act he shouldn't. They feel that the record and another made earlier this year called *Ol' Blue Eyes Is Back* are sad testimony that the once lustrous and inventive voice of Frank Sinatra has declined to the point of embarrassment and potential fraud. That and the contemptuous crudity of his recent public behaviour has made even some of his most passionate admirers concede that ego, money, power or whatever gratification stimulated his return to performing overshadowed good judgment and instead of calling women journalists "whores" – and worse – he should finally call it quits.'

Still on the charity trail . . . in the first picture (top right), taken in June 1979, Henry Kissinger (left) and ex-President Ford (right) are pictured with a group of diabetic children at an event in Denver held to raise funds for the Children's Diabetes Foundation. In the second picture, also from 1979, the scene changes to Monte Carlo, where Sinatra was flanked by Princess Grace and Sophia Loren at the Red Cross Ball. On the opposite page, it is Sinatra himself who is being honoured, at Las Vegas in December 1979. His songwriting buddy of old, Jule Styne, is about to give him the first Pied Piper award from ASCAP (the American Society of Composers, Authors and Publishers), and the others in attendance forming a rough half-circle from left to right are Paul Anka, Milton Berle, Glen Ford, Rich Little, Harry James, Sammy Cahn, Dionne Warwick and Henry Mancini.

There was much more in the same vein – the voice lacking in fluency, depth and certainty and communicating something like disdain, Sinatra groping for high notes, losing his attack, panting like a greyhound. And to complete this veritable season of Sinatra-bashing, there was his long-term commentator, George Frazier, writing now in the *Boston Globe*: 'The trouble with you, Frankie, is you got no style. All your life you wanted to be a big man but the wrong kind of big man. Look, Sinatra, Momo Giancana is just another version of Haldeman, and Agnew makes three. You're a sad case, Frankie. I think you're the best male vocalist who ever lived, but I also think you're a miserable failure as a human being.' It was no surprise he was voted, by the Lady Journalists of Hollywood, 'Sour Apple of the Year'. Yet the more surprising fact had been his level of industry in that first full unretired year – almost 100 concerts and three record albums – and although he moved into his sixtieth year with a quieter couple of months before taking up residence for three months at the Nevada venues of Harrah's, Lake Tahoe, and the Las Vegas old faithful, Caesar's Palace, he seemed determined to work just as hard in 1975.

With all the mixed feelings there were about him at this time, he was to find solace, as has so often been the case in his life, in London. He arrived in the British capital in May after an exhausting and sometimes uneasy North American tour – his offer of a million dollars to a photographer in Toronto if the man could prove his allegation that he'd been punched by a Sinatra bodyguard went unanswered – and a roasting from the German Press, treatment which was generally agreed to have been way way over the top. The German papers sneered at the empty seats at his concert. When a kidnap threat was received in Berlin, and he cancelled his show there, the papers implied it was a stunt and that he was afraid of having a flop. They raked over all the allegations from down the years as a matter of course, calling him both a pathetic alcoholic and a super gangster.

He had his revenge in London, where he was appearing on 29 and 30 May at the Royal Albert Hall, for the first time since 1970. It wasn't only that the audience of 7,000 cheered him to the top of that exotic Victorian dome as he said: 'I could have answered them and told reporters to look to the sins of their fathers. I could have mentioned Dachau. They are the gangsters.' Nor was it simply that Princess Margaret, Princess Anne, Princess Grace of Monaco, Ava Gardner, Mia Farrow and half the showbiz names of the world were sitting up front. Sweetest of all were the newspaper reviews, which were ecstatic, and I would go along with every one of them. If it were indeed true that Sinatra had wobbled along the way in 1974, which on the evidence I have is dubious except to critical ears determined to get a story that his voice was going, then he'd made the grade again at the end of May 1975.

'Is he now a 59-year-old short-winded has-been living on nostalgia?' asked Ray Wright in *The Evening Standard*. 'They needn't have worried. The voice is in great shape, the breath-control still extraordinary. The obituaries have been distinctly premature.' And this was Robert Shelton in *The Times*: 'One of the priciest spectaculars since the sacking of Car-

thage . . . It promised to be "Dad's Wood-stock" until Sinatra got into his vein, and then the accolades, memories, sentiment and sympathy made it all make sense. . . . When he sang *I've had my share of losing* in Paul Anka's *My Way* he became everyone's lonely uncle . . . A weeping, moving evening all round.'

Tickets priced at £30 were fetching £250. On both nights he received long and ecstatic standing ovations. No wonder he said on the first night, 'This is a marvellous night. It is one of the best nights of my entire career,' of which Robert Shelton commented: 'It may have been a stock testimonial, mouthed as facilely as his classic songs of beautiful lovers and losers, but you believed him as much as you believe his lyrics.' Shelton was wrong to doubt him. Sinatra really did mean every word, a judgement underlined by his astonishing statement in the middle of *The Lady Is a Tramp* on the second night: 'I'm very grateful for the marvellous reception in the way of criticism we have had from the British Press. It does mean a great deal because that's what we live on in our business. That and 40 million dollars a year.' Typical Sinatra, that, as typical as his MacArthur-like proclamation: 'I will return.' He was as good as his word. By November he was back

in London, at the Palladium, playing ten shows with Count Basie and Sarah Vaughan. For 15,000 tickets there had been 350,000 orders.

Something similar had occurred in August, when the dinner-jacketed Sinatra played a week of 'back-to-back' shows with the young folk-rocker, John Denver, in jeans, at Harrah's in Lake Tahoe. For once, the billing of the event as 'the entertainment coup of the decade' was almost true, and there were 672,412 requests for seats. Among other events of that hugely successful summer and fall of 1975 were his two weeks at the large Uris Theatre in New York, with Basie and Ella Fitzgerald, when the shows grossed more than one million dollars and the enthusiasm was such that the media agreed he was indeed the biggest attraction to play Broadway in modern times, and an appearance on Jerry Lewis's Labor Day Telethon to raise money for Muscular Dystrophy. This was, of course, another facet of Sinatra's immensely widespread charitable activities, and yet again to balance our portrait of the man it is time to record a few other examples.

During his Palladium season in London he was joined by Spiro Agnew, a regular member of his entourage at this time – Sinatra not letting even disgraced friends down, returning

131

favours he had once received. He and the ex-Vice President flew to Teheran to give a concert and on to Israel for two charity shows in aid of the Jerusalem Foundation for Arab and Jewish children. He was given the Jerusalem Medal by the City of Jerusalem as he pledged $250,000 in State of Israel Bonds in memory of 'Mrs Goldberg who was my parents' neighbour in Hoboken', the woman who had looked after him so often when he was a child and had, indeed, helped to shape his whole philosophy. These gestures of late 1975 were, as by now has become abundantly apparent, only the tip of the generous part of the complex Sinatra persona. Back in 1971, at his farewell concert in Los Angeles, where the audience included Ronald Reagan and Spiro Agnew, Princess Grace of Monaco and James Stewart, Pearl Bailey and Bob Hope, Barbra Streisand, Danny Kaye and Sammy Davis Junior, all at $250 a throw, he had given the entire proceeds of more than a million dollars, to the unemployed of Hollywood – or, to give it the formal name, the Motion Picture and Television Relief Fund. This was a gesture more in tune with the liberalism of his Democratic rather than his approaching Republican days. In that same year of 1971, in January, a Sinatra who was plainly much affected by the occasion attended the dedication ceremony of the Martin Anthony Sinatra Medical Center in Palm Springs, to which he had donated more than $800,000 dollars in memory of the father who had died in the same month of 1969, aged 74.

The list would grow tedious in full. Enough to say that Sinatra's generosity and charity, in matters large and small, have been quite overwhelming throughout his life. When, on 23 May 1976, the University of Nevada at Las Vegas conferred upon him an honorary Doctorate of Humane Letters for 'his charitable endeavours which have raised millions of dollars for humanitarian causes and deeds that have frequently been done anonymously', every word was true – except that the citation

might have read *millions upon millions* of dollars – and the honour stood for all the others he had received and was still to receive in his life. I think of Buddy Rich, 'given twenty-five grand and no strings attached' when the drummer told his ex-roommate of Dorsey days of his ambition to start a band. I remember Charlie Morrison of the Mocambo night club dying penniless and Sinatra moving into the club with Nelson Riddle for a two-week carnival until all the bills were paid and the widow had enough to keep the club going. I recall Earl Wilson's story of Toots Shor who said that he'd been given $150,000 by Sinatra down the years – years when that amount of money was worth well over a million (at least) today.'

And so Sinatra, ending 1975 on a high high, moved towards a period when life would be quieter and for some years far less controversial. The first step came two days after he had got that honour at the University of Nevada. On 25 May 1976, he married Barbara Marx, who had patiently awaited the event for five or so years, well aware of the history of previous attempts to push Sinatra towards altar or registry office. It was a relaxed affair, attended by old and new friends, like Ronald Reagan, Sammy Davis, Gregory Peck and Kirk Douglas, as well as his second grandchild, Amanda Catherine, aged two months. The next nine years of his life have appeared to validate what he said afterwards: 'I really have found a new kind of tranquillity. Barbara is a marvellous woman, and I have a different kind of life now.' That was true, more true than he knew, for one by one the lynchpins of his life were falling away, and he would need the love and support of his new wife.

Almost eight years after his father's death, on 6 January 1977, Dolly Sinatra was killed in an air crash, flying from Palm Springs to Las Vegas to see him perform. Only after a two-day search of the snowbound San Bernadino mountains was her body found. She was 82. At her funeral a week later, Sinatra was distraught. As one biographer, John Howlett, noted: 'Sinatra had remained in awe of his mother to the very end of her life. She was insistently proud of his success and he, according to close friends, always in need or in search of her approval and praise. The strong but often absent mother of his childhood had remained for ever part of his ceaseless and obsessive drive to succeed and dominate in his own right.' Gone, too, more than two years earlier, on 10 October 1974, was Sinatra's longtime business manager, Hank Sanicola, of whom Sinatra said: 'Of the five most important people in my life, Hank Sanicola was one. I couldn't have made it without him.'(Oddly, the number one on Sinatra's list was John Quinlan, a one-time Australian opera singer with whom he was named as co-author in a book Tommy Dorsey published in 1941, *Tips on Pop Singing*; Sinatra credited Quinlan's coaching with saving his voice during the late 1940s.) Sanicola was fulsome about Sinatra in return, proclaiming him 'probably the greatest phenomenon in the history of show business. I watched him for years doing things that no one has ever given him credit for ... acts of generosity that he would regard as bad manners to discuss ... There will never be another one like him. He made the word "Star" really mean something.'

Sinatra did not cease to continue behaving like a star, even though at a slower pace. Among the highlights of the next two years or so were journeys to sing in London in both 1977 and 1978, on the first of which he raised £60,000 for a National Advisory Centre on Battered Children, run by the National Society for the Prevention of Cruelty to Children. In September 1979, he gave a unique concert in Egypt on an open-air stage with the Pyramids as backcloth – part of a three-day gala which would raise $500,000 for charity. Sinatra was at his most relaxed, and witty. 'It's the biggest room I've ever played, and the toughest act I've ever followed,' he told the thousand guests, seated on Persian carpets.

Back home he was doing fine as well. Ignoring earlier statements of intent, he made a TV movie. His performance as an ageing cop fighting the Mob in a TV dramatisation of Philip Rosenberg's *Contract on Cherry Street* was widely praised for its intensity and conviction. Sinatra's gesture was a tribute to his mother, for this *Cherry Street* had been her favourite book. He was coming into line for any number of TV tributes as he moved towards his 65th birthday. The most memorable, perhaps, was in February 1978, a TV special called *Man of the Hour*, in which Ronald Reagan, emerging ever more clearly as the Republican Presidential choice for 1980, would say with some wit: 'I'm pleased to be here tonight honouring my very dear friend, Frank Sinatra. I must say that when this television programme was being planned the producer hadn't decided what political figures would participate. It was a choice between me and Governor Brown, and I lost again. Seriously, this is Frank's night and I'm here out of gratitude. Frank worked for me in all my campaigns. He was with me all the way to the Governor's mansion. Without his help, who knows, I might have been President.'

Sinatra followed that by joining a party of 150 celebrities on a visit to Israel in April 1978 for the dedication of the Frank Sinatra International Student Centre at the Mount Scopus campus of the Hebrew University in Jerusalem. He explained his donation thus: 'I had a street education, from the gutter to the curbstone. I am self-taught, but have learned a lot from listening to people with great knowledge. Education is what it is all about. I hope it will eventually wipe out the lack of tolerance, and that brotherhood and peace may spread throughout the world.' In March of the next year, his three-record album *Trilogy* came out, his first for five years, and apart from being nominated for six Grammy awards, the noted critic Leonard Feather bestowed upon it the description 'historic'. And so it was, not least for the survival of the voice, for the care and craftsmanship which Sinatra continued to lavish upon every song he sang, even on one

Three notable events of 1982 – again illustrating the verve with which Sinatra has continued to perform and live. In a remarkable concert at Radio City Music Hall, New York, in February 1982, Sinatra appeared with Luciano Pavarotti, the great operatic singer; from Pavarotti's gesture (right) he seems to be declaring Sinatra the winner. Another memorable double act was his performance with daughter Nancy at Caesar's Palace in Las Vegas in March 1982 when they performed their hit duet of the 1960s *Somethin' Stupid*. He celebrated with a monster cake, his 67th birthday on 12 December at the Golden Nugget Casino in Atlantic City with his wife, Barbara, looking on approvingly.

or two he might have been better advised not to attempt.

The critics continued to be kind, too. Here was Tom Sutcliffe in *The Guardian* (1977) saying: 'He's above hoarseness. It's the opposite of a look-no-strings approach, especially with orchestral arrangements like these. More a case of this is how it's done, and you love it.' And there was the author Ray Connolly, two decades and more behind Sinatra, laying it similarly on the line as well. 'He's been a giant hero of my lifetime – yet in no way has he been part of my generation's life-style . . . His magic is stylised and contrived . . . but he has a sense of theatre, which comes over on record, too, to make the lyrics of what may sometimes seem the most clichéd of songs an achingly meaningful experience in poetry. . . . Behind him he leaves three decades of beautifully sung songs, three decades of nostalgia and bucketfuls of maidenly tears. While Sinatra records are still being played around the world, we'll all be romantics from time to time.' And when, in September 1980, he was back in London to give a series of concerts at both the Royal Festival and the Royal Albert Hall, I was moved to observe in *The Sunday Times*: 'Sinatra has become the keeper of the flame for everyone from 40 to 80. His songs distil the youth, the nostalgia of millions. He also happens to be the best at it: an artist of colossal stature. He swings, he speaks, he shapes songs like no one else. That's genius.'

Sinatra was even given a relatively easy passage when, unexpectedly, in October 1980, he made a return to movies, with Faye Dunaway, in *The First Deadly Sin* – 'a deliberately old-fashioned detective thriller', as Nicholas Wapshott said of it in *The Times* of London, when it came to Britain in 1981. 'A well-upholstered vehicle for Sinatra and he takes a smooth ride, easing his way around a grubby New York, quietly investigating a motiveless murder. Sinatra deliberately underacts the part of a hardworking regular cop, a role which over a dozen years ago in *Tony Rome* and *The Detec-*

tive, he would have revelled in.' The *Daily Mail* emphasised the notable performance of Sinatra 'who makes you wonder how great an actor he'd have become if he hadn't been able to sing.'

Such pleasantries, however, were not alone to set the tone of the 1980s. This was a new decade, tougher and pricklier in many ways than either the 1960s or 1970s, a decade when dreams would end, when unemployment would settle like a blight on many nations as the world struggled with a second industrial (except that it was technological) revolution, when the young would get pushier in pursuit of a huge variety of goals, when concern about nuclear warfare, environmental damage and minority rights would verge on hysteria, when terrorists would give the lead in a new, undemocratic way of trying to achieve ends political, industrial, social and personal. It is not a world which Frank Sinatra much likes, I suspect, in common with many of his generation. So on the one side would be he, cut-

ting himself off increasingly from real life and his fans behind armies of security guards, except when he walked upon the platforms of performance. On the other side would be a new generation of media people, children of the rock age to whom Sinatra's music would mean little in terms of emotional and historical reference, younger writers who (many of them unmusical to boot) would see only the negative side of Sinatra – the dodgy image, the sometimes tetchy ageing man, the recluse behind his wall of muscle, all of which cannot be denied. Some of them have learned particular lessons well. They have brought the techniques of street warfare to journalism, and some laid in wait for Sinatra.

At first, criticisms were perfectly reasonable. 'Why,' asked the *Daily Star* of London in September 1980, 'should Frank Sinatra be allowed to come into this country with a pack of bodyguards? His heavy mob should be told to stay at home.' The *Sunday Express* commented adversely upon the entourage who occupied almost the entire sixth floor of The Savoy and the bodyguards who accompanied Sinatra's wife Barbara into the House of Commons and the House of Lords when she visited them. And even in a sea of warm concert reviews, the *Daily Mail*'s Jack Tinker quite rightly seized upon one well-known negative in Sinatra's style, criticising his 'impertinence' in rewriting Cole Porter on stage, and adding: 'Larry Hart's pen would have jumped up and stabbed him (Hart) in the eye had he had the bad form to write that the lady "loves the groovy super wind in her hair", tramp though she may have been.' Dave Gelly of *The Observer* thought Sinatra's concerts the best since he retired eight years ago; James Johnson of the *Evening Standard* agreed that the shows were brilliant – but: 'It is not easy to warm towards somebody who apparently likes to cast himself in the role of an arrogant and unpleasant individual offstage.'

The signs of the waning of the love affair between Sinatra and the Press of the mid-1970s

135

in Britain were there for all to see. Four years later, the British newspapers – a fair number of them, at least – were to explode into paeans of vituperation whose spite had to be tasted to be believed. In the interim Sinatra – despite continuing acts of generosity, and recognition for them, including the establishment of a Frank Sinatra Student Scholarship Fund in his hometown, Hoboken – had been engaged in some activities bound to enrage the radicals among the reporters and critics watching him, and to offend some who were not radicals. On 19 January 1981, he produced and directed the Inaugural Gala for the newly-elected President Reagan – and came up with a special version of *Nancy* for the President's lady. In July 1981, he flew to South Africa to give a series of concerts in Sun City, a vast new centre for entertainment and gambling in Bophuthatswana. For Sinatra, singing in this 'black homeland' was another step in his long campaign against apartheid. He said simply: 'I'll sing in South Africa. Why not? As long as there is no kind of segregation.' Many, naturally, did not accept this gloss upon the event. The British trade unions, Equity and the Musicians' Union, had banned their members appearing before South African audiences. Sinatra was, for a fee said to be over £1 million, ignoring the possibility of being blacklisted in a campaign being mounted through the United Nations to dissuade entertainers and actors from visiting South Africa.

Then came the Kitty Kelley affair, beginning in early 1983 and continuing for the next two years. A gossip-mongering writer, she announced the start of an unauthorised biography of Sinatra. The *Daily Mirror* quoted her as saying, 'Most journalists who even ask the mean, excitable Sinatra what he thinks of the weather are likely to find themselves in the Potomac River.' Sinatra circulated all his friends and enemies with a letter via his lawyers making it clear they would cooperate with Kelley at their peril. Asked what she was being paid for her research, she answered: 'A million

dollars plus a choice of funeral gown to be laid out in.' Against a background of reports during 1983 that Sinatra was writing his own 'official' autobiography, with the help of a professional author, the affair rumbled on. Sinatra's very costly legal attempts to stop her book soon started a national debate over the freedom of the Press in America. A body calling itself Reporters for Freedom of the Press and many top journalists entered the lists, claiming that Sinatra's suit was an attempt to intimidate anyone wanting to look into famous pasts. He was said to be especially alarmed by reports that Kelley's team were reopening the story of how he introduced Judith Exner to John F. Kennedy when she was a known girl-friend of the mobster Sam Giancana, murdered in 1975.

There were numerous attempts to serve a writ upon Kelley in a $2 million suit claiming she misrepresented herself as having his blessing to ask questions, and Sinatra's lawyers offered a reward for information on her whereabouts. He also claimed that his own company alone had the right to exploit his name and image. This enraged the National Writers' Union and the American Society of Journalists and Authors, who defended the woman's right to proceed with the book. 'This is a chilling example of how a powerful public figure, using money and influence, can orchestrate what the public shall know about him,' said Michael Wheland, president of the Washington Independent Writers' Society. The *Sunday Express* in London called his attempts to 'muzzle' Kitty Kelley a farce as the business rolled into and through 1984. She herself popped up to put her word in from time to time, claiming according to the *Daily Mirror* in June that many people asked by Sinatra not to speak to her had since telephoned offering information because they refused to be pushed around.

There was an explosive development in the saga towards the close of 1984 – widely interpreted by the media as an attempt to under-

mine Kitty Kelley's book – when Sinatra announced that he intended to tell his life story, warts and everything, in a six-hour multi-million dollar TV series, produced by his daughter Tina. It would be shown in the USA in 1986. 'I intend to put down what happened in my life, or maybe most of it. There will be plenty of warts.' We shall see. If Sinatra does produce something which even approaches the truth, the whole truth and nothing but the truth, he will be the most remarkable autobiographer (even on television) in history.

In the 1980s, he had other ups and downs. He was reported to have spent £200,000 on portable electronic devices designed to thwart telephone tappers. In 1981 there were further rumbles about alleged Mafia connections. President Reagan had been moved to write a letter in defence of his friend – auctioned in New York for $12,000, a world record price for a document by a living person. 'I have known Frank Sinatra for a number of years,' said Rea-

gan. 'I am aware of the incidents, highly publicised quarrels with photographers, night club scrapes, etc., and I admit it is not a life-style I emulate or approve. However, there is a less publicised side to Mr Sinatra which justice must recognise. I know of no one who has done more in the field of charity than Frank Sinatra.'

Sinatra made further headway in accentuating the positive in 1981 when he got back his gambling licence, in part, after a Nevada hearing. He was allowed to become an adviser to Caesar's Palace casino. 'Frank is one of the finest and most trustworthy, reliable and truthful men I have known,' said Gregory Peck at the hearing. 'He has a temperament, but that is what helps make him a performer.' Kirk Douglas weighed in with: 'He is the kind of man who does something good then runs away. I admire his guts. I am rather astounded at the number of investigations that take place on Frank Sinatra. I find him guilty of being impulsive and a great artist.' And Los Angeles county sheriff, Peter Pitchers, a former FBI man, really put the cream on the cake when he said he'd spent 40 years investigating unfounded allegations against Sinatra. 'If he's a member of the Mafia, I'm the Godfather!'

He continued to make great charitable gestures, too, with a trip to Buenos Aires in 1981 at a reported $2 million for four concerts, with a substantial part of the money going to homes and children in Argentina. He also played again in Brazil, where on his first visit in 1980 he had created a record for a concert by a single performer when he played to an audience of 175,000 people at the Maracana Stadium in Rio de Janeiro. With Sammy Davis Junior, he raised almost $500,000 at a concert in aid of the Atlanta murder task force who were seeking the monstrous killer who had slain 21 black children. One significant explosion during this period came at a private party when he fumed, according to the *Daily Mirror*, that he was becoming increasingly fed up with reports of his marital troubles. He said they'd been married for seven years, and planned to be married for another seven and another seven. . . . Then, during early 1984, it was confirmed that Sinatra would return to England in September to give six concerts at the Royal Albert Hall. Four years earlier, at the same venue, he had declared: 'I love Britain so much, I will try to return.'

Sinatra was about to keep his word, and pro-mised to give the first concert's proceeds of around £50,000 to the St John Ambulance Brigade. First, on 3 September, he went to Toronto to give an open air performance. It rained buckets, but 15,000 fans who had paid around $75 each waited in the downpour. Sinatra sang for 25 minutes, then went off. The furious crowd booed and shouted as the band packed up, but the promoter defended him stoutly. It was very dangerous, it was claimed, for him to appear. 'He took a hell of a risk singing in the rain with all that electrical equipment near him. His wife asked him not to go on, his advisers asked him not to go on, but he insisted. I felt thrilled when he did his set.'

Then, a few days before he was due to leave for London, Sinatra's name was yet again dragged into Mafia mud by a book – this one from Antoinette, daughter of mobster Sam Giancana, that dreaded name which had so often fallen like a deadly shadow across Sinatra's life. Reports on the book said that the FBI file on Sinatra now weighs 14 lbs – but that lawyers and others who have studied it say it is full of unsubstantiated allegations. That fact, however, has never worried some writers. As Sinatra flew in to England, the papers were full of news about the coming concerts, the Toronto scenes, the Kitty Kelley affair, the book by Giancana's daughter. . . . It was not surprising that the ramparts around Sinatra were fortified more intensively than ever.

'Unassailable, assailed'

0 CODA

IT WAS THE WALL OF UNATTRACTIVE MUSCLE and bone, the guardians of the master who apparently didn't want to get anywhere near his disciples, which more than anything else turned journalists and others off Sinatra in the month of September 1984, that should have been so emotional and wonderful a return to the city which has often seemed to love him most, as he loves London in return. Too much of the tone of the affair was set, as on other occasions in recent years, by Sinatra chuckling and flexing his shoulders while mouthing the phrase 'The Francis Albert Hall', by bodyguards sealing off every entrance of the place and one of the coarsest of them screaming at the stage door, 'Get back, get back . . . you'll only see him for three seconds.' Sinatra might be telling the crowds inside, 'I love you all – I mean it', but in the streets outside that was not the way it felt. So said witness after witness.

The faithful were very patient. The faithful always have been down the years. A woman who'd paid, by her standards, the earth for a ticket from a scalper had said on his previous visit: 'If I can just get in to see him, then I really don't mind dying.' And another: 'You know what they say – half the western world was conceived listening to one of his LPs. I just can't wait to see him.' Equally weighty, however, were the words of the fan who watched him dive without a wave into the big car that would take him back to the big suite on the big floor of the big hotel where big men in droves would keep away the little people of the world. 'We've made him a millionaire. He could have treated us better.' The papers could have treated Sinatra better too. They were pretty merciless. John Ryle of *The Sunday Times*, having been mirthfully refused an interview, rewrote a goodly selection of the nasties about him – the Kitty Kelley stuff, the New Jersey state commission the previous month calling him an 'obnoxious bully' after an incident at an Atlantic City casino, the 'Mafia Princess' book, and perspicaciously added: 'Sinatra's reputation has probably been enhanced, if anything, by

the shadow of The Mob. The likes of Giancana and Fischetti add a glint of danger to the tinsel of stardom'.

Of the concerts themselves, there were some good or at least equivocal reviews. In *The Sunday Times* George Melly began by observing: 'A mellow dignity, wryly exploited, has replaced the aggressive stance of yesterday . . . Courteous is what he's become, even, it would seem, modest. That dodgy edge, that sense of street-wise menace has evaporated.' On his actual singing, Melly was less enthusiastic: 'I can't believe that even the most cloth-eared and fanatical of his admirers could fool themselves into believing that his voice is what it was.

Hilary Bonner in *The Mail on Sunday* said some pleasant things. 'He is a creator of makebelieve. And his fans do not see an old man in the harsh glare of the arc light. They are aware only of the magic presence of a wizard who has cast a musical spell for nearly half a century.' By and large, however, the popular papers let him have it. 'Fairly boring performance,' said *The Star*'s Alasdair Buchan. Baz Bamigboye in the *Daily Mail* averred: 'At 68 his voice has gone, so for crooner read croaker.'

Even *The Times*, in the person of Max Bell, was hostile – typically this: 'Where once he climbed inside the skin of a song he is now content to address it politely like a half-remembered acquaintance.'

None of these words, though, reached the pitch of ferocity, the sound of vindictive delight, which one of the new urban guerrillas of Fleet Street brought to her work. She, an unknown called Adella Littman, could be observed metaphorically sharpening her razor between paragraphs, unable to forbear repeating some of the more offensive words:

'Francis Albert Sinatra's hair has been hand-sewn, patched and thatched. But there is nothing surgeons can do with a geriatric larynx. . . .

'His 68-year-old voice is cracked and jerks

about like a wayward needle on one of his LPs. He is a bloated caricature of a living legend. . . .

'He is an old-age pensioner bloated with a lifetime of birds, booze, brawls and four marriages, and so on . . . .

It was a piece so over the top that perhaps it was just meant to stir up the readership. It did. There were a lot of telephone calls demanding, apparently, her head on a spike, and many abusive letters too. The *Express* milked it for all it was worth.

You could scarcely help sympathising with Buddy Rich in *Metronome*, who felt like busting someone's face open – except that you don't do that to a woman. 'This broad that wrote about him is going to be old – I wouldn't be surprised if she's an old broad now.' Reading those dire words like 'bloated' (much in favour in *The People*, too, whose John Smith said, 'Bloated and croaky and forgetting his lines, the magic is gone. Francis Albert is yesterday's man with about as much sex appeal as an old sock') made one very sad for Sinatra if it was even true in part, but more so about the kind of spiteful nonsense which sometimes passes for journalism today.

Nonsense? Well, I cannot say for certain since I was not around to join in those merry days of 17 September *et seq* in 1984. The previous month, LA had proved no lady to me. Smitten with legionnaire's disease, confined in Hollywood for fourteen days on a life support machine, and then to a very slow recovery, I was scarcely in a position come September even to want to read the reviews very much, let alone go to the concerts. Hence why George Melly was covering in *The Sunday Times*. I was puzzled by the extremity of the criticisms, however, for what I *did* have was the album which Sinatra had recorded only a few months earlier in the spring, *LA Is My Lady*, and that showed little of the alarming diminution of powers which all those 'critics' appeared to have discovered. A touch of hoarseness, yes, some limitation in breathing and range compared with

the former Sinatra, the voice of an ageing man – but phrasing, adventurousness and, above all, *life* were intact in a record of impressive quality. The all-star band, with Quincy Jones to guide it and classic players like George Benson, Michael Brecker, Steve Gadd and the venerable Lionel Hampton to inspire it, gave Sinatra exactly the lift he needed to blend old-style swing punch with tangy modernism. All one had to do was *listen* to the joyous attack of *Mack the Knife* to hear that. This was Sinatra again wanting to test himself in a vital new context, not content to remix the old flavours and fade gently away. What I heard when I played that album after I *had* read the newspapers – and what I hear now, replaying it over and over, together with his other LP of the 1980s, *She Shot Me Down* – bore and bears little relationship to some of the criticisms about those Albert Hall concerts.

Within a week or so, Sinatra was on his travels again, giving a charity concert in Vienna, receiving a Boy Scouts of America Distinguished Citizen Award in Los Angeles for 'longtime support for scouting and deep concern for bettering the lives of children throughout the world' – which must have made his enemies fume and, in the 'support of scouting' section, surprised even some of his friends – singing for a record *low* fee (the union minimum, £515) at Reagan's second inaugural gala in Washington as January of a new year rolled around. Life seemed almost like usual with him in 1985, indeed. Before that inaugural gala, harassed by reporters dragging up the old gangland links stuff, he shouted at the press people yet again. 'You're dead, every one of you. You're dead', he said. The outburst was reported to be worrying to Reagan and his people – but that didn't stop him giving Sinatra the Medal of Freedom at the White House on 24 May, the same day Sinatra received an honorary doctorate in engineering (*engineering?*) at the Stevens Institute of Technology in Hoboken, the hometown where he hadn't graduated from high school. He said he regretted he hadn't furthered his education more and that he was enjoying the college ceremony better than the White House, because there was less fuss, despite the fact that 100 students had signed a petition protesting at the award to him – but then these days students will protest at anything. No demo materialised. Jokes about Sinatra's lean and hungry look were, amazingly, still being made – Bob Hope's crack: 'I hear Michael Jackson has bought him as a door chime' – and the entertainer himself was being decidedly modest. Having given up smoking after 50 years, and taken to swimming, skipping and bag-punching, he would say: 'I don't know what it means when people call me a legend. What is a legend? King Arthur was a legend. I can't relate to it.' That was all in the first half of 1985. It seemed we had not heard the last of Sinatra being nasty or Sinatra being nice. Business as usual. . . . Except for one thing. The voice, the concerts, the shows.

I do not know if I will ever hear him sing again in a hall or a club. I will miss that, but perhaps it does not matter. We have his records, and they are really the finest flower of his art, for as we have long since discovered the recording studio was the place where he put on his greatest shows – his true theatre, his real music room, the gallery where masterpieces were both made and then displayed. The nicest event of 1984, for example, was the availabililty in Britain of those sixteen reissued Capitol *chef d'œuvre* albums of the 1950s, all digitally remastered to bring out every note, nuance, consonant of his performances.

I believe, despite the extremities of some London journalists in September 1984, that Sinatra's musical reputation is virtually unassailable. It is more so than ever today, perhaps, since the current climate of greater catholicity and eclecticism in popular music favours that reputation. What can loosely be termed 'classic' popular music has made a powerful comeback in the last few years. The younger people at jazz concerts; the sudden fashion for danc-

ing to bebop in London clubs; the happiness of Joe Jackson with 'jump band' music, Linda Rondstadt so successfully selling old ballads with Nelson Riddle behind her, Alison Moyet in Britain trying to phrase like Billie Holiday all express this trend. Even *The Rolling Stone Encyclopaedia of Rock and Roll* would in 1983 include a long entry on Sinatra. 'His poised trombone-like phrasing, his nearly 100 hit singles and his career trajectory – from riot-inducing teen idol to movie star to pop elder statesman – have been the model and envy of rockers from the beginning.' Perhaps all of these things are a sign that the vitriolic battles between camps in popular music, and between generations, will subside.

No one, however, can know for certain. For myself, I am just very glad to have Frank Sinatra to celebrate. About the paradoxes of his character and the Mr Hyde side of his personality we have read enough in this book and elsewhere. I am sad that he has not behaved better at many times in his life. There are things that cannot be excused. I regret that one's heroes cannot always be perfect; but then I regret my own shortcomings, and those of many other friends. Life is life, art is art and, as Sinatra once said, 'I'm for anything that gets you through the night, be it prayer, tranquillisers or a bottle of Jack Daniels.' No musical artist this century, with the exception of his peer, Duke Ellington, has so crucially helped me through the nights and days of all the years, spring and summer, fall and winter, or has with his work and craft and dedication and total magic more sustained and delighted me. The same, I know, is true for millions of others who are nostalgic, perhaps, but who also instinctively recognise genius when they hear it. Sinatra was put on earth to achieve an artistic mission, it seems, rather than to be a saint – and in our imperfect world, who is to say that is not enough?

SINATRA ON RECORD

This is not a complete listing of Sinatra's recordings, although it certainly covers the majority of them. These are simply the albums which I believe are the best. There is some overlap between a few of the compilations. That's the annoying thing about compilations; you often want one of them because of particular songs when you already possess other songs on other records. Compilations, though, are often such good value that you have to include some, especially for those people who want to have a deal of Sinatra to hear without going the whole hog. I have to say, however, that I consider any decent popular music collection incomplete without the 16 albums conceived as "theme" records when Sinatra was with Capitol in the 1950s and very early 1960s. As a body of work those albums are simply superb; no other singer in history has left a memorial like it, and in the 1980s they were issued again, digitally remastered, to sound even better. Record labels given are those on the UK releases.

THE EARLY SINATRA

1940–42

The Dorsey/Sinatra Sessions 1940–42
(6-LP set) RCA Victor with Tommy Dorsey and his Orchestra
Arranged and/or conducted by Sy Oliver, Axel Stordahl, Paul Weston, Fred Stulce.
Notice on so many of these tracks, Sinatra's voice and Dorsey's trombone are almost like mirror images; light, soft, endlessly flowing. Sinatra's sweetness and tenderness of tone are already, at the beginning of his climb, noticeable, whilst his self-assurance is so marked one can well understand Dorsey's remark about standing on the bandstand 'so amazed I'd almost forget to take my own solos'. Even a lesser-known song like 'Say It' sounds great.
RECORD 1: The sky fell down, Too romantic, Shake down the stars, Moments in the moonlight, I'll be seeing you, Say it, Polka dots and moonbeams, The fable of the rose, This is the beginning of the end, Hear my song Violetta, Fools rush in, Devil may care, April played the fiddle, I haven't time to be a millionaire.
RECORD 2: Imagination, Yours is my heart alone, You're lonely and I'm lonely, East of the sun, Head on my pillow, It's a lovely day tomorrow, I'll never smile again*, All this and heaven too, Where do you keep your heart, Whisperin'*, Trade winds, The one I love*, The call of the canyon, Love lies.

RECORD 3: I could make you care, The world is in my arms, Our love affair, Looking for yesterday, Tell me at midnight, We three, When you awake, Anything, Shadows on the sand, You're breaking my heart all over again, I'd know you anywhere, Do you know why?, Not so long ago, Stardust*.
RECORD 4: Oh look at me now**, You might have belonged to another, You lucky people you, It's always you, I tried, Dolores*, Without a song, Do I worry?*, Everything happens to me, Let's get away from it all***, I'll never let a day pass by, Love me as I am, This love of mine.
RECORD 5: I guess I'll have to dream the rest*, You and I, Neiani*, Free for all*, Blue skies, Two in love, Pale moon, I think of you, How do you do without me?, A sinner kissed an angel, Violets for your furs, The sunshine of your smile, How about you, Snootie little cutie**.
RECORD 6: Poor you, I'll take Tallulah****, The last call for love, Somewhere a voice is calling, Just as though you were here*, Street of dreams*, Take me, Be careful it's my heart, In the blue of evening, Dig down deep*, There are such things*, Daybreak, It started all over again*, Light a candle in the chapel.
* with The Pied Pipers
** with Connie Haines and The Pied Pipers
*** with Connie Haines, Jo Stafford and The Pied Pipers
**** with Tommy Dorsey, Jo Stafford and The Pied Pipers

1939–52

Sinatra Plus
Fontana (double album)
Arranged and/or conducted by Axel Stordahl (except where indicated)
RECORD 1: The birth of the blues, The nearness of you, What makes the sunset?, I begged her, I've got a crush on you (trumpet solo by Bobby Hackett), Saturday night (is the loneliest night in the week), The things we did last summer, I concentrate on you, It's only a paper moon*, You go to my head, Bim bam baby, How deep is the ocean?, One for my baby, Bess, oh where's my Bess (from "Porgy and Bess").
RECORD 2: All or nothing at all**, Spring is here, S'posin'***, Time after time, Stormy weather****, All of me, The music stopped, September song, Sweet Lorraine*****, Try a little tenderness, My blue heaven*, When your lover has gone, I'm glad there is you, Ol' man river.
* with George Siravo and his Orchestra
** with Harry James and his Orchestra
*** with the André Previn Quartet
**** with the Ken Lane Singers
***** with the Metronome All-Stars

1939–52

The Essential Frank Sinatra
(3-LP set) CBS
Arranged and/or conducted by Andy Gibson, Harry James, Axel Stordahl, Xavier Cugat, Sy Oliver, Alvy West, Phil Moore, Hugo Winterhalter, George Siravo, Percy Faith.
Most tracks below are arranged and conducted by Stordahl with the exception of those indicated.
RECORD 1: From the bottom of my heart, Melancholy mood (both arr. Andy Gibson, with Harry James and his Orchestra), My buddy, These are the things I love (also known as Here comes the night) with Harry James and his Orchestra, Close to you (with the Bobby Tucker Singers), There's no you, The charm of you, When your lover has gone, I should care, A friend of yours (with the Ken Lane Singers), My shawl (with Xavier Cugot and his Orchestra), Nancy (with the laughing face), You are too beautiful, Why shouldn't I?, One love, Something old, something new.
RECORD 2: Blue skies, Guess I'll hang my tears out to dry, Why shouldn't it happen to us, It's the same old dream (with Four Hits and a Miss), You can take my word for it, Baby (with the Page Cavanaugh Trio), Sweet Lorraine (arr. Sy Oliver, with the Metronome All-Stars), My romance (duet with Dinah Shore), One for my baby, It all came true (with Alvy West and the Little Band, arr. Alvy West), Poinciana, Body and soul, I went down to Virginia, If I only had a match, Everybody loves somebody, Comme ci, comme ça, If you stub your toe on the moon (with the Phil Moore Four, arr. Phil Moore).
RECORD 3: The right girl for me, The huckle buck, If I ever love again (with the Double Daters, arr. and cond. by Hugo Winterhalter), Why remind me?, Sunshine cake (duet with Paula Kelly), (We've got a) Sure thing (with the Modernaires), It's only a paper moon, My blue heaven, Nevertheless (this and previous two tracks arr. and cond. by George Siravo), You're the one, Love me, I'm a fool to want you, The birth of the blues, Walkin' in the sunshine, Azure-te (Paris blues), Why try to change me now (arr. and cond. by Percy Faith – Sinatra's last record for CBS).

1943–51

In the Beginning, Frank Sinatra
(2-LP set) CBS
Arranged and conducted by Axel Stordahl
RECORD 1: I've got a crush on you, If you are but a dream (adapted from Rubinstein's Romance), Nancy, The girl that I marry, The house I live in, Mean to me, I have but one heart, The moon was yellow, Full moon and empty arms (based on Rachmaninoff's Piano Concerto No. 2), Put your dreams away.
RECORD 2: Day by day, I couldn't sleep a wink last

night, Ol' man river, Time after time, I'm a fool to want you, Saturday night (is the loneliest night of the week), Five minutes more, Sunday, Monday or always, The coffee song (They've got an awful lot of coffee in Brazil), Dream.

1944–50

Sinatra Souvenir
Fontana
Arranged and/or conducted by Axel Stordahl, except where indicated
Nancy, One for my baby, Embraceable you, Stella by starlight, The birth of the blues, I don't know why, Lover (with George Siravo and his Orchestra, arr. by George Siravo), September song, Begin the Beguine, Don't cry Joe (with Hugo Winterhalter and his Orchestra, arr. by Hugo Winterhalter), I only have eyes for you, Laura, Poinciana, I couldn't sleep a wink last night (with the Ken Lane Singers).

THE CAPITOL CLASSICS

1953–54

Songs for Young Lovers
Capitol
Arranged and/or conducted by Nelson Riddle
Sinatra's first LP for Capitol consisted of 8 songs on a 10″ record; later, the four starred songs were added to make it a 12″ album
The girl next door, They can't take that away from me, Violets for your furs, Someone to watch over me*, My one and only love*, Little girl blue, Like someone in love, A foggy day, It worries me*, I can read between the lines*, I get a kick out of you, My funny valentine.

1953–55

Swing Easy
Capitol
Arranged and/or conducted by Nelson Riddle, Heinie Beau, Axel Stordahl
This was Sinatra's second LP for Capitol and, like his first, was originally a 10″ album. It too was expanded with four extra songs at a later date. These songs are starred. All the arrangements are by Nelson Riddle – even "I love you" which was originally credited to Billy May – except for "Lean baby" which was arranged by Heinie Beau and conducted by Axel Stordahl.
Jeepers creepers, Taking a chance on love, Wrap your troubles in dreams, Lean baby*, I love you*, I'm going to sit right down and write myself a letter, Get happy, All of me, How could you do a thing like that to me?*, Why should I cry over you?*, Sunday, Just one of those things.

1955

In the Wee Small Hours
Capitol
Arranged and conducted by Nelson Riddle
In the wee small hours of the morning, Mood indigo, Glad to be unhappy, I get along without you very well, Deep in a dream, I see your face before me, Can't we be friends?, When your lover has gone, What is this thing called love?, Last night when we were young, I'll be around, Ill wind, It never entered my mind, Dancing on the ceiling, I'll never be the same, This love of mine.

1956

Songs for Swingin' Lovers
Capitol
Arranged and conducted by Nelson Riddle
You make me feel so young, It happened in Mon-

terey, You're getting to be a habit with me, You brought a new kind of love to me, Too marvellous for words, I've got you under my skin, I thought about you, Old devil moon, Pennies from heaven, Love is here to stay, We'll be together again, Makin' whoopee, Swingin' down the lane, Anything goes, How about you?

Close To You
Capitol
Arranged and conducted by Nelson Riddle, also featuring the Hollywood String Quartet
Close to you, P.S. I love you, Love locked out, Everything happens to me, It's easy to remember, Don't like goodbyes, With every breath I take, Blame it on my youth, It could happen to you, I've had my moments, I couldn't sleep a wink last night, The end of a love affair.

A Swingin' Affair!
Capitol
Arranged and conducted by Nelson Riddle
Night and day, I wish I were in love again, I got plenty o' nuttin', I guess I'll have to change my plan, Nice work if you can get it, Stars fell on Alabama, No one ever tells you, I won't dance, The lonesome road, At long last love, You'd be so nice to come home to, I got it bad and that ain't good, From this moment on, If I had you, Oh! look at me now.

1957

Where Are You?
Capitol
Arranged and conducted by Gordon Jenkins
Where are you?, The night we called it a day, I cover the waterfront, Maybe you'll be there, Laura, Lonely town, Autumn leaves, I'm a fool to want you, I think of you, Where is the one?, There's no you, Baby, won't you please come home?

Come Fly With Me
Capitol
Arranged and conducted by Billy May
Come fly with me, Around the world, Isle of Capri, Moonlight in Vermont, Autumn in New York, On the road to Mandalay*, Let's get away from it all, April in Paris, London by night, Brazil, Blue Hawaii, It's nice to go trav'ling.
* Because of objections by the Kipling Society "On the road to Mandalay" was omitted from the original version of this album, but has been reinstated on the latest digital remastered set of 1950s/1960s albums which was brought out in Britain during 1984.

1958

Only the Lonely
Capitol
Arranged and conducted by Nelson Riddle
Only the lonely, Angel eyes, What's new?, It's a lonesome old town, Willow weep for me, Goodbye, Blues in the night, Guess I'll hang my tears out to dry, Ebb tide, Spring is here, Gone with the wind, One for my baby.

Come Dance With Me
Capitol
Arranged and conducted by Billy May
Come dance with me, Something's gotta give, Just in time, Dancing in the dark, Too close for comfort, I could have danced all night, Saturday night, Day in day out, Cheek to cheek, Baubles, bangles and beads, The song is you, The last dance.

1953–58

Look to Your Heart
Capitol
Arranged and conducted by Nelson Riddle, except for "I'm gonna live till I die" arranged by Dick Reynolds, conducted by Ray Anthony
This is not a "concept" album but a collection of songs originally conceived as singles
Look to your heart, Anytime, anywhere, Not as a stranger, Our town, You, my love, Same old Saturday night, Fairy tale, The impatient years, I could have told you, When I stop loving you, If I had three wishes, I'm gonna live till I die.

1953–61

Frank Sinatra – 20 Golden Greats
Capitol
Arranged and conducted by Nelson Riddle, Billy May. A compendium, obviously
That old black magic, Love and marriage, Fools rush in, The lady is a tramp, Swingin' down the lane, All the way, Witchcraft, It happened in Monterey, You make me feel so young, Nice 'n' easy, Come fly with me, High hopes, Let's do it, I've got you under my skin, Chicago, Three coins in the fountain, It's nice to go trav'ling, Young at heart, In the wee small hours of the morning, The tender trap.

1958–65

Sinatra for the Sophisticated
Capitol
Arranged and conducted by Nelson Riddle, Billy May.
Another album put together from different "theme" albums
I get a kick out of you, Brazil, Always, Too close for comfort, I've heard that song before, Oh! look at me now, That old black magic, Baubles, bangles and beads, I love Paris, Just one of those things, Day by day, The lady is a tramp, I concentrate on you, Let's get away from it all.

1953–59

The Rare Sinatra
Capitol
Arranged and conducted by Nelson Riddle except where shown.
A real curiosity, odd tracks of songs mostly never before released until this 1978 compilation – some of them alternative versions from known sessions. The "Where or when" is a classic from 1958, especially the first 28 bars accompanied only by Bill Miller's stark piano! Sinatra has never sung with deeper feeling. "The song is you" (1958) is a fifth version done by Sinatra, the take not selected for the "Come dance with me" album, arranged by Billy May; "Memories of you" (1956) was recorded for the famous "Songs for swinging lovers", but not used. All these are gems – but one perfectly understands why "There's a flaw in my flue" was never used. How could Jimmy van Heusen and Sammy Cahn ever allow such a title on a plaintive ballad?
Don't make a beggar of me*, Ya better stop, Day in, day out, Memories of you, If it's the last thing I do (with the Hollywood String Quartet), I couldn't care less, Take a chance, There's a flaw in my flue (with the Hollywood String Quartet), The song is you**, Where or when, It all depends on you**, The one I love (Belongs to somebody else)***
* Arranged and conducted by Axel Stordahl
** Arranged and conducted by Billy May
*** Arranged and conducted by Gordon Jenkins

1959

No One Cares
Capitol
Arranged and conducted by Gordon Jenkins
When no one cares, A cottage for sale, Stormy weather, Where do you go?, I don't stand a ghost of a chance with you, Here's that rainy day, I can't get started, Why try to change me now?, Just friends, I'll never smile again, None but the lonely heart, The one I love (Belongs to somebody else).

1960

Nice 'n' Easy
Capitol
Arranged and conducted by Nelson Riddle
Nice 'n' easy, That old feeling, How deep is the ocean, I've got a crush on you, You go to my head, Fools rush in, Nevertheless, She's funny that way, Try a little tenderness, Embraceable you, Mam-'selle, Dream.

Sinatra's Swingin' Session
Capitol
Arranged and conducted by Nelson Riddle
When you're smiling, Blue moon, S'posin, It all depends on you, It's only a paper moon, My blue heaven, Should I?, September in the rain, Always, I can't believe that you're in love with me, I concentrate on you, You do something to me.

1957–60

All the Way
Capitol
Another collection of songs originally conceived as singles.
All the way, High hopes, Talk to me, French Foreign Legion, To love and be loved, River, stay 'way from my door, Witchcraft, It's over, it's over, it's over, Ol' MacDonald, This was my love, All my tomorrows, Sleep warm.

1961

Come Swing With Me!
Capitol
Arranged and conducted by Billy May
Day by day, Sentimental journey, Almost like being in love, Five minutes more, American beauty rose, Yes indeed!, On the sunny side of the street, Don't take your love from me, That old black magic, Lover, Paper doll, I've heard that song before.

1957–62

Sinatra Sings . . . of Love and Things!
Capitol
Arranged and conducted by Nelson Riddle, except for "Monique" (arranged and conducted by Felix Slatkin) and "I gotta right to sing the blues" (arranged and conducted by Skip Martin) which was the very last single recorded for Capitol by Sinatra.
This album is mostly a collection of songs originally conceived as singles, and put together here in a compilation during the period when Sinatra's relationship with Capitol had sharply deteriorated as he began to put out recordings through his own company.
The nearness of you, Hidden persuasion, The moon was yellow, I love Paris, Monique (song from movie, Kings Go Forth), Chicago, Love looks so well on you, Sentimental baby, Mister success, They came to Cordura, I gotta right to sing the blues, Something wonderful happens in summer.

1962

Point of No Return
Capitol
Arranged and conducted by Axel Stordahl.
This was the sixteenth and last of the Capitol albums which were conceived and produced as complete entities, as distinct from the many compilation albums which were put out from Sinatra's Capitol years. Appropriately for this album, Sinatra returned to work with his friend Axel Stordahl, who had been so influential in making Sinatra's early career as a soloist.
When the world was young, I'll remember April, September song, A million dreams ago, I'll see you again, There will never be another you, Somewhere along the way, It's a blue world, These foolish things, As time goes by, I'll be seeing you, Memories of you.

REPRISE: THE EXPERIMENTAL YEARS

1960

Ring-a-Ding Ding!
Reprise
Arranged and conducted by Johnny Mandel
This was the first album by Sinatra for his own Reprise label. It also marked the beginning of a decade of records which were much more experimental than those of the 1950s. In particular, Sinatra began to use jazz arrangers and musicians. Later were to come records with Count Basie, Duke Ellington and others, but on this album he used one of the "hottest" of the younger jazz-based arrangers, Johnny Mandel. There were also in the band which accompanied him jazz musicians as well-known as Bud Shank (flute), Frank Rosolino (trombone), Don Fagerquist (trumpet), Emil Richards (vibraphone) and his long-time pianist, Bill Miller. They are heard in solos or obbligati at various points of the album.
Ring-a-ding ding!, Let's fall in love, Be careful, it's my heart, A foggy day, A fine romance, In the still of the night, The coffee song, When I take my sugar to tea, Let's face the music and dance, You'd be so easy to love, You and the night and the music, I've got my love to keep me warm.

1961

Sinatra Swings
Reprise
Arranged and conducted by Billy May
Falling in love, The curse of an aching heart, Don't cry Joe, Please don't talk about me when I'm gone, Love walked in, Granada, I never knew, Don't be that way, Moonlight on the Ganges, It's a wonderful world, Have you met Miss Jones?, You're nobody till somebody loves you.

I Remember Tommy . . .
Reprise
Arranged and conducted by Sy Oliver
I'm getting sentimental over you, Imagination, There are such things, East of the sun, Daybreak, Without a song, I'll be seeing you, Take me, It's always you, Polka dots and moonbeams, It started all over again, The one I love (Belongs to somebody else).

Sinatra and Strings
Reprise
Arranged and conducted by Don Costa
I hadn't anyone till you, Night and day, Misty, Stardust, Come rain or shine, It might as well be spring, Prisoner of love, That's all, All or nothing at all, Yesterdays.

1962

Sinatra and Swingin' Brass
Reprise
Arranged and conducted by Neal Hefti
Goody Goody, They can't take that away from me, At long last love, I'm beginning to see the light, Don'cha go 'way mad, I get a kick out of you, Tangerine, Love is just around the corner, Ain't she sweet, Serenade in blue, I love you, Pick yourself up.

Sinatra Sings Great Songs from Great Britain
Reprise
Arranged and conducted by Robert Farnon
The very thought of you, We'll gather lilacs, If I had you, Now is the hour, The gipsy, A nightingale sang in Berkeley Square, A garden in the rain, London by night, We'll meet again, I'll follow my secret heart.

Sinatra – Basie
Reprise
Arranged and conducted by Neal Hefti, with the Count Basie Orchestra
Pennies from heaven, Please be kind, The tender trap, Looking at the world through rose-coloured glasses, My kind of girl, I only have eyes for you, Nice work if you can get it, Learnin' the blues, I'm gonna sit right down and write myself a letter, I won't dance.

1963

Sinatra's Sinatra
Reprise
Arranged and conducted by Nelson Riddle
I've got you under my skin, In the wee small hours of the morning, The second time around, Nancy, Witchcraft, Young at heart, All the way, How little we know, Pocketful of miracles, Oh what it seemed to be, Call me irresponsible, Put your dreams away.

1964

Frank Sinatra Sings Days of Wine and Roses
Reprise
Arranged and conducted by Nelson Riddle
Days of wine and roses, Moon river, The way you look tonight, Three coins in the fountain, In the cool cool cool of the evening, Secret love, Swinging on a star, It might as well be spring, The continental, Love is a many splendoured thing, All the way.

It Might As Well Be Swing
Reprise
Arranged and conducted by Quincy Jones
Fly me to the moon, I wish you love, I believe in you, More, I can't stop loving you, Hello Dolly, I wanna be around, The best is yet to come, The good life, Wives and lovers.

1964 *(partly recorded in 1962)*

Softly As I Leave You
Reprise
Arranged and conducted by Nelson Riddle, Marty Paich, Don Costa, Billy May and Ernie Freeman
Emily, Here's to the losers, Dear heart, Come blow your horn, Love isn't just for the young, I can't believe I'm losing you, Pass me by, Softly, as I leave you, Then suddenly love, Available, Talk to me baby, The look of love.

1965

September of My Years
Reprise
Arranged and conducted by Gordon Jenkins
The September of my years, How old am I, Don't

wait too long, It gets lonely early, This is all I ask, Last night when we were young, The man in the looking glass, It was a very good year, When the wind was green, Hello young lovers, I see it now, Once upon a time, September song.

Moonlight Sinatra
Reprise
Arranged and conducted by Nelson Riddle
Moonlight becomes you, Moon song, Moonlight serenade, Reaching for the moon, I wished on the moon, Oh you crazy moon, The moon got in my eyes, Moonlight mood, Moon love, The moon was yellow.

1966

Strangers in the Night
Reprise
Arranged and conducted by Nelson Riddle, except for title track
Strangers in the night, Summer wind, All or nothing at all, Call me, You're driving me crazy, On a clear day, My baby just cares for me, Down town, Yes sir, that's my baby, The most beautiful girl in the world.

Sinatra at The Sands
Reprise (double album)
With Count Basie and his Orchestra, in concert
Come fly with me, I've got a crush on you, I've got you under my skin, Shadow of your smile, Street of dreams, One for my baby, Fly me to the moon, One o'clock jump (instrumental), Monologue, You make me feel so young, All of me (instrumental), The September of my years, Get me to the church on time, It was a very good year, Don't worry 'bout me, Makin' whoopee (instrumental), Where or when, Angel eyes, My kind of town, Monologue, My kind of town.

1967

Francis Albert Sinatra and Antonio Carlos Jobim
Reprise
Arranged and conducted by Claus Ogerman
The girl from Ipanema*, Dindi, Change partners, Quiet nights of quiet stars, Meditation, If you never come to me, How insensitive*, I concentrate on you*, Baubles, bangles and beads, Once I loved.
* with Antonio Carlos Jobim

Francis A and Edward K
Reprise
Arranged by Billy May, with the Duke Ellington Orchestra
Follow me, Sunny, All I need is the girl, Indian summer, I like the sunrise, Yellow days, Poor butterfly, Come back to me.

Frank Sinatra and the World We Knew
Reprise
Arranged and/or conducted by Billy Strange, Gordon Jenkins, Ernie Freeman, H. B. Barnum
The world we knew, Somethin' stupid (with Nancy Sinatra), This is my love, Born free, Don't sleep in the subway, This town, This is my song, You are there, Drinking again, Some enchanted evening.

1968

Cycles
Reprise
Arranged and produced by Don Costa, conducted by Bill Miller
Rain in my heart, From both sides now, Little green apples, Pretty colours, Cycles, Wandering, By the time I get to Phoenix, Moody river, My way of life, Gentle on my mind.

1968–69

My Way
Reprise
Arranged and conducted by Don Costa
Watch what happens, Didn't we?, Hallelujah, I love her so, Yesterday, All my tomorrows, My way, A day in the life of a fool, For once in my life, If you go away, Mrs Robinson.

A Man Alone
Reprise
Arranged and conducted by Don Costa
A man alone, Night, I've been to town, From promise to promise, The single man, The beautiful strangers, Lonesome cities, Love's been good to me, Empty is, Out beyond the window, Some travelling music, A man alone.

Watertown
Reprise
A love story composed by Bob Gaudio and Jake Holmes, produced and arranged by Bob Gaudio, Charles Callelo and Joe Scott
Watertown, Goodbye, For a while, Michael and Peter, I would be in love, Elizabeth, What a funny girl, What's now is now, She says, The train.

1960–65

Frank Sinatra: A Man and his Music
Reprise, double album
Narrated and sung by Frank Sinatra, with the Orchestras of Nelson Riddle, Gordon Jenkins, Billy May, Sy Oliver, Count Basie, Ernie Freeman, Johnny Mandel and Don Costa, with other highlights of Sinatra's career.
RECORD 1: Put your dreams away, All or nothing at all, I'll never smile again, There are such things, I'll be seeing you, The one I love belongs to somebody else, Polka dots and moonbeams, Night and day, Oh, what it seemed to be, Soliloquy, Nancy, The house I live in, From here to eternity (extract from film, with Montgomery Clift and Frank Sinatra).
RECORD 2: Come fly with me, How little we know, Learnin' the blues, In the wee small hours of the morning, Young at heart, Witchcraft, All the way, Love and marriage, I've got you under my skin, Ring-a-ding ding!, The second time around, The summit (comedy routine – Sinatra, Dean Martin, Sammy Davis Junior), The oldest established (permanent floating crap game) (Sinatra, Bing Crosby, Dean Martin), Luck be a lady, Call me irresponsible, Fly me to the moon, Softly as I leave you, My kind of town, The September of my years.

1967–70

Sinatra and Company
Reprise
One side arranged by Eumir Deodato, conducted by Morris Stoloff, the other side arranged by Don Costa
Drinking water*, Someone to light up my life, Triste, Don't ever go away, This happy madness*, Wave, One note samba*, I will drink the wine, Close to you, Sunrise in the morning, Bein' green, My sweet lady, Leaving on a jet plane, Lady day.
* with Antonio Carlos Jobim.

THE AUTUMN YEARS

1973

Ol' Blue Eyes is Back
Reprise
Arranged by Don Costa and Gordon Jenkins, conducted by Gordon Jenkins
You will be my music, You're so right, Winners, Nobody wins, Send in the clowns, Dream away, Let me try again, There used to be a ball park, Noah.

1973–74

Some Nice Things I've Missed
Reprise
Arranged by Don Costa and Gordon Jenkins
You turned my world around, Sweet Caroline, The summer knows, I'm gonna make it all the way, Tie a yellow ribbon round the ole oak tree, Satisfy me, One more time, If, You are the sunshine of my life, What are you doing the rest of your life, Bad, bad Leroy Brown.

1973
(compilation of songs recorded in 1961)

Frank
Reprise, double album
Arranged and conducted by Sy Oliver and Don Costa
RECORD 1: I hadn't anyone till you, Night and day, Misty, Stardust, Come rain or come shine, It might as well be spring, Prisoner of love, That's all, All or nothing at all, Yesterdays.
RECORD 2: I'm getting sentimental over you, Imagination, There are such things, East of the sun, Daybreak, Without a song, I'll be seeing you, Take me, It's always you, Polka dots and moonbeams, It started all over again, The one I love belongs to somebody else, I'm getting sentimental over you.

1974

Sinatra – the Main Event
Reprise
With Woody Herman and the Young Thundering Herd, in concert
The lady is a tramp, I get a kick out of you, Let me try again, Autumn in New York, I've got you under my skin, Bad, bad Leroy Brown, Angel eyes, You are the sunshine of my life, The house I live in, My kind of town, My way.

1963–75

Sinatra – the Reprise Years
Reprise (4-album set)
Arranged and/or conducted by Don Costa, Nelson Riddle, Billy May, Johnny Mandel, Duke Ellington, Neal Hefti, Count Basie, Robert Farnon, Gordon Jenkins, Claus Ogerman, Bill Miller, Sy Oliver, etc. A superb compilation.
RECORD 1: In the still of the night, Granada, I'm getting sentimental over you, Without a song, I get a kick out of you, Night and day, Come rain or come shine, All or nothing at all, A nightingale sang in Berkeley Square, All alone, I want to dance, Ol' man river.
RECORD 2: I've got you under my skin, In the wee small hours of the morning, Nancy, The way you look tonight, Fly me to the moon, Softly as I leave you, All the way, Luck be a lady, I'll only miss her when I think of her, The September of my years, This is all I ask, It was a very good year.
RECORD 3: Strangers in the night, Call me irresponsible, Moon love, Don't worry 'bout me, One for my baby, My kind of town, Poor butterfly, How insensitive, Dindi, By the time I get to Phoenix, Cycles, Didn't we?, Somethin' stupid.
RECORD 4: Love's been good to me, A man alone, Going out of my head, Something, The train, Lady day, Drinking again, Send in the clowns, Let me try again, What are you doing the rest of your life? If, Put your dreams away, My way.

Portrait of Sinatra (40 Songs from the Life of a Man)

Reprise, double album

Another compilation using many of the same conductors and arrangers as in the previous set

RECORD 1: Let's face the music, Nancy, I've got you under my skin, Let me try again, Fly me to the moon, All or nothing at all, For once in my life, Bonita, My kind of town, Call me irresponsible, All the way, Strangers in the night, Didn't we?, Come fly with me, The second time around, In the wee small hours of the morning, Bad, bad Leroy Brown, Softly, as I leave you, Cycles, Send in the clowns.

RECORD 2: That's life, Little green apples, Song of the Sabia, Goody goody, Empty tables, I believe I'm gonna love you, Star gazer, I sing the songs, You are the sunshine of my life, It was a very good year, Somethin' stupid, Young at heart, You make me feel so young, Yesterday, Pennies from heaven, If, Something, Star, Love's been good to me, My way.

Trilogy (Past Present Future)

Reprise, three album set

RECORD 1: The Past, arranged and conducted by Billy May

The song is you, But not for me, I had the craziest dream, It had to be you, Let's face the music and dance, Street of dreams, My shining hour, All of you, More than you know, They all laughed.

RECORD 2: The Present, arranged and conducted by Don Costa

You and me, Just the way you are, Something, MacArthur park, Theme from New York, New York, Summer me, winter me, Song sung blue, For the good times, Love me tender, That's what God looks like.

RECORD 3: The Future, a musical fantasy in three tenses, composed, arranged and conducted by Gordon Jenkins, with the Philharmonic Symphony Orchestra and Chorus

What time does the next miracle leave?, World war none! The future (The future, I've been there, Song without words), Before the music ends.

She Shot Me Down

Reprise

Arranged and conducted by Gordon Jenkins, Don Costa; the final track arranged by Nelson Riddle, conducted by Vincent Falcone Junior

Good thing going, Hey look, no crying, Thanks for the memory, A long night, Bang bang (My baby shot me down), Monday morning quarterback, South – to a warmer place, I loved her, The gal that got away/It never entered my mind (medley).

L.A. is My Lady

Reprise

Produced and conducted by Quincy Jones, featuring George Benson, Lionel Hampton, Bob James, Ray Brown, Steve Gadd, Joe Newman and Urbie Green

L.A. is my lady, The best of everything, How do you keep the music playing?, Teach me tonight, It's all right with me, Mack the knife, Until the real thing comes along, Stormy weather, If I should lose you, A hundred years from today, After you've gone.

Acknowledgements

This book was mostly written during a period of 12 months which encompassed a near-fatal illness that finally felled me in Los Angeles (viral pneumonia, virus unknown, probably legionella) and, later, a heart problem stemming from a muscle weakened by that illness. So that the book has been completed at all owes almost everything to the care of Liz, my wife, and my family and many friends, and especially to the care, skills and probably prayers of the doctors, nurses, staff and sisters of the St Joseph Medical Center in Burbank, California, a place with a view of the NBC studios, the Walt Disney Studios and the famed Forest Lawn cemetery, loose model of the place in Evelyn Waugh's 'The Loved One'. The showbusiness views kept me thinking of Sinatra; the other view kept my mind on living. In the difficult months of 1985, the tolerant encouragement of my publisher, Colin Webb – he who also did *Duke* with me – was much appreciated. He is always a pleasure to work with and so is my old friend and co-author, George Perry. To the secretarial skills of Joan Brooke, the researches of Jenny Prior, Jenny de Gex, and Ted Nunn of the Sinatra Music Society I also owe much; and my debt to all those many journalists and authors who have written on Sinatra since he began his climb the best part of half a century ago is great. The estimation of Sinatra's singing, his general artistry, his place in the twentieth century is utterly my own; so, too, are many observations of the artist at work and play. But for the crucial facts (and sometimes suppositions) covering years when I did not personally observe the man, I have plainly had to turn to the work of others. Over the last twenty years or so there have inevitably been many biographies which, although varying to some extent, effectively repeat or improvise upon virtually every key episode in Sinatra's life. Through this repetition an archive of accepted history about Sinatra has become established with the years. Nonetheless, I am indebted to the valuable material provided in these books, and in the text I have endeavoured clearly to indicate sources. The key books for everyone interested in further study of the astonishing Sinatra phenomenon are these:

The Voice: The Story of an American Phenomenon, by E J Kahn Jr
(Musicians Press Ltd., London;
Harper & Brothers, New York, 1947)

Sinatra,
by Robin Douglas-Home
(Grosset & Dunlap, New York, 1962)

Sinatra, Retreat of the Romantic
by Arnold Shaw
(W H Allen, London;
Holt, Rinehart & Winston, New York, 1968)

The Great American Popular Singers
by Henry Pleasants
(Victor Gollancz, London;
Simon & Schuster, New York, 1974)

Frank Sinatra
by Anthony Scudato
(Michael Joseph, London, 1976)

Sinatra
by Earl Wilson
(W H Allen, London;
Macmillan, New York, 1976)

Frank Sinatra
by John Howlett
(Plexus, London;
Simon & Schuster/Wallaby Books, New York, 1980)

The Frank Sinatra Scrapbook
by Richard Peters
(Pop Universal/Souvenir Press, London;
St Martin's Press, New York, 1982)

Sinatra: An American Classic
by John Rockwell
(Elm Tree Books, London;
Rolling Stone Press, New York, 1984)

SINATRA ON FILM

by George Perry

Sinatra made his first appearance in a feature film in 1941 and his last, to date, in 1980, which would be a considerable span for any screen actor, encompassing, as it does, 57 films. His record with the Academy of Motion Picture Arts and Sciences is commendable – he won an Oscar in 1953, a nomination as best actor in 1955, the Jean Hersholt award in 1970, and three times aided James van Heusen and Sammy Cahn's success in winning the Best Song award. Alongside his remarkable life as a singer he has been able to maintain a productive film career that in terms of sheer output would not shame any film star who had dedicated all his working life to the making of movies.

Yet given all that, and his overwhelming talent as a performer, it is disappointing that only a handful of his films amount to anything more than a way of killing time. It is easy enough to blame Hollywood politics, but Sinatra was one of the few able to reach a position where he could call the shots, and the ascent to such heights did not seem to improve his judgment. It is unarguable that many of the works disparaged by the critics were successful at the box office, but whereas, for example in the case of Elvis Presley, the films were nothing more than formula entertaiments to display his songs, Sinatra was able quite rapidly to move away from such a limiting notion, and in several pictures demonstrated an extraordinary dramatic talent.

Discounting lost footage in two-reelers made in 1936–7 when he was singing with the Hoboken Four as part of the entourage of that arch-discoverer of amateur talent, Major Bowes, his debut in films was almost accidental. It happened during the first year that he was on the road with the Tommy Dorsey Orchestra as the band singer. Their appearance in a modest Hollywood musical designed for the bottom half of a double bill and called *Las Vegas Nights* gave Sinatra an onscreen opportunity to sing 'I'll Never Smile Again', a number that was getting plenty of spots on the radio. Sinatra was already generating attention through Dorsey recordings and air time, but the pot-boiling film was not a crowd-puller. Another minor effort, *Ship Ahoy*, in the following year, fared better, having Eleanor Powell, Virgina O'Brien and Red Skelton as its stars, and far more opportunities for Dorsey. Sinatra was able to join the Pied Pipers (Chuck Lowry, Jo Stafford, Clark Yokum and Hal Hopper) for a couple of numbers, but he was still merely part of the Dorsey outfit. In September 1942 he made his big breakout from Dorsey, feeling sufficiently confident to succeed as a singer on his own, and went out to California where he was given a spot *Reveille with Beverly*, in a vacuous wartime musical starring the whirlwind tap-dancer, Ann Miller. She played a girl disc jockey mesmerising the boys at a nearby army camp with her wake-up programme, and Sinatra in this unmemorable epic sang Cole Porter's *Night and Day* surrounded by piano-playing, violin-strumming girls in evening gowns.

On New Year's Eve, 1942, he filled the Paramount Theatre on Times Square with swooning teenage females in one of the great moments of show business. The movie was *Star-Spangled Rhythm*, Paramount's patriotic musical with all the stars on the lot. The stage show was Benny Goodman and his Orchestra, and Sinatra was his extra vocalist. Nothing could ever be the same for him after that. Sinatra was the sensation of the age, and only had to appear on stage for hundreds of bobby-soxers, as the teenagers of the day were called on account of their taste in hosiery, to scream, faint or climax, to the disgust of the righteous and those whose duty it was to ready the theatre for the next performance. The publicity for the wretched *Reveille with Beverly* was hastily recast and Sinatra given star billing for his three-minute appearance. Hollywood now became interested in the slight, sunken-cheeked crooner, who now had his network radio show, *Your Hit Parade*, and RKO-Radio Pictures won the race to sign a contract with

'Frankie' hits the movies. Below, his brief band spot with
Tommy Dorsey for *Ship Ahoy*. Above right, an MGM
portrait made when he appeared in *Till the Clouds Roll By*.
Below right, with Anne Jeffreys in *Step Lively*, a remake
of the Marx Brothers' *Room Service*.

Had his career continued in this vein it is unlikely that it would have lasted for much longer, once the Frankie phenomenon was over. Clearly the studio had no real idea how to use him, and were unaware of his versatility, but there were some critics who, while not liking the films very much, had discerned that here was an interesting screen persona waiting to be developed.

Sinatra's own frustration was expressed in one of his earliest intemperate remarks to a newspaper reporter. He said, having been caught at an unguarded moment on a heavy day, that 'pictures stink', and went on to make

him. He was known throughout the teenage world as 'Frankie', and an early practitioner of hype nicknamed him 'The Voice'.

The first film in which Sinatra was called upon to play a role, and not merely be the incidental vocalist, was *Higher and Higher*, which had originally been a Rodgers and Hart musical on Broadway. Characteristically, Hollywood felt that the score could be improved upon, and new words and music by Jimmy McHugh and Harold Adamson were commissioned, including *I Couldn't Sleep a Wink Last Night*, a mighty Sinatra song hit. The film itself, in which Sinatra played the rich young man next door to a household where the servants are attempting to pass off a maid as an heiress, was poor, and Sinatra was not exactly stretched.

It was followed by *Step Lively*, an ill-advised musical remake of the Marx Brothers' *Room Service*, which, in any case, was not one of their best films. Again the main attraction was Sinatra's singing, and there was little chance for a real performance.

...med with Gene Kelly in *Anchors Aweigh* (left) as
...ors on shore leave in Hollywood, Sinatra held his own
... as a hoofer. In *It Happened in Brooklyn* (below) he
... a returned GI, here with Gloria Grahame. If *The
...acle of the Bells* (right) was a disaster, *The Kissing
...dit* was a nightmare.

a few cynical comments on the moviemaking system. However, it was still the time when Hollywood believed itself to be wonderful, and there was a widely-regarded convention not to knock it. For the critic who was biting the hand of opportunity to be a neophyte actor, who had received his break through the good fortune of a magnetic singing voice, was considered outrageously ungrateful. There was a brief hullabaloo, and the public became aware of the prickly side of Sinatra's nature where films were concerned which, as it happened at that stage in his progress, may have been no bad thing. Certainly there was a great improvement in his work and a chance to display talents that had hitherto been overlooked.

He was fortunate that his contract enabled him to make one picture a year for another studio. In 1945 a wise old producer, Joe Pasternak, signed him for a Gene Kelly musical at MGM and it was the turning point.

In *Anchors Aweigh*, which was directed by

155

George Sidney, Kelly and Sinatra played shipmates on shore leave in Los Angeles. Kelly is brash, extrovert, a wow with the women. Sinatra is shy, earnest, sincere. Kelly tries to help his friend win a movie bit player (Kathryn Grayson) who has hopes of becoming a singing star, and ends up falling for her himself. The film is overlong but very likeable. It is also very much Kelly's film – not only does he get the girl (Sinatra meets a nice waitress from Brooklyn) but he has the spectacular numbers, including a dance with the mouse half of MGM's animated *Tom and Jerry*. But Sinatra is able to sing some effective numbers, and dance as well, holding his own in a duet with Kelly that takes place in a hostel and which requires some energetic leaping over beds.

The film was a success and MGM bought out the RKO contract with the intention of setting Sinatra up in more of their musicals. It guaranteed him $1.5 million over seven years and a chance to make one non-MGM film a year, and

did not interfere with radio and recording work.

He then squeezed in a ten-minute short for Mervyn LeRoy on racial intolerance, called *The House I Live In*, and it won a special Academy Award. Some critics felt that his brief appearance in MGM's ludicrous star-studded biography of the composer, Jerome Kern, who died even as the cameras turned, negated the good work in the short. For part of the final sequence of *Till the Clouds Roll By*, Sinatra stood on a pedestal in all-white tuxedo in front of an equally-gleaming orchestra and sang the great Kern ballad, *Ol' Man River*, the lyrics of which are a black man's lament at white man's exploitation. But in spite of the dreadful taste of the production designer, Sinatra delivered the song with power and feeling.

He then starred in a minor, but occasionally charming black-and-white comedy with music, called *It Happened in Brooklyn*, where he played a returned GI finding it hard to get back to his roots. Once again he failed to win Kathryn

156

sby Berkeley's lively *Take Me Out to the Ball Game*
him back with Gene Kelly (left), and led to the great
GM musical *On the Town*. Sinatra is seen (below) in the
ehistoric Man' number with Ann Miller, Betty Garrett,
ne Kelly, Jules Munshin and unidentified dinosaur, and
axing between takes in a harem outfit for the Coney
and finale.

Grayson, a high school teacher who wants to be a singer, but Gloria Grahame as a nurse from Brooklyn proved a more compatible mate. Sinatra also sang an engaging duet with Jimmy Durante in which he performed an acceptable take-off of the old vaudevillian's distinctive delivery. Although the film's box-office returns were modest, critics did at least note Sinatra's greater ease and assurance.

He then insisted, against the wishes of many MGM colleagues, on returning to RKO to play a priest in *The Miracle of the Bells*, which was the sort of sentimental anecdote best left on paper. Bing Crosby had won an Academy Award playing a priest in *Going My Way*, but Sinatra, in spite of a suitably contrite performance, was less fortunate, and the film was a failure. In Wardour Street, the marketing centre of film distribution in England, there is a superstition that any film with 'Miracle' in the title is foredoomed, and this was an example subscribing to the myth.

Next came the feeblest of his MGM films, *The Kissing Bandit*, a costume musical set in Spanish California. Its dismal box-office performance came as Sinatra's singing career had entered the doldrums. The euphoric bobby-sox era had passed, his hit parade radio show had become lack-lustre, the Axel Stordahl style of arrangement sounded distinctly old-fashioned alongside the more aggressive singers such as Frankie Laine who were coming up in popularity, and Sinatra was suffering from marital problems, fatigue and a constant bad press. In 1949 he quit the hit parade show.

Meanwhile, MGM put him into a cheerful Technicolor musical with his old shipmate, Gene Kelly, which was to be directed by Busby Berkeley, creator of the great Warner musicals of the early Thirties. The result, the exuberant *Take Me Out to the Ball Game*, had a flimsy plot to overcome, being about a baseball team at the turn-of-the-century which acquires a new owner who turns out to be Esther Williams in one of her dry roles. Sinatra, as usual, doesn't win her with the brash Kelly around, but is paired off with Betty Garrett. There was something about the teaming that appealed to the studio, for she, with Kelly and Sinatra, and the third of the principal ball players, comedian Jules Munshin, remained together for the next film, *On the Town*, where they were joined by dancers Vera-Ellen and Ann Miller.

Unarguably, *On the Town* is Sinatra's best musical, and a landmark in the genre. The simple plotline concerns three sailors hitting New York with a 24-hour pass. Kelly is the leader, intent on finding Vera-Ellen, whom he believes to be a celebrity, but in reality is a girl from his home town working her way through dance class by appearing at Coney Island. The others are suborned into the search – the clownish Munshin, paired with Ann Miller acting the part of an unlikely anthropologist, and Sinatra, who appears to be overwhelmed and devoured by Garrett, as a voracious female cab-driver.

The film broke new ground in musical cinema with its opening sequence. *New York, New York*, which was filmed in a variety of locations throughout the city. In order to perform a musical number a pre-recorded playback is necessary, enabling the performers to lip-sync and move in correct tempo. This is feasible in a static location, but much harder when the principals are on the open top of a double-decker bus, for example. Sound equipment in 1949 was bulky, cumbersome and ill-suited for busy Manhattan streets. It took some persuading of the studio executives to take the first unit to New York, and the time at the disposal of the film-makers was tight. But they created one of the most breathtaking numbers in film musical history, and paved the way for countless sequences in realistic settings in musical films to follow.

Sinatra, although by now his hollow-cheeked youthful looks were disappearing, was still treated in the script as a frail, insubstantial wraith, evoking the maternal instincts of the lady cabbie. He is the member of the trio who persists long after the others have abandoned any pretence, and gone girl-hunting, in continuing the sightseeing, armed with a woefully out-of-date guide book. One of his most amusing duets with Garrett, *Come Up to My Place*, exploits this conflict of interest.

Sadly, while *On the Town* received superb notices as well as being a box-office success, it did little to assist Sinatra's flagging career. He was merely a member of the team, and the main credit inevitably went to Kelly, who also co-directed with Stanley Donen. In spite of Kelly's entreaties Sinatra decided to pull out of MGM and go his way. But his sagging fortunes were not helped by Howard Hughes, the boss of RKO, who released in 1951 a Sinatra film made in 1948, then considered so bad that the studio had put it on the shelf, rather than lose more money trying to market it. When it was called *It's Only Money* Sinatra had top billing, but now he was relegated to third place and the title changed to *Double Dynamite*, a cheap reference, as the advertising was to make clear, to his co-star, Jane Russell's most prominent assets. Also attending these dire proceedings was Groucho Marx. The film was a 'programmer', designed to fit half of a double-bill, and inevitably was a flop. Although Sinatra was not to blame, the dread label, 'box-office poison', was beginning to be applied to him. He was now noisily pursuing Ava Gardner, then approaching the crest of her stardom, and during this period he made *Meet Danny Wilson*. In this he played a nightclub singer owing his progress to the patronage of a gangster, who then threatened him for a half-share of his earnings. Although Sinatra was able to sing a number of well-known standards such as *How Deep is the Ocean?*, *She's Funny that Way* and *All of Me* the film was unsuccessful, and the Press drew parallels betweem the storyline and Sinatra's own life, with its colourful headlines referring to his dubious underworld acquaintances.

Now came the nadir. His recording contract

Sinatra made a classic comeback from the ropes playing Maggio in Fred Zinnemann's *From Here to Eternity*, his Academy Award-winning performance settling for ever any lingering doubts about his acting ability.

with Columbia was not renewed, and CBS dropped his television show. He even had the humiliation of being fired by his agent, when MCA announced that they would no longer represent him, claiming that he owed $40,000 in commission. His divorce from Nancy Sinatra finalised, he married Ava Gardner in November 1951 and found himself in the back seat watching her film career flourish. He went with her on location to Kenya for *Mogambo*, which she was making with Clark Gable, mainly because there was little else for him to do. He had tried to interest Harry Cohn, the autocratic head of Columbia, in giving him the part of Angelo Maggio in the forthcoming film of the best-selling novel by James Jones, *From Here to Eternity* and had been told that Eli Wallach was the preferred choice. The film was expected to be one of the big ones of the forthcoming year, and was to be filmed on location in Hawaii as well as in the Gower Street studios.

In Africa Sinatra's life suddenly changed. He made a decision to fight for the part. He returned to Hollywood and offered to play Maggio for a thousand dollars a week, a fraction of his former film earnings. Cohn let him have a screen test, although he was still unconvinced. The director, Fred Zinnemann, was so excited with the result that he argued on Sinatra's behalf, and the deciding factor was that Wallach had become unavailable, having signed to appear on Broadway in a Tennessee Williams play.

Sinatra played the rebellious Maggio – an Italian-American slum-kid with a grudge against the army, who dies after a brutal confrontation with a sadistic stockade sergeant – with an extraordinary intensity and feeling, a performance far exceeding the mere $8,000 he was paid to do it. The film was a huge financial success, but what made the difference to Sinatra's fortunes was that he was given the Academy Award for Best Supporting Actor. Such an honour, coming at the time it did, was worth infinitely more than mere dollars.

160

Suddenly, directed by Lewis Allen (page 150), Sinatra
[pla]yed a killer attempting to assassinate the President. It's
[a m]odest film, but he was able to collect more respectful
[not]ices than before *Eternity*.

Sinatra was suddenly back in favour. He had made a classic comeback from the ropes, the kind of renaissance that could not fail to make good newspaper copy.

Sinatra lost out with Harry Cohn for the lead in *On the Waterfront* which went instead to Marlon Brando, and thus did not make two Oscar winners in a row. He sued Columbia, and won modest compensation. Meanwhile, his marriage to Ava Gardner was disintegrating in a public and spectacular fashion.

Although *Suddenly*, a programmer made quickly after *From Here to Eternity*, was not a huge success, Sinatra got good notices for it, and in *Young at Heart* he co-starred with Doris Day, renewing their rostrum partnership from the time of *Your Hit Parade* on the radio. In those days the relationship had been warm and friendly, but now it was fraught with temperament and quarrels. The resulting film, however, a remake with music of a 1938 tear-jerker called *Four Daughters*, was a box-office success and contained several Sinatra numbers, including the title song which became a No. 1 single.

He followed as a fast-talking young doctor in *Not as a Stranger*, a long, but undistinguished Stanley Kramer film, which gave him the chance to act with Robert Mitchum. Sinatra and Kramer got on badly, but Mitchum generously claimed that the sardonic performance of his co-star saved the film from total disaster.

Sinatra was a founder member and pack master of a small, exclusive Hollywood group of Holmby Hills residents called the 'Rat Pack', dedicated to the hedonistic principle of relieving boredom, open to individuals who were unconcerned by what others thought of them. Other members included the Bogarts, Sid Luft and Judy Garland, Joey Bishop, Sammy Cahn, Ernie Kovacs and Nathaniel Benchley. Such diversionary activity made the grind more interesting, and fulfilled some atavistic yearning on Sinatra's part for circles or courts. But to those on the outside it was seen as an elitist and irresponsible group of boozers and boors.

Hit title songs assisted the dramatic *Young at Heart* **(centre), with Doris Day, and the comedy** *The Tender Trap* **(bottom), with Debbie Reynolds. Perhaps the long-winded** *Not as a Stranger*, **with Robert Mitchum, could also have used one.**

In 1954 Sinatra, having recorded the title song for *Three Coins in the Fountain*, assisted Sammy Cahn and Jule Styne, who wrote the lyrics, to win the Oscar for Best Song. He returned to MGM to appear in *The Tender Trap*, with another hit title song by James van Heusen and Sammy Cahn, playing a womanising Broadway agent believing that he is deftly avoiding being lured into marriage while having the pick of any number of satisfying young actresses at his whim. He is, of course, eventually snared by the ingenue, Debbie Reynolds, who pretends to be much dumber than she really is. It was the first of his cynical swinging bachelor parts and the public showed its approval of the casting by ensuring a healthy box-office return.

The next film to be released was *Guys and Dolls*, the long-awaited film version of Frederick Loesser's hit Broadway musical, based on characters and stories by Damon Runyon, which was produced by Samuel Goldwyn and directed by Joseph L. Mankiewicz, although actually shot before *The Tender Trap*. Sinatra would have preferred to have played the role of Sky Masterson, the gambler who bets that he can take the demure mission girl, played by Jean Simmons, on a trip to Havana, and for the second time he saw a plum role pass to Marlon Brando. Instead, he took the part of Nathan Detroit, the proprietor of the oldest established permanent floating crap game in New York, and long-time fiancé of cabaret singer Miss Adelaide, with Vivian Baine in that role repeating her stage performance. Sinatra's instinct was right on this occasion – he would have made a better Sky Masterson than Brando, and his portrayal of Nathan Detroit turned out to be more Sicilian than Jewish. Brando and Sinatra did not hit it off readily, both professionally and off-screen, and the Method, requiring an intense period of working into a role, was not to Sinatra's taste.

Nevertheless, he was well capable of projecting himself into a characterisation, as he proved spectacularly in his next film, which

In spite of miscasting, Sinatra did what he could as Nathan Detroit in *Guys and Dolls*, but had difficulty working with Marlon Brando in the role of Sky Masterson, particularly as it was the part that he had hankered after himself.

got him an Oscar nomination as Best Actor in 1955, the year that the award went to Ernest Borgnine for *Marty*. In *The Man with the Golden Arm* he played a drug-addicted poker dealer, and scene in which he underwent the 'cold turkey' withdrawal process aroused considerable controversy, being for its day the most explicit sequence relating to hard drugs that had ever been seen on the screen. Otto Preminger's direction was heavy-handed, and the film, for all the attention it received at the time, including the withholding of the Production Code Seal of Approval – a surefire way of achieving box office success – has not lasted all that well, although Sinatra's performance does retain its integrity.

It served the purpose of establishing his position as a serious screen actor, and he was able to bankroll his own production of *Johnny Concho*, which was directed by Don McGuire. Sinatra played the leading role of a cowardly cowboy, forced to take action after his brother has been gunned down. It was almost as though he was getting out of his system a childhood urge to play cowboys, and the film did nothing to enhance his reputation.

Sinatra was then supposed to take the leading role in *Carousel*, directed by Henry King, but demurred on arriving in Maine when he found that the film was being made in two systems, Todd-AO and CinemaScope, which meant that each set-up had to be filmed twice. He had a preference for shooting his scenes wherever possible in only one take, and had always disliked working with people like Brando who required several opportunities to play themselves in. After two days of long-distance wrangling with the studio back in Hollywood, Sinatra walked off the set in a rage. Twentieth Century-Fox first replaced him with Gordon Macrae, then started a lawsuit for a million dollars. However, after a decision was made to shoot the film in only one system after all, the action was dropped. Regrettably, posterity was still denied what might have been a memorable Sinatra performance.

He did have the satisfaction of appearing in another musical, which turned out to be more successful than *Carousel. High Society*, directed at MGM by Charles Walters, was a remake of *The Philadelphia Story*, a justly celebrated 1940 upper-crust marital comedy starring Cary Grant and Katharine Hepburn. Turned into a Technicolor spectacular with songs written by Cole Porter, its location switched to Rhode Island so that Louis Armstrong, en route to the Newport Jazz Festival, could be included, and given a cast that also featured Grace Kelly and Bing Crosby in the Hepburn-Grant roles, the film was sprightly and entertaining. It was the first time that Sinatra and Crosby, his teenage idol, had been in a film with each other, and they made the most of their song together, a drinking number, *Well, Did you Evah?*, with a Porter lyric rich in double entendres and colourful imagery.

Along with most of Hollywood, Sinatra had a bit part in Michael Todd's extravaganza, *Around the World in Eighty Days*, as the piano player in a San Francisco saloon presided over by Marlene Dietrich. He went from that into another film for Stanley Kramer, and the experience was even less satisfactory than *Not as a Stranger*. Allegedly, Kramer only asked Sinatra to play a Spanish guerilla leader in *The Pride and the Passion* because he was unable to get Brando. The film was from a C. S. Forester novel set in the Peninsular Wars, and described how an enormous gun was manhandled across Spain to lift the siege of Avila. It was a hard film to make, in rugged, dusty locations, and while everyone else made do with shabby accommodation, sometimes even sleeping in tents, Sinatra, going through the trauma of divorce from Ava Gardner, insisted on staying in comfort in Madrid, driving vast distances to and from the set each day, and then proved unwilling to rehearse with his co-stars, Cary Grant and Sophia Loren.

His next film was *The Joker is Wild*, directed by Charles Vidor, which was the story of a friend, Joe E. Lewis, who had been a nightclub singer in the Prohibition era and had fallen foul of gangsters who slashed his vocal chords. After a long self-pitying wallow in alcohol he made it back to the top as a comedian. As with *Meet Danny Wilson*, there were hints of Sinatra's own story, but he performed creditably, pushing one of the numbers, *All the Way* by James van Heusen and Sammy Cahn, towards that year's Oscar for Best Song. He also owned a percentage of this film and the next, which was *Pal Joey*.

Ironically, Sinatra was now able to achieve a part that Brando had really wanted, the nightclub heel of the last of the Rodgers and Hart Broadway musicals, and the stage vehicle which had made a star of Gene Kelly in 1940. *Pal Joey* was a less than satisfactory film – Hollywood shifted the location to San Francisco for purely photogenic reasons, discarded much of the score and put in songs from other Rodgers and Hart shows. While Rita Hayworth was well-suited to the role of the ex-stripper transformed by a good marriage into a Nob Hill socialite, Kim Novak, who had been Sinatra's co-star in *The Man with the Golden Arm*, floundered as a young singer. But there is one superb Sinatra song, his one-to-one performance of *The Lady is a Tramp*, sung in the empty nightclub to Rita Hayworth, his profile etched against a spotlight and each line of the lyric given an insolent caress.

His friend Humphrey Bogart died early in 1957, just before *Pal Joey* went into production, and it deeply affected him. There was a brief period when the gossip columns forecast that he would marry Bogie's widow, Lauren Bacall, but Sinatra himself terminated the idea. Yet in spite of the box-office success of *Pal Joey* he had difficulty in getting a new film under way, and *Kings Go Forth*, his next, was one of his poorer efforts, an improbable war story divided between mountain fighting and Riviera relaxing, with Natalie Wood as a half-caste.

Then followed *Some Came Running*, another adaptation of a James Jones best-seller, with Shirley MacLaine playing one of her early

High Society was a hoot to make, with co-stars Bing Crosby and Grace Kelly, seen (top) with director Charles Walters and producer Sol C. Siegel. Sinatra even danced with the future princess. He played a cameo role as a saloon pianist in Michael Todd's ambitious *Around the World in Eighty Days* (above), but appeared less happily with Cary Grant and Sophia Loren in *The Pride and the Passion* (right).

floosies. It was a difficult shoot, and the townspeople of Madison, Indiana, the chosen location, were much put out by the behaviour of the Hollywoodites who descended in their midst, and particularly by Sinatra and his co-starring friend, Dean Martin. The film, in spite of direction by Vincente Minnelli, is about on the level of the average television mini-series.

Another Oscar-winning song by van Heusen and Cahn, *High Hopes*, was featured in Frank Capra's *A Hole in the Head*, Sinatra's next, which was filmed on location in the more sophisticated climate of Miami Beach, where nevertheless the Press lurked awaiting more salacious anecdotes of boorish behaviour and, on not finding them, invented a few. Such was Capra's skill, in spite of his eight-year absence from the screen, that the flimsiness of the storyline was scarcely noticed. Sinatra played a hotelier whose premises are about to be taken over by the bank unless he can raise some quick money, and Edward G. Robinson was his rich, but unhelpful, brother in New York.

Now Sinatra made a war film, set in Burma, called *Never So Few*, another undistinguished work. By now the old Rat Pack had faded, but

a new circle succeeded it known as the Clan. One of its founder members, Sammy Davis Junior, blotted his copybook by openly criticising Sinatra on a television show, referring to the way he stepped on people. He was punished by not being given a part in *Never So Few*, being replaced by a little-known actor from television called Steve McQueen, who turned out to be one of the few satisfactory elements of the film.

Another disappointment was a laboured, expensive musical made from a Cole Porter Broadway hit, *Can-Can*, which bore a stale scent throughout, with Maurice Chevalier and Louis Jourdan resurrecting their double act from *Gigi* and Shirley MacLaine generally over-acting. The film secured one particular place in the annals of Hollywood legend in that it was the production deemed worthy of a visit from Mr Khrushchev, the Russian premier, to demonstrate that the film capital was not so decadent as Soviet propaganda would suggest. The scene being shot was a chorus number which turned out to be a frothy riot of raised skirts, high kicks, flashing thighs, taut garters, transparent panties and plunging necklines, a

Rodgers and Hart's musical *Pal Joey* (left) put Sinatra in a triangle with Rita Hayworth (above) and Kim Novak, both seen in a dream sequence. *Kings Go Forth* (below), with Tony Curtis, was a so-so war film, and the good folk of Madison, Indiana took a while to forget *Some Came Running* (bottom) which he made with Martha Hyer (left) and Shirley MacLaine (right).

display watched grimly by the puritanical guest.

The Clan came into its own with *Ocean's Eleven*, a caper film, its plot very similar to that of a British thriller of the same period, *The League of Gentlemen*, in that Sinatra played a ringleader who calls in his old army buddies to enact a spectacular heist, in this instance the takings of five Las Vegas casinos on New Year's Eve. In spite of the incessant clowning of Sinatra, Dean Martin, Peter Lawford, Joey Bishop, the reinstated Sammy Davis Junior, and other Clan members, the film was better than those that followed.

Sinatra guested in the lamentable *Pepe*, and then appeared with Spencer Tracy in one of the latter's worst films, *The Devil at Four O'Clock*. Tracy's rare ill-at-ease performance was compounded by Sinatra's refusal to play off-camera to him in his one-shots, a professional lapse which hurt the elder man.

The Clan reassembled for *Sergeants Three*, a tedious reworking of the *Gunga Din* story as a western, which thwarted the critics by doing surprisingly well at the box office. Sinatra's next film, however, while collecting the best notices of any of his later works, was a relative and undeserved failure with the public.

John Frankenheimer's *The Manchurian Candidate* was adapted by George Axelrod from a Richard Condon novel about a Korean War veteran and ex-prisoner who through advanced brainwashing techniques has been programmed to carry out a political assassination in America. He was played by Laurence Harvey, with Sinatra as his ex-comrade who discovers the secret. Frankenheimer's dazzling technique overcame inconsistencies and downright implausibilities in the plot, but when a few months after it was released President Kennedy was shot and killed in Dallas, United Artists, the distributors, withdrew the film.

Come Blow Your Horn was another of Sinatra's swinging bachelor forays, and in spite of its provenance as an early Neil Simon stage play was a tired work. Next came John

Sinatra starred with Edward G. Robinson (left) and Eleanor Parker (below left) in Frank Capra's *A Hole in the Head*, which had another Oscar-winning song. *Never So Few* with Gina Lollobrigida (right) was poor, and Sinatra, angry with Sammy Davis Jr, gave his part to a newcomer, Steve McQueen (below right).

Huston's thriller, *The List of Adrian Messenger*, which was a self-indulgent joke for a number of stars, including Sinatra, Tony Curtis, Burt Lancaster, Kirk Douglas and Robert Mitchum, who appeared so heavily masked by latex make-up that they were unrecognisable, and their identities were revealed in a lengthy coda in which they stripped off their masks.

There followed two more 'Clan' movies, the mildly funny *4 for Texas*, with Sinatra and Dean Martin as rival saloon owners deep into double – and triple-crossing each other, and *Robin and the Seven Hoods*, which ought to have been a great deal better, having at its heart the engaging idea of transposing the legend of Robin Hood to Chicago in the 1920s. There were one or two good songs, however, including *My Kind of Town (Chicago is)*.

Sinatra next succumbed to a vanity that

attacks so many actors, and directed as well as starred in his next film, *None but the Brave*, which was a war story. A group of Americans are forced down on a remote Pacific island that is held by the Japanese, and for the sake of mutual survival the enemies come to terms, on the understanding that once they are back in the war hostilities resume. The film was an American–Japanese co-production and made in Hawaii. It was to Sinatra's credit that this only directing effort should be a serious anti-war film rather than some further confectionery featuring the Clan, but it was not particularly successful, and the dialogue sequences had a flatness about them and might have been handled more adroitly.

For *Von Ryan's Express*, directed by Mark Robson, Sinatra was again in the war, this time as the sole American inmate of a prisoner-of-war camp in Italy who concocts a wildly ambitious escape plot involving the seizure of a German train. Although a conventional war adventure, it maintained an exciting pace, and went down well with the public. *Marriage on the Rocks*, which followed, was another disappointment, a laboured marital comedy with Deborah Kerr and Dean Martin. And then, *Cast a Giant Shadow*, the next film, was an ambitious biography of David Marcus, one of the founders of modern Israel, but like everything else Sinatra was in during this period, it was not up to standard. He played the part of a soldier-of-fortune, a pilot who dropped soda-water bottles on the Arabs, there being no bombs available. He then made another tiny guest appearance in a bad film, as himself in *The Oscar*, a Hollywood story. After that he starred with Tony Franciosa in *Assault on a Queen*, a dismal caper movie in which the Cunard liner, *Queen Mary*, is the target of a hijack attempt. It was made in the year in which he married Mia Farrow, and passed the age of 50. He had met the young actress two years earlier, and almost as soon as they were wed their hitherto pleasant relationship soured.

Sinatra made his next film in England, a

thriller called *The Naked Runner*, in which he played an American businessman in London whose son is kidnapped. Later he discovers that he has been framed by British intelligence in order to carry out an assignment. Sidney Furie directed it in a modish Sixties style, but it was a less than satisfactory work. He returned to America to make another film in Miami, *Tony Rome*, in which he played a hard-boiled private eye whose tacky home was a boat. The intricate, erotic, violent plot seemed vaguely reminiscent of the Howard Hawks movie version of Raymond Chandler's *The Big Sleep*, but spiced with the frankness that a more permissive age allowed. The director was his friend, Gordon Douglas, who was to go on to

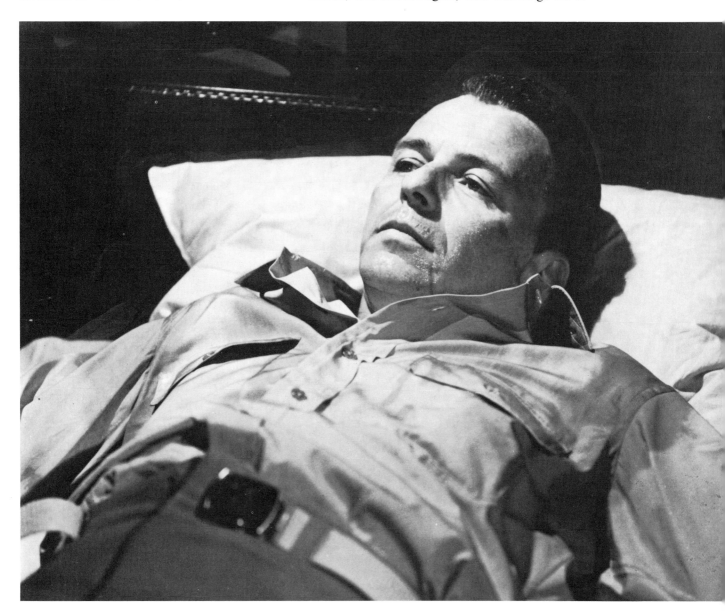

make three films for Sinatra in a row.

But before the next film could begin, his brief third marriage was finished. The part that Mia Farrow was to have had in *The Detective* was awarded to Jacqueline Bisset. Sinatra raced through the film with an angry rage that seems to explode from the screen. The character he played is a New York police detective whose swift, effective methods have sent an innocent man to the electric chair. It is a sordid film, and caused anguish in the gay community on account of its condemnatory attitudes. Not that they should have worried over much, for none of humankind came out of it smelling of roses. The other film Gordon Douglas directed was a rapid sequel to *Tony Rome*, called *Lady in Cement*. It was much the same mix as before, but with an extra polish acquired through practice.

Sinatra now decided that he was past the agonies of regular film-making and announced that *Dirty Dingus Magee* would be his last. It

was an absurd misjudgement on his part to build a farewell performance around a raucous spoof western laced with crude and vulgar jokes. Accordingly, he received a vigorous critical lambasting and the film was savaged so violently that even the public, as well as his friends, stayed away from it. There was no appetite for this sort of thing until Mel Brooks, a Sinatra fan as it happens, made *Blazing Saddles* four years later. Sinatra was tempted by, but finally turned down, a role in *The Little Prince* which was later made by his old colleague of *On the Town*, Stanley Donen, but it turned out to be a dispiriting, dismal flop, so at least one dose of anguish for him was spared.

Sinatra *did* reappear, both times playing a tired, grudge-bearing, hard-nosed cop. In 1977 he made a television film called *Contract on Cherry Street*, spending three hours of airtime tracking down and killing Mafia mobsters who shot his best friend. And in 1980 he appeared in *The First Deadly Sin*, a thriller directed by

Robin and the Seven Hoods (**opposite**) **was Sinatra's second film with Bing Crosby, a gangster comedy. He directed** *None But the Brave* (**left**) **himself, as well as starring, and played the escaping GI prisoner-of-war in** *Von Ryan's Express* (**right**), **a crazy flier in** *Cast a Giant Shadow* (**below left**) **and a heist man with his eye on the Queen Mary in** *Assault on a Queen* (**below right**).

In his last films Sinatra tended to play detectives. The hard-nosed Miami private eye *Tony Rome* was the first of these characterizations, and the style of the film recalled the Chandleresque *film noirs* of the Forties.
Sinatra played a tough New York cop in *The Detective* (top left), with Jackie Bisset, and reprised Tony Rome in *Lady in Cement* (bottom left and overleaf top) with Raquel Welch.

Brian G. Hutton, in which he was a police officer tracking down a killer in the weeks before he has to retire. As an additional complication, his wife, played by Faye Dunaway, is lying in hospital dying, having suffered inept surgery. It is curious that in five of the last six Sinatra films, made over a 13-year period, he should be either a private eye or a police detective.

The next question inevitably is whether Sinatra, as he reaches his 70s, will ever make another film. There is, of course, absolutely no need that he should, and few of his later films are of much value. At the beginning of the 1970s he had decided that he should quit rather than face the humiliation of rejection, and twice he broke his own promise. The temptation now, one suspects, will be easier to resist.

Looking at the sum total of his screen work it is certainly disappointing that so little of it is of outstanding value. Of his excellence as song-and-dance man, light comedian and serious dramatic actor, there can be no dispute. His presence has even made bearable films that were otherwise below par. The man was always a paradox, alternately a monster and the biggest-hearted giver in the world. His anger, scorn and impatience often unnerved fellow artists, yet just as many will testify to the extraordinary loyalty and kindness he could muster, with no intention of making such gestures in public. As an actor he was a 'natural', an instinctive performer to whom being on the button came viscerally. Hence his dislike of rehearsals and retakes, and his lack of ease with those who created their characterisations cerebrally.

There are, in that long career, a small number of performances that have the uniqueness, the special quality of a great star, the inspired electric presence. With Gene Kelly in *Anchors Aweigh* he was a superb junior partner, giving just enough to assert his personality without ever being guilty of upstaging. In *From Here to Eternity* he deservedly won an Oscar, and made a major contribution to the success of the film. In film after film he rose above the basic

Sinatra's Western, *Dirty Dingus Magee* (below) went largely unappreciated. His last film was *The First Deadly Sin* (below right) in which he played a police detective near retirement with a deadly killer to nab.

material – *The Man with the Golden Arm*, *Pal Joey*, even, let it be said, *Ocean's Eleven*. The last of his really good films was *The Manchurian Candidate*, but we ought not dismiss Von Ryan and Tony Rome and Mike Connor and Alfred Boone and Charlie Reader and Barney Sloan and Tony Manetta out of hand, even if we have reservations about the overall quality of the pictures in which they appear. The man who gave those characters to the film-going public was never dull, always watchable, and sometimes was more brilliant than even he was able to appreciate.

Stars must be exceptional, unique, untouchable. Unquestionably, Sinatra was a star.

ILMOGRAPHY

1941

1 Las Vegas Nights (Paramount)
DIRECTOR Ralph Murphy
CAST Constance Moore (Norma Jennings);
Bert Wheeler (Stu Grant); Phil Regan (Bill
Stevens); Lillian Cornell (Mildred
Jennings); Virginia Dale (Patsy Lynch);
Hank Ladd (Hank Bevis); Katy (Betty
Brewer); Tommy Dorsey and his Orchestra.
ORIGINAL SCREENPLAY Ernest Pagano,
Harry Clark
ADDITIONAL DIALOGUE Eddie Welch
MUSICAL DIRECTOR Victor Young
MUSICAL ADVISOR Arthur Franklin
MUSICAL NUMBERS STAGED BY LeRoy Prinz
INCIDENTAL SCORE Phil Boutelje and Walter
Scharf
MUSICAL ARRANGEMENTS Axel Stordahl,
Victor Young, Charles Bradshaw, Leo
Shuken, Max Terr
PHOTOGRAPHY William C. Mellor
EDITOR Arthur Schmidt
ART DIRECTION Hans Dreier, Earl Hedrick
RUNNING TIME 89 minutes
PRODUCED BY William LeBaron

A so-so comedy about a comedian and a girl
singing trio stranded in Las Vegas, starting
a night club on winnings, seeing it wrecked,
and eventually claiming an inheritance.
Sinatra appears as the band singer with
Tommy Dorsey and his Orchestra, and performs 'I'll Never Smile Again'.

1942

2 Ship Ahoy (MGM)
DIRECTOR Edward Buzzell
CAST Eleanor Powell (Tallulah Winters);
Red Skelton (Merton K. Kibble); Bert Lahr
(Skip Owens); Virginia O'Brien (Fran
Evans); William Post Jr (H. U. Bennett);
Tommy Dorsey and his Orchestra.
SCREENPLAY Harry Clork
ADDITIONAL MATERIAL Harry Kurnitz,
Irving Brecher
Based on story by Matt Brooks, Bradford
Ropes, Bert Kalmar
MUSIC SUPERVISED AND CONDUCTED BY
George Stoll
MUSICAL ARRANGEMENTS Axel Stordahl, Sy
Oliver, Leo Arnaud, George Bassman, Basil
Adlam
INCIDENTAL SCORE George Bassman, George
Stoll, Henry Russell

PHOTOGRAPHY Leonard Smith, Robert
Planck
EDITOR Blanche Sewell
ART DIRECTION Cedric Gibbons, Harry
McAfee
DANCE NUMBERS STAGED BY Bobby Connolly
RUNNING TIME 95 minutes
PRODUCED BY Jack Cummings

A mindless, but entertaining musical, with
Eleanor Powell as a dancer, on board a ship
with her troupe and the Tommy Dorsey
Orchestra en route to open a floating night
club in Puerto Rico. She inadvertently carries a magnetic mine in her luggage, but
unmasks the enemy spies by dancing out a
Morse message in a big number. Sinatra
again appears as the band singer, and sings
two numbers, 'The Last Call for Love' and
'On Moonlight Bay', with The Pied Pipers
(Chuck Lowry, Jo Stafford, Clark Yokum
and Hal Hopper) and 'Poor You' with Red
Skelton and Virginia O'Brien. Also performing are Buddy Rich on drums, Ziggy Elman
on trumpet and Joe Bushkin on piano.

1943

3 Reveille with Beverly (Columbia)
DIRECTOR Charles Barton
CAST Ann Miller (Beverly Ross); William
Wright (Barry Lang); Dick Purcell (Andy
Adams); Franklin Pangborn (Vernon
Lewis); Tim Ryan (Mr Kennedy); Larry
Parks (Eddie Ross); Barbara Brown (Mrs
Ross); Douglas Leavitt (Mr Ross); Adele
Mara (Evelyn Ross); Bob Crosby and his
Orchestra; Freddie Slack and his Orchestra,
with Ella Mae Morse; Duke Ellington and
his Orchestra; Count Basie and his
Orchestra; Frank Sinatra; the Mills
Brothers; the Radio Rogues.
ORIGINAL SCREENPLAY Howard J. Green,
Jack Henley, Albert Duffy
MUSICAL DIRECTOR Morris Stoloff
PHOTOGRAPHY Philip Tannura
EDITOR James Sweeney
ART DIRECTION Lionel Banks
RUNNING TIME 78 minutes
PRODUCED BY Sam White

A salesgirl in a record shop becomes a radio
station announcer and soups up a dawn
request programme with popular songs
aimed at an army camp, with consequent
popularity. In spite of the big names the film

is a mess, although it has a certain period
curiosity value. Sinatra only performs one
number, Cole Porter's 'Night and Day'.

1944

4 Higher and Higher (RKO)
DIRECTOR, PRODUCER Tim Whelan
CAST Michele Morgan (Millie); Jack Haley
(Mike); Frank Sinatra (Frank); Leon Errol
(Drake); Marcy McGuire (Mickey); Victor
Borge (Fitzroy Wilson); Mary Wickes
(Sandy); Elizabeth Risdon (Mrs Keating);
Barbara Hale (Catherine Keating); Mel
Torme (Marty); Paul Hartman (Byngham);
Grace Hartman (Hilda); Dooley Wilson
(Oscar).
ASSOCIATE PRODUCER George Arthur
SCREENPLAY Jay Dratler and Ralph Spence
ADDITIONAL DIALOGUE William Bowers,
Howard Harris
Based on play by Gladys Hurlbut and
Joshua Logan
MUSICAL DIRECTOR Constantin
Bakaleinikoff
ORCHESTRAL ARRANGEMENTS Gene Rose
MUSICAL ARRANGEMENTS FOR FRANK SINATRA
Axel Stordahl
INCIDENTAL SCORE Roy Webb, orchestrated
by Maurice de Packh
VOCAL ARRANGEMENTS Ken Darby
MUSICAL NUMBERS STAGED BY Ernst Matray
PHOTOGRAPHY Robert DeGrasse
EDITOR Gene Milford
ART DIRECTION Albert S. D'Agostino, Jack
Okey
RUNNING TIME 90 minutes

SINATRA'S NUMBERS 'You Belong in a Love
Song', 'I Couldn't Sleep a Wink Last
Night', 'A Lovely Way to Spend an
Evening', 'The Music Stopped', 'I Saw You
First' (Jimmy McHugh and Harold
Adamson).

A scullery maid poses as a bankrupt's
debutante daughter in the hope that she can
entrap a rich husband and pay the wages of
a household of servants. Sinatra in his first
acting role plays the wealthy young man next
door, but she ends up marrying the butler.
Sinatra's shy appeal for bobbysoxers comes
across in this slight film, which started out
as a Rodgers and Hart musical on Broadway, the score of which Hollywood threw
away.

1944

5 Step Lively (RKO)
DIRECTOR Tim Whelan
CAST Frank Sinatra (Glen); George Murphy (Miller); Adolphe Menjou (Wagner); Gloria De Haven (Christine); Walter Slezak (Gribble); Eugene Pallette (Jenkins); Wally Brown (Binion); Alan Carney (Harry); Grant Mitchell (Dr Glass); Anne Jeffreys (Miss Abbott); Frances King (Mother); Harry Noble (Father); George Chandler (Country Yokel); Rosemary La Planche (Louella); Shirley O'Hara (Louise); Elaine Riley (Lois); Dorothy Malone (Telephone Operator); Frank Mayo (Doorman).
SCREENPLAY Warren Duff, Peter Milne
Based on play *Room Service* by John Murray and Allen Boretz
MUSICAL DIRECTOR Constantin Bakaleinikoff
ORCHESTRAL ARRANGEMENTS Gene Rose
MUSICAL ARRANGEMENTS FOR FRANK SINATRA Axel Stordahl
VOCAL ARRANGEMENTS Ken Darby
MUSICAL NUMBERS CREATED AND STAGED BY Ernst Matray
PHOTOGRAPHY Robert DeGrasse
EDITOR Gene Milford
ART DIRECTION Albert S. D'Agostino, Carroll Clark
RUNNING TIME 88 minutes
PRODUCED BY Robert Fellows

SINATRA'S NUMBERS 'Come Out, Come Out, Wherever You Are', 'Where Does Love Begin?', 'As Long as There's Music', 'Some Other Time' (Jule Styne and Sammy Cahn).

In this musical remake of the Marx Brothers' *Room Service* Sinatra is an aspiring playwright who has fallen into the clutches of an indigent revue producer, holed up in a hotel with his cast and unpaid bill. On discovering that he can sing he persuades Sinatra to take over the lead and the show is a hit. Sinatra now had top billing, and the film was really an excuse to enable him to sing.

1945

6 Anchors Aweigh (MGM)
DIRECTOR George Sidney
CAST Frank Sinatra (Clarence Doolittle); Kathryn Grayson (Susan Abbott); Gene Kelly (Joseph Brady); José Iturbi (Himself); Dean Stockwell (Donald Martin); Girl from Brooklyn (Pamela Britton); Rags Ragland (Police Sergeant); Billy Gilbert (Cafe Manager); Henry O'Neill (Admiral Hammond); Carlos Ramirez (Carlos); Edgar Kennedy (Police Captain); Grady Sutton (Bertram Kraler); Leon Ames (Admiral's Aide); Sharon McManus (Little Girl Beggar); James Flavin (Radio Cop); James Burke (Studio Cop); Henry Armetta (Hamburger Man); Chester Clute (Iturbi's Assistant); William Forrest (Movie Director); Ray Teal (Assistant Director); Milton Kibbee (Bartender); Charles Coleman (Butler); Garry Owen, Steve Brodie (Soldiers).
SCREENPLAY Isabel Lennart

Based on story by Natalie Marcin
MUSIC SUPERVISED AND CONDUCTED BY George Stoll
FRANK SINATRA'S VOCAL ARRANGEMENTS Axel Stordahl
KATHERINE GRAYSON'S VOCAL ARRANGEMENTS Earl Brent
INCIDENTAL SCORE George Stoll, Calvin Jackson
ORCHESTRATIONS Ted Duncan, Joseph Nussbaum, Robert Franklyn, Wally Heglin
DANCE SEQUENCES Gene Kelly
PHOTOGRAPHY Robert Planck, Charles Boyle
EDITOR Adrienne Fazan
ART DIRECTION Cedric Gibbons, Randall Duell
"Tom and Jerry" cartoon by Fred Quimby
Technicolor
RUNNING TIME 143 minutes
PRODUCED BY Joe Pasternak

SINATRA'S NUMBERS 'We Hate to Leave', 'What Makes the Sunset?', 'The Charm of You', 'I Begged Her', 'I Fall in Love Too Easily' (Jule Styne and Sammy Cahn), Brahms' 'Lullaby'.

A large-scale MGM musical heavily influenced by Gene Kelly in the first of several sailor characterisations. He and Sinatra play shipmates on shore leave in Hollywood who become involved with an aspiring singer, and attempt to get her an audition with Jose Iturbi. Sinatra has several excellent Styne-Cahn songs (plus a snatch of 'If You Knew Susie') and performs some vigorous dancing alongside Kelly in the 'I Hate to Leave' number.

7 The House I Live In (RKO)
DIRECTOR Mervyn LeRoy
ORIGINAL SCREENPLAY Albert Maltz
MUSICAL DIRECTION Axel Stordahl
INCIDENTAL SCORE Roy Webb
EDITOR Philip Martin Jr
RUNNING TIME 10 minutes
PRODUCED BY Frank Ross

SINATRA'S NUMBERS 'If You Are But a Dream' (Nathan J. Bonx, Jack Fulton, Moe Jaffe), 'The House I Live In' (Earl Robinson, Lewis Allan).

A short extolling the virtues of tolerance and freedom of speech and religion. Sinatra steps out from a recording studio for a break and finds a number of young boys bullying another because they don't like his church. He separates them and sings 'The House I Live In'. This small propaganda film won a Special Academy Award.

1946

8 Till the Clouds Roll By (MGM)
DIRECTOR Richard Whorf
CAST June Allyson (Guest Star); Lucille Bremer (Sally); Judy Garland (Marilyn Miller); Kathryn Grayson (Magnolia); Van Heflin (James I. Hessler); Lena Horne (Julie); Van Johnson (Band Leader); Angela Lansbury (Guest Star); Tony

Martin (Gaylord Ravenal); Virginia O'Brien (Ellie); Dinah Shore (Julie Sanderson); Frank Sinatra (Guest Star); Robert Walker (Jerome Kern); Dorothy Patrick (Mrs Jerome Kern); Gower Champion (Dance Specialty); Cyd Charisse (Dance Specialty); Harry Hayden (Charles Frohman); Paul Langton (Oscar Hammerstein); Paul Maxey (Victor Herbert); Ray McDonald (Dance Specialty); Mary Nash (Mrs Muller); Caleb Paterson (Joe); William 'Bill' Phillips (Hennessey); The Wilde Twins (Specialty); Rex Evans (Cecil Keller); Maurice Kelly (Dance Specialty); Ray Teal (Orchestra Conductor); Byron Foulger (Frohman's Secretary); William Halligan (Captain Andy).
SCREENPLAY Myles Connolly, Jean Holloway
ADAPTATION George Wells, from an original story by Guy Bolton
MUSIC SUPERVISED AND CONDUCTED BY Lenny Hayton
ORCHESTRATIONS Conrad Salinger
VOCAL ARRANGEMENTS Kay Thompson
MUSICAL NUMBERS STAGED AND DIRECTED BY Robert Alton
PHOTOGRAPHY Harry Stradling, George Folsey
EDITOR Albert Akst
ART DIRECTION Cedric Gibbons, Daniel B. Cathcart
Technicolor
RUNNING TIME 137 minutes
PRODUCED BY Arthur Freed

Sinatra performs 'Ol' Man River' (Jerome Kern and Oscar Hammerstein II).

An amazing saccharin Hollywood biography of Jerome Kern, with an incredible melange of stars. Sinatra's contribution is a notable climax, singing the great song about darkies totin' bales, bodies all achin' and racked with pain, in an immaculate white suit on a pedestal in front of a huge, snow-white orchestra – but visuals aside, he is in tremendous voice.

1947

9 It Happened in Brooklyn (MGM)
DIRECTOR Richard Whorf
CAST Frank Sinatra (Danny Webson Miller); Kathryn Grayson (Anne Fielding); Peter Lawford (Jamie Shellgrove); Jimmy Durante (Nick Lombardi); Gloria Grahame (Nurse); Marcy McGuire (Rae Jakobi); Aubrey Mather (Digby John); Tamara Shayne (Mrs Kardos); Billy Roy (Leo Kardos); Bobby Long (Johnny O'Brien); William Haade (Police Sergeant); Lumsden Hare (Canon Green); Wilson Wood (Fodderwing); Raymond Largay (Mr Dobson); William Tannen (Captain); Al Hill (Driver); Dick Wessel (Cop); Lennie Bremen (Corporal); Bruce Cowling (Soldier); Mitchell Lewis (Printer).
SCREENPLAY Isabel Lennart
Based on original story by John McGowan
MUSICAL DIRECTION, SUPERVISION, INCIDENTAL SCORE Johnny Green

ORCHESTRATIONS Ted Duncan
FRANK SINATRA'S VOCAL ORCHESTRATIONS
Axel Stordahl
MUSICAL NUMBERS STAGED AND DIRECTED BY
Jack Donohue
PIANO SOLOS Andre Previn
PHOTOGRAPHY Robert Planck
EDITOR Blanche Sewell
RUNNING TIME 104 minutes
PRODUCED BY Jack Cummings

SINATRA'S NUMBERS 'Brooklyn Bridge', 'I Believe', 'Time after Time', 'The Song's Gotta Come from the Heart', 'It's the Same Old Dream' (Jule Styne and Sammy Cahn), 'La Ci Darem la Mano' (Mozart), 'Black Eyes' (Russian).

Sinatra plays a GI returned from the war, who stays with an old pal, Durante, who is a high school janitor. A teacher at the school is also, like him, an aspiring singer, she falls for an English heir instead, and the hero pairs off with a Brooklyn girl. It's a small-scale picture, but Sinatra hits his stride, particularly in a comic duet with Durante.

1948

10 The Miracle of the Bells (RKO)
DIRECTOR Irving Pichel
CAST Fred MacMurray (Bill Dunnigan); Alida Valli (Olga Treskovna); Frank Sinatra (Father Paul); Lee J. Cobb (Marcus Harris); Harold Vermilye (Orloff); Charles Meredith (Father Spinsky); Jim Nolan (Tod Jones); Veronica Pataky (Anna Klovna); Philip Ahn (Ming Gow); Frank Ferguson (Dolan); Frank Wilcox (Dr Jennings); Ray Teal (Koslick); Dorothy Sebastian (Katy); Billy Wayne (Tom Elmore); Syd Saylor (Fred Evans); Tom Stevenson (Milton Wild); Ian Wolfe (Gravedigger); Oliver Blake (Slenzka); George Chandler (Max); Regina Wallace (Martha); Franklyn Farnum, Snub Pollard, Beth Taylor (Worshippers); Quentin Reynolds (Narrator).
SCREENPLAY Ben Hecht, Quentin Reynolds
ADDITIONAL MATERIAL FOR SINATRA
SEQUENCES: DeWitt Bodeen
Based on novel by Russell Janney
MUSIC Leigh Harline
PHOTOGRAPHY Robert de Grasse
EDITOR Elmo Williams
ART DIRECTION Ralph Berger
RUNNING TIME 120 minutes
PRODUCED BY Jesse L. Lasky, Walter MacEwan

Sinatra sings 'Ever Homeward' (Kasimierz Lubomirski, Jule Styne and Sammy Cahn).

Bing Crosby had won an Academy Award portraying a priest, but Sinatra was less fortunate. A press agent arranges for a deceased film star to be buried in her gritty small town and for the bells to ring out, but the studio head refuses to release her film. Then statues in the church turn to face the coffin. Sinatra, playing the young cleric in charge, does his best, but the film is cloyingly sentimental, and doesn't come off.

11 The Kissing Bandit (MGM)
DIRECTOR Laslo Benedek
CAST Frank Sinatra (Ricardo); Kathryn Grayson (Teresa); J. Carroll Naish (Chico); Mildred Natwick (Isabella); Mikhail Rasumny (Don Jose); Billy Gilbert (General Torro); Sono Osato (Bianca); Clinton Sundberg (Colonel Gomez); Carleton Young (Count Belmonte); Edna Skinner (Juanita); Vincente Gomez (Guitarist); Henry Mirelez (Pepito); Nick Thompson (Pablo); Jose Dominguez (Francisco); Albert Morin (Lotso); Pedro Regas (Esteban); Julian Rivero (Postman); Mitchell Lewis (Fernando); Byron Foulger (Grandee); Ricardo Montalban, Ann Miller, Cyd Charisse (Dancers).
ORIGINAL SCREENPLAY Isabel Lennart, John Briard Harding
MUSIC SUPERVISED AND CONDUCTED BY George Stoll
MUSICAL ARRANGEMENTS Leo Arnaud
INCIDENTAL SCORE George Stoll, Albert Sendrey, Scott Bradley, Andre Previn
DANCE DIRECTOR Stanley Donen
PHOTOGRAPHY Robert Surtees
EDITOR Adrienne Fazan
ART DIRECTION Cedric Gibbons, Randall Duell
Technicolor
RUNNING TIME 102 minutes
PRODUCED BY Joe Pasternak

SINATRA'S NUMBERS 'What's Wrong With Me?', 'If I Steal a Kiss', 'Senorita' (Nacio Herb Brown and Edward Heyman), 'Siesta' (Nacio Herb Brown and Earl Brent).

A woeful disaster, with Sinatra as a wimpish eastern college graduate attempting to live up to his late father's reputation as a womanising thief in 1830s California. The post-production injection of a flashy dance sequence fails to lift it out of the morass.

1949

12 Take Me Out to the Ball Game
(Everybody's Cheering U.K.) (MGM)
DIRECTOR Busby Berkeley
CAST Frank Sinatra (Dennis Ryan); Esther Williams (K. C. Higgins); Gene Kelly (Eddie O'Brien); Betty Garrett (Shirley Delwyn); Edward Arnold (Joe Lorgan); Jules Munshin (Nat Goldberg); Richard Lane (Michael Gilhuly); Tom Dugan (Slappy Burke); Murray Alper (Zalinka); Wilton Graff (Nick Donford); Mack Gray (Henchman); Charles Regan (Henchman); Saul Gorss (Steve); Douglas Fowley (Carl); Eddie Parks (Dr Winston); James Burke (Cop in Park); The Blackburn Twins (Specialty); Gordon Jones (Senator Catcher); Henry Kulky (Acrobat); William Tannen (Photographer); Ed Cassidy (Teddy Roosevelt); Dick Wessel (Umpire); Pat Flaherty (Umpire); Virginia Bates, Joi Lansing (Girls on Train).
SCREENPLAY Harry Tugend, George Wells
Based on story by Gene Kelly and Stanley Donen
MUSIC SUPERVISED AND CONDUCTED BY Adolph Deutsch

INCIDENTAL SCORE Roger Edens
ORCHESTRAL ARRANGEMENTS Adolph Deutsch, Conrad Salinger, Robert Franklyn, Paul Marquardt, Alexander Courage, Axel Stordahl, Leo Arnaud
VOCAL ARRANGEMENTS Robert Tucker
DANCE DIRECTION Gene Kelly, Stanley Donen
PHOTOGRAPHY George Folsey
EDITOR Blanche Sewell
ART DIRECTION Cedric Gibbons, Daniel B. Cathcart
Technicolor
RUNNING TIME 93 minutes
PRODUCED BY Arthur Freed

SINATRA'S NUMBERS 'Take Me Out to the Ball Game' (Albert von Tilzer and Jack Norworth), 'Yes, Indeedy', 'O'Brien to Ryan to Goldberg', 'The Right Girl for Me', 'It's Fate, Baby, It's Fate' (Roger Edens, Betty Comden and Adolph Green), 'Strictly U.S.A.' (Roger Edens).

A cheerful turn-of-the-century musical blend of baseball and vaudeville, with Sinatra and Kelly battling for the favours of the club's new owner, played by Esther Williams, who hardly has a chance to get wet. The plot is off the back of an envelope, but the musical numbers are excellent.

13 On the Town (MGM)
DIRECTORS Gene Kelly, Stanley Donen
CAST Gene Kelly (Gabey); Frank Sinatra (Chip); Betty Garrett (Brunhilde Esterhazy); Ann Miller (Claire Huddesen); Jules Munshin (Ozzie); Vera-Ellen (Ivy Smith); Florence Bates (Madame Dilyovska); Alice Pearce (Lucy Schmeeler); George Meader (Professor).
SCREENPLAY Adolph Green, Betty Comden from their musical play, based on an idea by Jerome Robbins
MUSIC SUPERVISED AND CONDUCTED BY Lennie Hayton
ORCHESTRAL ARRANGEMENTS Conrad Salinger, Robert Franklyn, Wally Heglin
VOCAL ARRANGEMENTS Saul Chaplin
INCIDENTAL SCORE Roger Edens, Saul Chaplin, Conrad Salinger
Music for 'Miss Turnstiles' and 'A Day in New York' by Leonard Bernstein
PHOTOGRAPHY Harold Rossen
EDITOR Ralph E. Winters
ART DIRECTION Cedric Gibbons, Jack Martin Smith
Technicolor
RUNNING TIME 98 minutes
PRODUCED BY Arthur Freed

SINATRA'S NUMBERS 'New York, New York', 'Come Up to My Place' (Leonard Bernstein, Adolph Green and Betty Comden), 'You're Awful', 'On the Town', 'Count on Me' (Roger Edens, Adolph Green and Betty Comden).

A classic screen musical, it derived from a Broadway ballet called *Fancy Free* which in turn was enlarged into a hit stage show. The film set new standards in pace, freshness and vigour, and is the best of all servicemen-on-leave pictures. The opening sequence was shot on location in New York itself, a daring innovation in a musical, only half-trusted by the studio who only permitted two week's filming there.

1951

14 Double Dynamite (RKO)
DIRECTOR Irving Cummings
CAST Jane Russell (Mildred Goodhug); Groucho Marx (Emile J. Keck); Frank Sinatra (Johnny Dalton); Don McGuire (Bob Pulsifer Jr); Howard Freeman (R. B. Pulsifer Sr); Nestor Paiva (Bookie); Frank Orth (Mr Kofer); Harry Hayden (J. L. McKissack); William Edmunds (Baganucci); Russell Thorson (Tailman); Joe Devlin (Fankie Boy); Lou Nova (Max); Charles Coleman (Santa Claus); Ida Moore (Little Old Lady); Hal K. Dawson (Mr Hartman); George Chandler (Messenger); Jean De Briac (Maitre D').
SCREENPLAY Melville Shavelson
ADDITIONAL DIALOGUE Harry Crane
From original story by Leo Rosten, based on a character created by Manni Manheim
MUSIC Leigh Harline
PHOTOGRAPHY Robert de Grasse
EDITOR Harry Marker
ART DIRECTION Albert S. D'Agostino, Feild M. Gray
RUNNING TIME 80 minutes
PRODUCED BY Irving Cummings Jr

SINATRA'S NUMBERS 'Kisses and Tears', 'It's Only Money' (Jule Styne and Sammy Cahn).

The title is a cheap reference to Jane Russell's distinctive features. It is a dire comedy in which Sinatra plays a bank teller afraid to confess to his good fortune on the racetrack because a discrepancy of a similar amount has been discovered in his fiancee's accounts. The film contributed to Sinatra's box-office decline in the early Fifties

15 Meet Danny Wilson
(Universal-International)
DIRECTOR Joseph Pevney
CAST Frank Sinatra (Danny Wilson); Shelley Winters (Joy Carroll); Alex Nicol (Mike Ryan); Raymond Burr (Nick Driscoll); Tommy Farrell (Tommy Wells); Vaughn Taylor (T. W. Hatcher); Donald McBride (Sergeant); Barbara Knudson (Marie); Carl Sklover (Cab Driver); John Day (Gus); Jack Kruschen (Heckler); Tom Dugan (Turnkey); Danny Welton (Joey Thompson); Pat Flaherty (Mother Murphy); Carlos Molina (Bandleader); George Eldridge (Lieutenant Kelly); Bob Donnelly (Emerson); John Idrisano (Truck Driver); Tony Curtis (Nightclub Patron).
ASSOCIATE PRODUCER, ORIGINAL SCREENPLAY Don McGuire
MUSICAL DIRECTOR Joseph Gershenson
MUSICAL NUMBERS STAGED BY Hal Belfer
PHOTOGRAPHY Maury Gertsman
EDITOR Virgil Vogel
ART DIRECTION Bernard Herzbrun, Nathan Juran
RUNNING TIME 88 minutes

PRODUCED BY Leonard Goldstein

SINATRA'S NUMBERS 'You're a Sweetheart' (Jimmy McHugh and Harold Adamson), 'Lonesome Man Blues' (Sy Oliver), 'She's Funny that Way' (Richard Whiting and Neil Moret), 'A Good Man is Hard to Find' (Eddie Green), 'That Old Black Magic' (Harold Arlen and Johnny Mercer), 'When You're Smiling' (Mark Fisher, Joe Goodwin and Larry Shay), 'All of Me' (Seymour Simons and Gerald Marks), 'I've Got a Crush on You' (George and Ira Gershwin), 'How Deep is the Ocean?' (Irving Berlin).

An edgy nightclub singer is assisted to the top by a gangster boss, who then threatens mayhem if he does not get a half-share of the earnings. There's an uneasy suggestion of *roman-à-clef* about this film, mixing mobster melodrama with a number of coolly-delivered standards in Sinatra's easy style.

1953

16 From Here to Eternity (Columbia)
DIRECTOR Fred Zinnemann
CAST Burt Lancaster (Sgt Milton Warden); Montgomery Clift (Robert E. Lee Prewitt); Deborah Kerr (Karen Holmes); Donna Reed (Lorene); Frank Sinatra (Angelo Maggio); Philip Ober (Capt. Dana Holmes); Mickey Shaughnessy (Sgt Leva); Harry Bellaver (Mazzioli); Ernest Borgnine (Sgt 'Fatso' Judson); Jack Warden (Cpl Buckley); John Dennis (Sgt Ike Galovitch); Merle Travis (Sal Anderson); Tim Ryan (Sgt Pete Karelsen); Arthur Keegan (Treadwell); Barbara Morrison (Mrs Kipfer); Jean Willes (Annette); Claude Akins (Sgt Baldy Dhom); Robert Karnes (Sgt Turp Thornhill); Robert Wilke (Sgt Henderson); Douglas Henderson (Cpl Champ Wilson); George Reeves (Sgt Maylon Stark); Don Dubbins (Friday Clark); John Carson (Cpl Paluso); Kristine Miller (Georgette); John Bryant (Capt. Ross); Joan Shawlee (Sandra); Angela Stevens (Jean); Willis Bouchey (Lieut. Colonel); Tyler McVey (Major Stern).
SCREENPLAY Daniel Taradash
Based on novel by James Jones
MUSIC SUPERVISED AND CONDUCTED BY Morris Stoloff
BACKGROUND MUSIC George Duning
ORCHESTRATIONS Arthur Morton
Song 'Re-enlistment Blues' by James Jones, Fred Karger and Robert Wells
PHOTOGRAPHY Burnett Guffey
EDITOR William Lyon
ART DIRECTION Cary Odell
RUNNING TIME 118 minutes
PRODUCED BY Buddy Adler

James Jones' sprawling best-seller about life in a Honolulu army barracks at the time of the Pearl Harbor attack is smoothly directed by Zinneman. Sinatra pleaded to play the dramatic role of the soldier murdered in the stockade, and won the Academy Award for Best Supporting Actor, one of eight Oscars that went to the film.

1954

17 Suddenly (United Artists)
DIRECTOR Lewis Allen
CAST Frank Sinatra (John Baron); Sterling Hayden (Tod Shaw); James Gleason (Pop Benson); Nancy Gates (Ellen Benson); Willis Bouchey (Dan Carney); Kim Charney (Pidge Benson); James Lilburn (Jud Hobson); Paul Frees (Benny Conklin); Christopher Dark (Bart Wheeler); Paul Wexler (Slim Adams); Ken Dibbs (Wilson); Clark Howatt (Haggerty); Charles Smith (Bebob); Dan White (Burge); Richard Collier (Hawkins); Roy Engel (First Driver); Ted Stanhope (Second Driver); Charles Waggenheim (Kaplan); John Berardino (Trooper).
ORIGINAL SCREENPLAY Richard Sale
MUSIC David Raskin
PHOTOGRAPHY Charles C. Clarke
EDITOR John F. Schreyer
ART DIRECTION Frank Sylos
RUNNING TIME 77 minutes
PRODUCED BY Robert Bassler

A thriller, with Sinatra as the leader of a trio who descend on a small Californian town with the intention of assassinating the president, who is passing through. They take over and terrorize a household. The film is a 'programmer', one designed for a double-bill, and while it maintains the suspense effectively, it is somewhat overwritten.

1955

18 Young at Heart (Warner)
DIRECTOR Gordon Douglas
CAST Doris Day (Laurie Tuttle); Frank Sinatra (Barney Sloan); Gig Young (Alex Burke); Ethel Barrymore (Aunt Jessie); Dorothy Malone (Fran Tuttle); Robert Keith (Gregory Tuttle); Elisabeth Fraser (Amy Tuttle); Alan Hale Jr (Robert Neary); Lonny Chapman (Ernest Nichols); Frank Ferguson (Bartell); Marjorie Bennet (Mrs Ridgefield); John Maxwell (Doctor); William McLean (Husband); Barbara Pepper (Wife); Robin Raymond (Girl); Tito Vuolo (Fat Man); Grazia Narciso (Fat Man's Wife); Ivan Browning (Porter); Joe Forte (Minister); Cliff Ferre (Bartender); Harte Wayne (Conductor).
ADAPTATION Liam O'Brien from screenplay *Four Daughters* by Julius J. Epstein and Lenore Coffee
Based on Cosmopolitan story *Sister Act* by Fannie Hurst
MUSIC SUPERVISED, ARRANGED, CONDUCTED BY Ray Heindorf
PIANO SOLOS Andre Previn
PHOTOGRAPHY Ted McCord
EDITOR William Ziegler
ART DIRECTION John Beckman
Warnercolor
RUNNING TIME 117 minutes
PRODUCED BY Henry Blanke

SINATRA'S NUMBERS 'Young at Heart' (Johnny Richards and Carolyn Leigh), 'Someone to Watch Over Me' (George and Ira Gershwin), 'Just One of Those Things'

(Cole Porter), 'One for my Baby' (Harold Arlen and Johnny Mercer), 'You, My Love' (Mack Gordon and James van Heusen).

A small town sentimental drama with music, in which Sinatra plays a cynical arranger called in by a composer to assist a musical comedy he is writing. He falls in love with one of the daughters in a household, although she is engaged to the other man, and on the wedding day elopes. But life is tough and unable to accept that she loves him he attempts to kill himself in a deliberate car crash. Freely adapted from a 1938 Michael Curtiz film, the overly-romantic story is made endurable by the singing of Sinatra and Day.

19 Not as a Stranger (United Artists)
DIRECTOR, PRODUCER Stanley Kramer
CAST Olivia de Havilland (Kristina Hedvigson); Robert Mitchum (Lucas Marsh); Frank Sinatra (Alfred Boone); Gloria Grahame (Harriet Lang); Broderick Crawford (Dr Aarons); Charles Bickford (Dr Runkleman); Myron McCormick (Dr Snider); Lon Chaney (Job Marsh); Jesse White (Ben Cosgrove); Harry Morgan (Oley); Lee Marvin (Brundage); Virginia Christine (Bruni); Whit Bissell (Dr Dietrich); Jack Raine (Dr Lettering); Mae Clarke (Miss O'Dell).
SCREENPLAY Edna and Edward Anhalt
Based on novel by Morton Thompson
MUSIC COMPOSED AND CONDUCTED BY George Antheil
ORCHESTRATIONS Ernest Gold
PHOTOGRAPHY Franz Planer
EDITOR Fred Knudtson
PRODUCTION DESIGN Rudolf Sternad
ART DIRECTION Howard Richmond
RUNNING TIME 135 minutes

An inordinately long adaptation of a best-selling novel about young doctors in training and their romantic complications. It takes some believing that many of the characters are young enough to be medical students. Sinatra has another cynical role which he trips through with customary ease.

20 The Tender Trap (MGM)
DIRECTOR Charles Walters
CAST Frank Sinatra (Charlie Y. Reader); Debbie Reynolds (Julie Gillis); David Wayne (Joe McCall); Celeste Holm (Sylvia Crewes); Jarma Lewis (Jessica Collins); Lola Albright (Poppy Matson); Carolyn Jones (Helen); Howard St John (Sam Sayers); Joey Faye (Sol Z. Steiner); Tom Helmore (Mr Loughran); Willard Sage (Director); Marc Wilder (Ballet Actor); Jack Boyle (Audition Dancer); James Drury (Eddie); Benny Rubin (Mr Wilson); Reginald Simpson (Stage Manager); Gil Harman (TV Announcer); Madge Blake (Society Reporter).
SCREENPLAY Julius J. Epstein
Based on play by Max Shulman and Robert Paul Smith
MUSIC COMPOSED AND CONDUCTED BY Jeff Alexander
ORCHESTRATIONS Will Beittel

PHOTOGRAPHY Paul C. Vogel
EDITOR John Dunning
ART DIRECTION Cedric Gibbons, Arthur Lonergan
Eastman Color
CinemaScope
RUNNING TIME 111 minutes
PRODUCED BY Lawrence Weingarten

Sinatra sings 'Love is the Tender Trap' (James van Heusen and Sammy Cahn).

An amusingly flippant comedy, with an engaging title song sung by Sinatra who is cast as a philandering theatrical agent half-hankering after the married life, lately enjoyed by his friend, David Wayne. He is eventually snared by an apparently naive, nubile young actress, Debbie Reynolds, who is smarter than he is. The pre-permissive age blunts many of the jokes.

21 Guys and Dolls (MGM)
DIRECTOR Joseph L. Mankiewicz
CAST Marlon Brando (Sky Masterson); Jean Simmons (Sarah Brown); Frank Sinatra (Nathan Detroit); Vivian Blaine (Miss Adelaide); Robert Keith (Lt Brannigan); Stubby Kaye (Nicely-Nicely Johnson); B. S. Pully (Big Jule); Johnny Silver (Benny Southstreet); Sheldon Leonard (Harry the Horse); Dan Dayton (Rusty Charlie); George E. Stone (Society Max); Regis Toomey (Arvid Abernathy); Kathryn Givney (General Cartwright); Veda Ann Borg (Laverne); Mary Alan Hokanson (Sister Agatha); Joe McTurk (Angie the Ox); Kay Kuter (Brother Calvin); The Goldwyn Girls.
SCREENPLAY Joseph L. Mankiewicz
From musical, book by Jo Swerling and Abe Burrows, music and lyrics by Frank Loesser
Based on story *The Idyll of Sarah Brown* by Damon Runyon
MUSIC SUPERVISED AND CONDUCTED BY Jay Blackton
ORCHESTRAL ARRANGEMENTS Skip Martin, Nelson Riddle (for Sinatra), Alexander Courage, Albert Sendrey
PHOTOGRAPHY Harry Stradling
EDITOR Daniel Mandell
PRODUCTION DESIGN Oliver Smith
ART DIRECTION Joseph Wright
Eastman Color
CinemaScope
RUNNING TIME 150 minutes
PRODUCED BY Samuel Goldwyn

SINATRA'S NUMBERS 'The Oldest Established Crap Game in New York', 'Guys and Dolls', 'Adelaide', 'Sue Me'.

Frank Loesser's brilliant Runyonesque Broadway musical about an underworld gambler taking on the unlikeliest bet that he can take the Save-a-Soul mission girl to dinner in Havana is given an over-respectful and rather ponderous treatment in Mankiewicz's studio-bound production. Sinatra is miscast as the Jewish crapgame proprietor, Nathan Detroit, and plays uneasily with Blaine and Kaye repeating their stage roles.

22 The Man with the Golden Arm
(United Artists)
DIRECTOR, PRODUCER Otto Preminger
CAST Frank Sinatra (Frankie Machine); Eleanor Parker (Zosh); Kim Novak (Molly); Arnold Stang (Sparrow); Darren McGavin (Louie); Robert Strauss (Schwiefka); John Conte (Drunky); Doro Merande (Vi); George E. Stone (Markette); George Matthews (Williams); Leonid Kinskey (Dominowski); Emile Meyer (Bednar); Shorty Rogers (Himself); Shelley Manne (Himself).
SCREENPLAY Walter Newman, Lewis Meltzer
Based on novel by Nelson Algren
MUSIC COMPOSED AND CONDUCTED BY Elmer Bernstein
ORCHESTRATIONS Frederic Steiner
PHOTOGRAPHY Sam Leavitt
EDITOR Louis R. Loeffler
ART DIRECTION Joseph Wright
RUNNING TIME: 119 minutes

Sinatra's performance as a lowlife poker dealer with a crippled wife and a massive drug addiction problem earned him an Academy Award nomination, but the film looks pretentious, muddled and overblown by modern standards. There is a harrowing 'cold turkey' sequence in which he undergoes withdrawal, a sensation in its day. Sinatra's performance is excellent, the film less so.

1956

23 Meet Me in Las Vegas
(Viva Las Vegas!) U.K.) (MGM)
DIRECTOR Roy Rowland
CAST Dan Dailey (Chuck Rodwell); Cyd Charisse (Maria Corvier); Jerry Colonna (Emcee); Paul Henreid (Maria's manager); Lena Horne (Guest star); Frankie Laine (Guest star); Mitsuko Sawamura (Japanese Girl); Agnes Moorehead (Miss Hattie); Lili Darvas (Sari Havany); Jim Backus (Tom Culdane); Oscar Karlweis (Lotsi); Liliane Montivecchi (Lilli); Cara Williams (Kelly Donavan); George Chakhiris (Young Groom); Betty Lynn (Young Bride); Frank Sinatra, Debbie Reynolds, Tony Martin, Peter Lorre, Vic Damone, Elaine Stewart (Unbilled guest appearances).
ORIGINAL SCREENPLAY Isabel Lennart
MUSIC SUPERVISED AND CONDUCTED BY George Stoll
PHOTOGRAPHY Robert Bronner
EDITOR Albert Akst
ART DIRECTION Cedric Gibbons, Urie McCleary
Eastman Color
CinemaScope
RUNNING TIME 112 minutes
PRODUCED BY Joe Pasternak

Sinatra plays a slot player in The Sands hotel who gapes in astonishment when Dan Dailey puts a coin in his machine and wins the jackpot, an appearance lasting only seconds.

24 Johnny Concho (United Artists)
DIRECTOR Don McGuire
CAST Frank Sinatra (Johnny Concho); Keenan Wynn (Barney Clark); William

Conrad (Tallman); Phyllis Kirk (Mary Dark); Wallace Ford (Albert Dark); Christopher Dark (Walker); Howard Petrie (Hegelson); Harry Bartell (Sam Green); Dan Russ (Judge Tyler); Willis Bouchey (Sheriff Henderson); Robert Osterloh (Duke Lang); Leo Gordon (Mason); Dorothy Adams (Sarah Dark); Jean Byron (Pearl Lang); Claude Akins (Lem); John Qualen (Jake); Wilfred Knapp (Pearson); Ben Wright (Benson); Joe Bassett (Bartender).
ASSOCIATE PRODUCER Henry Sanicola
SCREENPLAY David P. Harmon, Don McGuire
Based on story *The Man Who Owned the Town* by David P. Harmon
MUSIC COMPOSED AND CONDUCTED BY Nelson Riddle
ORCHESTRATIONS Arthur Morton
PHOTOGRAPHY William Mellor
EDITOR Eda Warren
ART DIRECTION Nicolai Remisoff
RUNNING TIME 84 minutes
PRODUCED BY Frank Sinatra

Sinatra plays the brother of an Arizona gun-man expected to avenge his shooting, but unable to face the challenge until persuaded by a girl and a preacher. Sinatra produced this low-key western, as well as playing the leading role. His main handicap is that the first part of the film builds him up as an unpleasant character, making his redemption all the more difficult.

25 High Society (MGM)
DIRECTOR Charles Walters
CAST Bing Crosby (C. K. Dexter-Haven); Grace Kelly (Tracy Lord); Frank Sinatra (Mike Connor); Celeste Holm (Liz Imbrie); John Lund (George Kittredge); Louis Calhern (Uncle Willie); Sidney Blackmer (Seth Lord); Louis Armstrong (Himself); Margalo Gilmore (Mrs Seth Lord); Lydia Reed (Caroline Lord); Gordon Richards (Dexter-Haven's Butler); Richard Garrick (The Lords' Butler); Reginald Simpson (Uncle Willie's Butler); Richard Keene (Mac); Paul Keast (Editor); Hugh Boswell (Parson); Ruth Lee, Helen Spring (Matrons).
SCREENPLAY John Patrick
Based on play *The Philadelphia Story* by Philip Barry
MUSIC SUPERVISED AND ADAPTED BY Johnny Green and Saul Chaplin
ORCHESTRA CONDUCTED BY Johnny Green
ORCHESTRAL ARRANGEMENTS Conrad Salinger, Nelson Riddle
MUSICAL NUMBERS STAGED BY Charles Walters
PHOTOGRAPHY Paul C. Vogel
EDITOR Ralph E. Winters
ART DIRECTION Cedric Gibbons, Hans Peters
Technicolor
VistaVision
RUNNING TIME 107 minutes
PRODUCED BY Sol C. Siegel

SINATRA'S NUMBERS 'Who Wants to be a Millionaire?', 'You're Sensational', 'Well, Did You Evah?', 'Mind If I Make Love to You?' (Cole Porter).

This is a jovial remake of a Grant–Hepburn comedy hit of 1940, enlivened with a superb Cole Porter score, plus Louis Armstrong ostensibly en route to the Newport Jazz Festival, hence the switch of location to Rhode Island. Sinatra, playing the reporter role filled earlier by James Stewart, at last gets to sing a duet with Bing Crosby, his teenage idol, who slips in the crack 'You must be the new fella!' It is one of the better musicals of its period.

26 Around the World in Eighty Days (United Artists)
DIRECTOR Michael Anderson
CAST David Niven (Phileas Fogg); Cantinflas (Passepartout); Shirley MacLaine (Princess Aouda); Robert Newton (Inspector Fix); plus cameo performances by Charles Boyer, Joe E. Brown, Martine Carol, John Carradine, Charles Coburn, Ronald Colman, Melville Cooper, Noël Coward, Finlay Currie, Reginald Denny, Andy Devine, Marlene Dietrich, Luis Miguel Dominguin, Fernandel, John Gielgud, Hermione Gingold, José Greco, Cedric Hardwicke, Trevor Howard, Glynis Johns, Buster Keaton, Evelyn Keyes, Beatrice Lillie, Peter Lorre, Edmund Lowe, A. E. Matthews, Mike Mazurki, Tim McCoy, Victor McClaglen, John Mills, Robert Morley, Alan Mowbray, Jack Oakie, George Raft, Gilbert Roland, Cesar Romero, Frank Sinatra, Red Skelton, Ronald Squire, Basil Sydney, Harcourt Williams.
PROLOGUE NARRATION Edward R. Murrow
SCREENPLAY James Poe, John Farrow, S. J. Perelman
Based on novel by Jules Verne
ASSOCIATE PRODUCER William Cameron Menzies
PHOTOGRAPHY Lionel Lindon
EDITORS Paul Weatherwax, Gene Ruggiero
ART DIRECTION James Sullivan
Eastman Color
Todd-AO
RUNNING TIME 178 minutes
PRODUCED BY Michael Todd

Sinatra plays a piano player in a saloon on the Barbary Coast presided over by Marlene Dietrich, in this ambitious version of the celebrated Jules Verne book. Todd engaged a galaxy of actors, some, such as Ronald Colman, making their farewell screen appearance, to play tiny parts, adding the thrill of star-spotting to the entertainment.

1957

27 The Pride and the Passion (United Artists)
DIRECTOR, PRODUCER Stanley Kramer
CAST Cary Grant (Anthony Trumbull); Frank Sinatra (Miguel); Sophia Loren (Juana); Theodore Bikel (General Jouvet); John Wengraf (Sermaine); Jay Novello (Balinger); Jose Nieto (Carlos); Carlos Larranga (Jose); Philip Van Zandt (Vidal); Paco El Laberinto (Manolo); Julian Ugarte (Enrique).
SCREENPLAY Edna and Edward Anhalt

Based on novel *The Gun* by C. S. Forester
MUSIC George Antheil
ORCHESTRATION Ernst Gold
PHOTOGRAPHY Franz Planer
EDITORS Frederic Knudtson, Ellsworth Hoagland
PRODUCTION DESIGN Rudolph Sternad
ART DIRECTION Fernando Carrere, Gil Parrondo
Technicolor
VistaVision
RUNNING TIME 132 minutes

Sinatra plays the leader of a group of Spanish guerillas in the Peninsular Wars, who throws in his lot with a British naval captain, Cary Grant, to drag a monumental abandoned gun to Avila and the fight against Napoleon. Much of the film is taken up with the epic journey. The result is laboured in every sense, although Sinatra manages to die heroically.

28 The Joker is Wild (Paramount)
DIRECTOR Charles Vidor
CAST Frank Sinatra (Joe E. Lewis); Mitzi Gaynor (Martha Stewart); Jeanne Crain (Letty Page); Eddie Albert (Austin Mack); Beverly Garland (Cassie Mack); Jackie Coogan (Swifty Morgan); Barry Kelley (Capt. Hugh McCarthy); Ted De Corsia (Georgie Parker); Leonard Graves (Tim Coogan); Valerie Allen (Flora); Hank Henry (Burlesque Comedian); Harold Huber (Harry Bliss); Ned Glass (Johnson); Sophie Tucker (Herself).
SCREENPLAY Oscar Saul
Based on book by Art Cohn
MUSIC COMPOSED AND CONDUCTED BY Walter Scharf
ORCHESTRATIONS Leo Shuken, Jack Hayes
ORCHESTRATION OF SONGS Nelson Riddle
PHOTOGRAPHY Daniel L. Fapp
EDITOR Everett Douglas
ART DIRECTION Hal Pereira, Roland Anderson
VistaVision
RUNNING TIME 126 minutes
PRODUCED BY Samuel J. Briskin

SINATRA'S NUMBERS 'I Cried for You' (Arthur Freed, Gus Arnheim, Abe Lyman), 'If I Could Be With You' (Jimmy Johnson and Harry Creamer), 'Chicago' (Fred Fisher), 'All the Way' (James van Heusen and Sammy Cahn).

Sinatra plays Joe E. Lewis, a nightclub singer in the Twenties whose career is halted by a gangland attack in which his vocal chords are slashed. He makes a comeback as a droll comedian after everyone has suffered his alcoholism and gloom. Although the film is over-long Sinatra handles the part with characteristic verve, and it is alleged that he achieves a convincing impersonation of the real Lewis mannerisms. His rendering of 'All of Me' helped it to win the Academy Award for Best Song.

29 Pal Joey (Columbia)
DIRECTOR George Sidney
CAST Rita Hayworth (Vera Simpson);

Frank Sinatra (Joey Evans); Kim Novak (Linda English); Barbara Nichols (Gladys); Bobby Sherwood (Ned Galvin); Hank Henry (Mike Miggins); Elizabeth Patterson (Mrs Casey); Robin Morse (Bartender); Frank Wilcox (Col. Langley); Pierre Watkin (Mr Forsythe); Barry Bernard (Anderson); Ellie Kent (Carol); Mara McAfee (Sabrina); Betty Utey (Patsy); Bek Nelson (Lola); Frank Sully (Barker); Henry McCann (Shorty); John Hubbard (Stanley); James Seay (Livingstone); Hermes Pan (Choreographer); Ernesto Molinari (Chef Tony).
SCREENPLAY Dorothy Kingsley
Based on musical by John O'Hara, Richard Rodgers and Lorenz Hart
MUSIC SUPERVISED AND CONDUCTED BY Morris Stoloff
MUSICAL ARRANGEMENTS Nelson Riddle
MUSIC ADAPTATION George Duning, Nelson Riddle
ORCHESTRATIONS Arthur Morton
PHOTOGRAPHY Harold Lipstein
EDITORS Viola Lawrence, Jerome Thoms
CHOREOGRAPHY Hermes Pan
ART DIRECTION Walter Holscher
Technicolor
RUNNING TIME 111 minutes
PRODUCED BY Fred Kohlmar

SINATRA'S NUMBERS 'I Didn't Know What Time it Was?', 'There's a Small Hotel', 'I Could Write a Book', 'The Lady is a Tramp', 'Bewitched, Bothered and Bewildered', 'What Do I Care for a Dame?' (Rodgers and Hart).

A free adaptation of the last great Rodgers and Hart musical, with Sinatra playing superbly the Gene Kelly role of the smalltime heel who through the patronage of a rich woman becomes the proprietor of a night club. The film setting is San Francisco, and it was obviously thought that the original score was inadequate since a number of other Rodgers and Hart standards such as 'The Lady is a Tramp' and 'My Funny Valentine' were interpolated.

1958

30 Kings Go Forth (United Artists)
DIRECTOR Delmer Daves
CAST Frank Sinatra (Lt Sam Loggins); Tony Curtis (Sgt Britt Harris); Natalie Wood (Monique Blair); Leora Dana (Mrs Blair); Karl Swenson (Colonel); Anne Codee (Madame Brieux); Edward Ryder (Cpl Lindsay); Jackie Berthe (Jean Francois); Marie Isnard (Old Frenchwoman); Red Norvo, Pete Candoli, Mel Lewis, Richie Kamuca, Red Wooten, Jimmy Weible (Jazz Musicians).
ASSOCIATE PRODUCER Richard Ross
SCREENPLAY Merle Miller
Based on the novel by Joe David Brown
MUSIC COMPOSED AND CONDUCTED BY Elmer Bernstein
ORCHESTRATIONS Leo Shuken, Jack Hayes
PHOTOGRAPHY Daniel L. Fapp
EDITORIAL SUPERVISOR William B. Murphy
ART DIRECTION Fernando Carrere

RUNNING TIME 109 minutes
PRODUCED BY Frank Ross

Movies about the 'champagne war', the campaign to liberate the south of France, are rare. In this one Sinatra is a lieutenant in love with the same girl in Nice as his sergeant, except that his intentions are less than honourable. The situation is exacerbated when the girl confesses she is half-black. It is a somewhat melodramatic work, and Sinatra ends the war with one arm and his rival killed by the Germans.

31 Some Came Running (MGM)
DIRECTOR Vincente Minnelli
CAST Frank Sinatra (Dave Hirsh); Dean Martin (Barma Dillert); Shirley MacLaine (Ginny Moorehead); Martha Hyer (Gwen French); Arthur Kennedy (Frank Hirsh); Nancy Gates (Edith Barclay); Leora Dana (Agnes Hirsh); Betty Lou Keim (Dawn Hirsh); Carmen Phillips (Rosalie); Steven Peck (Raymond Lanchak); Connie Gilchrist (Jane Barclay); John Brennan (Wally Dennis); Larry Gates (Prof. Robert Haven French); Ned Wever (Smitty); Denny Miller (Dewey Cole); Don Haggerty (Ted Harperspoon); William Schallert (Al); Geraldine Wall (Mrs Stevens); Janelle Richards (Virginia Stevens); George E. Stone (Slim); Anthony Jochim (Judge Bastin); Marion Ross (Sister Mary Joseph); Ric Roman (Joe); Roy Engel (Sheriff); Elmer Petersen (Radio Announcer).
SCREENPLAY John Patrick, Arthur Sheekman
Based on the novel by James Jones
MUSIC COMPOSED AND CONDUCTED BY Elmer Bernstein
ORCHESTRATIONS Leo Shuken, Jack Hayes
PHOTOGRAPHY William H. Daniels
EDITOR Adrienne Fazan
ART DIRECTION William A. Horning, Urie McCleary
MetroColor
CinemaScope
RUNNING TIME 127 minutes
PRODUCED BY Sol C. Siegel

A GI and aspiring novelist returns to his small town in Indiana with his easy girl friend and an unpublished book. A college teacher is attracted and tries to help his writing, but when he falls in love with her refuses to marry him. It is a long and somewhat melodramatic saga, the James Jones book reduced to soap opera level. It is also Sinatra's first film with Dean Martin.

1959

32 A Hole in the Head (United Artists)
DIRECTOR, PRODUCER Frank Capra
CAST Frank Sinatra (Tony Manetta); Edward G. Robinson (Mario Manetta); Eleanor Parker (Mrs Rogers); Carolyn Jones (Shirl); Thelma Ritter (Sophie Manetta); Keenan Wynn (Jerry Marks); Eddie Hodges (Ally Manetta); Dorine (Joi Lansing); George De Witt (Mendy); Jimmy Komack (Julius Manetta); Dub Taylor (Fred); Connie Sawyer (Miss Wexler); Benny Rubin (Mr Diamond); Ruby

Dandridge (Sally); B. S. Pully (Hood); Joy Nizzari (Alice); Pupi Campo (Master of Ceremonies).
SCREENPLAY Arnold Schulman, from his play
MUSIC Nelson Riddle
PHOTOGRAPHY William H. Daniels
EDITOR William Hornbeck
ART DIRECTION Eddie Imazu
Color by DeLuxe
CinemaScope
RUNNING TIME 120 minutes

SINATRA'S NUMBERS 'All My Tomorrows', 'High Hopes' (James van Heusen and Sammy Cahn).

A Capra comedy, with Sinatra as the owner of a tatty Miami hotel that is about to be seized by the bank. His rich brother in New York will only help him if he turns over his 11-year-old son to him and his wife. The story is slight, but Capra's skill is considerable and the work has an engaging charm. The song 'High Hopes' won the Academy Award for Best Song.

33 Never So Few (MGM)
DIRECTOR John Sturges
CAST Frank Sinatra (Capt. Tom C. Reynolds); Gina Lollobrigida (Carla Vesari); Peter Lawford (Capt. Grey Travis); Steve McQueen (Bill Ringa); Richard Johnson (Capt. Danny De Mortimer); Paul Henried (Nikko Regas); Brian Donlevy (General Sloan); Dean Jones (Jim Norby); Charles Bronson (Sgt John Danforth); Philip Ahn (Nautang); Robert Bray (Col. Fred Parkson); Kipp Hamilton (Margaret Fitch); John Hoyt (Col. Reed); Whit Bissell (Capt. Alofson); Richard Lupino (Mike Island); Aki Aleong (Billingsly); Ross Elliott (Dr Barry); Leon Lontoc (Laurel).
SCREENPLAY Millard Kaufman
Based on novel by Tom T. Chamales
MUSIC Hugo Friedhofer
ORCHESTRATION Robert Franklyn
PHOTOGRAPHY William H. Daniels
EDITOR Ferris Webster
ART DIRECTION Hans Peters, Addison Hehr
MetroColor
CinemaScope
RUNNING TIME 124 minutes
PRODUCED BY Edmund Grainger

Set in Burma during the Second World War, this long and rather dull film has Sinatra and Johnson commanding a guerilla force which becomes mixed up with the scurrilous activities of a Chinese warlord. Gina Lollobrigida makes no concessions to the film's period, Sinatra performs the action well enough, and Steve McQueen is impressive in an early role.

1960

34 Can-Can (Twentieth Century-Fox)
DIRECTOR Walter Lang
CAST Frank Sinatra (Francois Durnais); Shirley MacLaine (Simone Pistache); Maurice Chevalier (Paul Barrière); Louis Jordan (Phillippe Forestier); Juliet Prowse

(Claudine); Marcel Dalio (André); Leon Belasco (Orchestra Leader); Nestor Paiva (Bailiff); John A. Neris (Jacques); Jean Del Val (Judge Merceaux); Ann Codee (League President); Eugene Borden (Chevrolet); Jonathan Kidd (Recorder); Marc Wilder (Adam); Ambrogio Malerba (Apache Dancer); Carole Bryan (Gigi); Barbara Carter (Camille); Jane Earl (Renée); Ruth Earl (Julie); Laura Fraser (Germaine); Vera Lee (Gabrielle); Lisa Mitchell (Fifi); Wanda Shannon (Maxine); Darlene Tittle (Gisèle); Wilda Taylor (Lili); Peter Coe (Gendarme Dupont).
ASSOCIATE PRODUCER Saul Chaplin
SCREENPLAY Dorothy Kingsley, Charles Lederer
Based on musical by Abe Burrows, songs by Cole Porter
MUSIC ARRANGED AND CONDUCTED BY Nelson Riddle
VOCAL SUPERVISION Bobby Tucker
PHOTOGRAPHY William H. Daniels
EDITOR Robert Simpson
ART DIRECTION Lyle Wheeler, Jack Martin Smith
DANCES STAGED BY Hermes Pan
Technicolor
Todd-AO
RUNNING TIME 130 minutes
PRODUCED BY Jack Cummings

SINATRA'S NUMBERS 'I Love Paris', 'C'est Magnifique', 'Let's Do It', 'It's All Right With Me' (Cole Porter).

A lively, but somewhat sanitised version of the Broadway musical set in the Belle Epoque in Paris in which a new member of the judiciary attempts to force a nightclub where the infamous can-can is performed to close. This film is notable mainly for the notoriety ensuing when the Russian premier, Khrushchev, visited the set during the filming of a saucy number.

35 Ocean's Eleven (Warner)
DIRECTOR, PRODUCER Lewis Milestone
CAST Frank Sinatra (Danny Ocean); Dean Martin (Sam Harmon); Sammy Davis Jr (Josh Howard); Peter Lawford (Jimmy Foster); Angie Dickinson (Beatrice Ocean); Richard Conte (Anthony Bergdorf); Cesar Romero (Duke Santos); Patrice Wymore (Adele Ekstrom); Joey Bishop (Mushy O'Conners); Akim Tamiroff (Spyros Acebos); Henry Silva (Roger Corneal); Ilka Chase (Mrs Restes); Buddy Lester (Vincent Massler); Richard Benedict (George Steffens); Jean Willes (Grace Bergdorf); Norman Fell (Peter Rheimer); Clem Harvey (Louis Jackson); Hank Henry (Mr Jackson); Lew Gallo (Young Man); Robert Foulk (Sheriff Wimmer); Charles Meredith (Mr Cohen); Ronnie Dapo (Timmy Bergdorf); George E. Stone (Store Proprietor); Louis Quinn (De Wolfe); John Indrisano (Texan); Carmen Phillips (Hungry Girl); Murray Alper (Deputy); Hoot Gibson (Road Block Deputy); Gregory Gay (Freeman); Don 'Red' Barry (McCoy); Red Skelton (Casino Client);

George Raft (Jack Strager); Shirley MacLaine (Tipsy Girl).
SCREENPLAY Harry Brown, Charles Lederer
Based on the original story by George Clayton Johnson and Jack Golden Russell
MUSIC COMPOSED AND CONDUCTED BY Nelson Riddle
ORCHESTRATIONS Arthur Morton
PHOTOGRAPHY William H. Daniels
EDITOR Philip W. Anderson
ART DIRECTION Nicolai Remisoff
Technicolor
Panavision
RUNNING TIME 127 minutes

One of the first Hollywood 'caper' movies, in which an assorted group of former army chums are called together by Sinatra to rob five Las Vegas casinos simultaneously on New Year's Eve. The robbery depends on intricate, ingenious planning and split second timing. It's entertaining, but too long winded.

36 Pepe (Colombia)
DIRECTOR, PRODUCER George Sidney
CAST Cantinflas (Pepe); Dan Dailey (Ted Holt); Shirley Jones (Suzie Murphy); Carlos Montalban (Auctioneer); Vickie Trickett (Lupita); Matt Mattox (Dancer); Hank Henry (Manager); Suzanne Lloyd (Carmen); Stephen Bekassy (Jewellery Salesman); Carol Douglas (Waitress); Francisco Reguerra (Priest); Joe Hyams (Charro); William Demarest (Studio Gateman); Ernie Kovacs (Immigration Inspector); Jay North (Dennis the Menace); Bunny Waters (Bunny).
Guest stars as themselves: Joey Bishop, Billie Burke, Maurice Chevalier, Charles Coburn, Richard Conte, Bing Crosby, Tony Curtis, Bobby Darin, Sammy Davis Jr, Jimmy Durante, Jack Entratter, Col E. E. Fogelson, Zsa Zsa Gabor, Greer Garson, Hedda Hopper, Peter Lawford, Janet Leigh, Jack Lemmon, Dean Martin, Kim Novak, Andre Previn, Donna Reed, Debbie Reynolds, Carlos Rivas, Edward G. Robinson, Cesar Romero, Frank Sinatra.
SCREENPLAY Dorothy Kingsley, Claude Binyon
From a story by Leonard Spigelgass and Sonia Lieven, based on the play *Broadway Magic* by Ladislas Bush-Fekete
MUSIC SUPERVISION, BACKGROUND SCORE: Johnny Green
PHOTOGRAPHY Joe MacDonald
EDITORS Viola Lawrence, Al Clark
ART DIRECTION Ted Haworth
Technicolor
Sequences in CinemaScope
RUNNING TIME 195 minutes

An interminable extravaganza in which a Mexican peasant pursues a horse bought by a Hollywood director who has outbid him and ends up in the film capital, where he meets hordes of stars playing themselves. Sinatra, with Joe Bishop and Cesar Romero, advises him how to gamble and win enough money to produce his own picture. It is an unbearably tedious work.

1961

37 The Devil at Four O'Clock (Columbia)
DIRECTOR Mervyn LeRoy
CAST Spencer Tracy (Father Matthew Doonan); Frank Sinatra (Harry); Kerwin Matthews (Father Joseph Perrau); Jean Pierre Aumont (Jacques); Gregoire Aslan (Marcel); Alexander Scourby (Governor); Barbara Luna (Camille); Cathy Lewis (Matron); Bernie Hamilton (Charlie); Martin Brandt (Dr Wexler); Lou Mewrrill (Aristide); Marcel Dalio (Gaston); Tom Middleton (Paul); Ann Duggan (Clarisse); Louis Mercier (Corporal); Michele Monteau (Margot); Nanette Tanaka (Fleur); Tony Maxwell (Antoine); Jean Del Val (Louis); Moki Hana (Sonia); Warren Hsieh (Napoleon); William Keulani (Constable); 'Lucky' Luck (Captain Olsen); Norman Josef Wright (Fouquette); Robin Shimatsu (Marianne).
SCREENPLAY Liam O'Brien
Based on the novel by Max Catto
MUSIC George Duning
PHOTOGRAPHY Joseph Biroc
EDITOR Charles Nelson
ART DIRECTION John Beckman
Eastman Color
RUNNING TIME 126 minutes
PRODUCED BY Fred Kohlmar

Tracy plays a drink-sodden missionary who with the assistance of three convicts saves children in a Pacific leper colony from an erupting volcano. Sinatra is one of the convicts. It is another overlong, tedious film, and the gloomy ending is unfair compensation for those who have patiently sat through it.

1962

38 Sergeants Three (United Artists)
DIRECTOR John Sturges
CAST Frank Sinatra (1st Sgt Mike Merry); Dean Martin (Sgt Chip Deal); Sammy Davis Jr (Jonah Williams); Peter Lawford (Sgt Larry Barrett); Joey Bishop (Sgt Major Roger Boswell); Henry Silva (Mountain Hawk); Ruta Lee (Amelia Parent); Buddie Lester (Willie Shapknife); Phillip Crosby (Cpl Ellis); Dennis Crosby (Pvt. Page); Lindsay Crosby (Pvt. Wills); Hank Henry (Blacksmith); Richard Simmons (Col. Collingwood); Michael Pate (Watanka); Armand Alzamora (Caleb); Richard Hale (White Eagle); Mickey Finn (Morton); Sonny King (Corporal); Eddie Littlesky (Ghost Dancer); 'Ceffie' (Herself); Rodd Redwing (Irregular); James Waters (Colonel's Aide); Madge Balke (Mrs Parent); Dorothy Abbott (Mrs Collingwood); Walter Merrill (Telegrapher).
EXECUTIVE PRODUCER Howard W. Koch
ORIGINAL SCREENPLAY W. R. Burnett
MUSIC Billy May
PHOTOGRAPHY Winton C. Hoch
EDITOR Ferris Webster
ART DIRECTION Frank Hotaling
Technicolor
Panavision

RUNNING TIME 112 minutes
PRODUCED BY Frank Sinatra

A 'Clan' film parodying *Gunga Din* as a western , it features three US cavalry sergeants sorting out hostile Indians, aided by their bugler, an emancipated slave. It's all somewhat laboured and self-indulgent, and the 1939 film is infinitely to be preferred.

39 The Road to Hong Kong (United Artists)
DIRECTOR Norman Panama
CAST Bing Crosby (Harry Turner); Bob Hope (Chester Babcock); Joan Collins (Diane); Dorothy Lamour (Herself); Robert Morley (The Leader); Walter Gotell (Dr Zorbb); Roger Delgardo (Jhinnah); Felix Aylmer (Grand Lama); Peter Madden (Loma); Julian Sherrier (Doctor); Guy Standeven (Photographer); John McCarthy (Messenger); Simon Levy (Servant); Jacqueline Jones (Lady at Airport); Mei Ling (Chinese Girl); Katya Douglas (Receptionist).
Unbilled guests stars: Jerry Colonna, Dean Martin, David Niven, Peter Sellers, Frank Sinatra .
RUNNING TIME 91 minutes
PRODUCED BY Melvin Frank

Sinatra plays Joan Collins' boy friend in outer space and appears briefly at the end of the film, the last of the 'Road' series, and by far the worst.

40 The Manchurian Candidate (United Artists)
DIRECTOR John Frankenheimer
CAST Frank Sinatra (Bennett Marco); Laurence Harvey (Raymond Shaw); Janet Leigh (Rosie); Angela Lansbury (Raymond's Mother); Henry Silva (Chunjin); James Gregory (Sen. John Iselin); Leslie Parrish (Jocie Jordan); John McGiver (Sen. Thomas Jordan); Khigh Dhiegh (Yen Lo); James Edwards (Cpl Melvin); Douglas Henderson (Colonel); Albert Paulsen (Zilkov); Madame Spivy (Berezovo's Lady Counterpart); Barry Kelley (Secretary of Defence); Joe Adams (Psychiatrist); Lloyd Corrigan (Mr Gaines); Whit Bissell (Medical Officer); Mimi Dillard (Melvin's Wife); Anton Van Stralen (Officer); John Laurence (Gossfeld); Tom Lowell (Lembeck); Richard La Pore (Mavole); Nick Bolin (Berezovo); Nicky Blair (Silvers); William Thourlby (Little); Irving Steinberg (Freeman); John Francis (Haiken); Robert Riordan (Nominee); Reggie Nalder (Gomel); Miyoshi Jingu (Miss Gertrude); Anna Shin (Korean Girl); Bess Flowers (Gomel's Lady Counterpart).
EXECUTIVE PRODUCER Howard W. Koch
SCREENPLAY George Axelrod
Based on the novel by Richard Condon
MUSIC COMPOSED AND CONDUCTED BY David Amram
PHOTOGRAPHY Lionel Lindon
EDITOR Ferris Webster
ART DIRECTION Richard Sylbert
RUNNING TIME 126 minutes
PRODUCED BY George Axelrod, John Frankenheimer

John Frankenheimer was Hollywood's most promising director when he made this extraordinary thriller about a man brainwashed after capture in Korea who comes back to America as an assassination machine, timed to kill a presidential candidate at his nomination in order that control can be seized by a communist puppet. Sinatra plays the fellow captive who uncovers the far-fetched plot. Brilliant direction disguises the many loopholes in the story, and it is one of Sinatra's best films.

1963

41 Come Blow Your Horn (Paramount)
DIRECTOR Bud Yorkin
CAST Frank Sinatra (Alan Baker); Lee J. Cobb (Papa Baker); Molly Picon (Mama Baker); Barbara Rush (Connie); Jill St John (Peggy); Tony Bill (Buddy Baker); Dan Blocker (Mr Eckman); Phyllis McGuire (Mrs Eckman); Herbie Faye (Waiter); Romo Vincent (Barber); Charlotte Fletcher (Manicurist); Greta Randall (Tall Girl); Vinnie De Carlo (Max); Jack Nestle (Desk Clerk); Eddie Quillan (Elevator Operator); Grady Sutton (Manager); Joyce Nizzari (Snow Eskanazi); Carole Wells (Eunice); John Indrisano (Cab Driver); Dean Martin (Wino).
EXECUTIVE PRODUCER Howard W. Koch
SCREENPLAY Norman Lear, based on a play by Neil Simon
MUSIC COMPOSED AND CONDUCTED BY Nelson Riddle
ORCHESTRATIONS Gil Grau
PHOTOGRAPHY William H. Daniels
EDITOR Frank P. Keller
ART DIRECTION Hal Periera, Roland Anderson
Technicolor
Panavision
RUNNING TIME 112 minutes
PRODUCED BY Norman Lear, Bud Yorkin

SINATRA SINGS 'COME BLOW YOUR HORN' (James van Heusen and Sammy Cahn).

This is Neil Simon's first Hollywood success, a deftly-written Broadway comedy about a philandering New York bachelor who accommodates his younger brother from out-of-town and introduces him to girls and booze. The screenplay shifts the emphasis on to the older man and, as usual, Sinatra plays him to a tee.

42 The List of Adrian Messenger (Universal)
DIRECTOR John Huston
CAST George C. Scott (Anthony Gethryn); Dana Wynter (Lady Jocelyn Bruttenholm); Clive Brook (Marquis of Gleneyre); Gladys Cooper (Mrs Karoudjian); Herbert Marshall (Sir Wilfrid Lucas); Jacques Roux (Raoul Le Borg); John Merivale (Adrian Messenger); Marcel Dalio (Anton Karoudjian); Bernard Archard (Inspector Pike); Walter Anthony Houston (Derek); Roland D. Long (Carstairs); Anita Sharp-Bolster (Mrs Slattery); Alan Caillou (Inspector Seymour); John Huston (Lord

Ashton); Noel Purcell (Countryman); Richard Peel (Sergeant Flood); Bernard Fox (Lynch); Nelson Welch (White); Tim Durant (Hunt Secretary); Barbara Morrison (Nurse); Jennifer Raine (Student Nurse); Constance Cavendish (Maid); Eric Heath (Orderly); Anna Van Der Heide (Stewardess); Delphi Lawrence (Airport Stewardess); Stacy Morgan (Whip Man); Joe Lynch (Cyclist); Mona Lilian (Proprietress); Tony Curtis (Italian); Kirk Douglas (George Brougham); Burt Lancaster (Woman); Robert Mitchum (Jim Slattery); Frank Sinatra (Gypsy Stableman).
SCREENPLAY Anthony Veiller
Based on the novel by Philip MacDonald
MUSIC Jerry Goldsmith
PHOTOGRAPHY Joe MacDonald
EDITOR Terry Morse
ART DIRECTION Alexander Golitzen, Stephen Grimes, George Webb
RUNNING TIME 98 minutes
PRODUCED BY Edward Lewis

Huston's intricate whodunit involving murder among the British landed gentry uses the gimmick of a number of guest stars in cameo roles, so heavily-disguised as to be unrecognisable. Sinatra, accordingly, plays a swarthy gypsy, peeling off the latex make-up at the end of the film with his fellow superstars, who are obviously enjoying the whole experience, although audiences found it rather tiresome.

1964

43 4 for Texas (Warner)
DIRECTOR, PRODUCER Robert Aldrich
CAST Frank Sinatra (Zack Thomas); Dean Martin (Joe Jarratt); Anita Ekberg (Elya Carson); Ursula Andress (Maxine Richter); Charles Bronson (Matson); Victor Buono (Harvey Burden); Edric Connor (Prince George); Nick Dennis (Angel); Richard Jaeckel (Mancini); Mike Mazurki (Chad); Wesley Saddy (Trowbridge); Marjorie Bennett (Miss Adeline); Virginia Christine (Brunhilde); Ellen Corby (Widow); Jack Elam (Dobie); Jesslyn Fax (Widow); Fritz Feld (Maitre D'); Percy Helton (Ansel); Jonathan Hole (Renee); Jack Lambert (Monk); Paul Langton (Beauregard); Keith McConnell (Sweeney); Michel Monteau (Helene); Maidie Norman (Maid); Bob Steele (Customer); Mario Siletti (Bedoni); Eva Six (Mrs Burden); Pulaski (Abraham Sofaer); Michael St Angel (Williams); Grady Sutton (Secretary); Ralph Vokie (Bartender); Max Wagner (Bartender); William Washington (Doorman); Deave Willock (Alfred); Arthur Godfrey (Croupier); The Three Stooges, Teddy Buckner and his All-Stars (Guest stars).
EXECUTIVE PRODUCER Howard W. Koch
ORIGINAL SCREENPLAY Teddi Sherman, Robert Aldrich
MUSIC COMPOSED AND CONDUCTED BY Nelson Riddle
ORCHESTRATIONS Gil Grau
PHOTOGRAPHY Ernst Laszlo
EDITOR Michael Luciano

ART DIRECTION William Glasgow
Technicolor
RUNNING TIME 124 minutes

A 'Clan' western, with Sinatra and Dean Martin swanning their way through a tedious plot in which they become rival saloon owners, and double-cross each other for the proceeds of a stagecoach hold-up. Aldrich opens in his characteristically violent style, but thereafter gets bogged down by their self-indulgence.

44 Robin and the Seven Hoods (Warner)
DIRECTOR Gordon Douglas
CAST Frank Sinatra (Robbo); Dean Martin (John); Sammy Davis Jr (Will); Peter Falk (Guy Gisborne); Barbara Rush (Marian); Victor Buono (Sheriff Potts); Hank Henry (Six Seconds); Allen Jenkins (Vermin); Jack La Rue (Tomatoes); Robert Foulk (Sheriff Glick); Phillip Crosby (Robbo's Hood); Robert Carricart (Bluejaw); Phil Arnold (Hatrack); Sonny King (Robbo's Hood); Richard Simmons (Prosecutor); Harry Swoger (Soupmeat); Harry Wilson (Gisborne's Hood); Richard Bakalyan (Robbo's Hood); Bernard Fein (Charlie Bananas); Carol Hill (Cocktail Waitress); Joseph Ruskin (Twitch); Sig Ruman (Hammacher); Barry Kelley (Police Chief); Hans Conried (Mr Ricks); Edward G. Robinson (Big Jim); Bing Crosby (Allen A. Dale).
EXECUTIVE PRODUCER Howard W. Koch
ORIGINAL SCREENPLAY David R. Schwartz
MUSIC COMPOSED AND CONDUCTED BY Nelson Riddle
ORCHESTRATIONS Gil Grau
PHOTOGRAPHY (AND ASSOCIATE PRODUCER) William H. Daniels
EDITOR Sam O'Steen
ART DIRECTION LeRoy Deane
Technicolor
Panavision
RUNNING TIME 123 minutes
PRODUCED BY Frank Sinatra

SINATRA'S NUMBERS 'My Kind of Town', 'Style', 'Mr Booze', 'Don't Be a Do-Badder' (James van Heusen and Sammy Cahn).

The idea of shifting the Robin Hood legend to prohibition Chicago is an interesting one, but unfortunately it is fumbled in this laboured film which is larded with guest star cameos. It is fair to say that there are some cheerful songs and several good moments. Sinatra does in fact lay down a great standard: 'My Kind of Town'.

1965

45 None but the Brave (Warner)
DIRECTOR, PRODUCER Frank Sinatra
CAST Frank Sinatra (Chief Pharmacist Mate Maloney); Clint Walker (Captain Dennis Bourke); Tommy Sands (2nd Lt Blair); Brad Dexter (Sgt Bleeker); Tony Bill (Air Crewman Keller); Tatsuya Mihashi (Lt Kuroki); Takeshi Kato (Sgt Tamura); Sammy Jackson (Cpl Craddock); Richard Bakalyan (Cpl Ruffino); Rafer Johnson

(Private Johnson); Jimmy Griffin (Private Dexter); Christopher Dark (Private Searcy); Don Dorell (Private Hoxie); Phillip Crosby (Private Magee); John H. Young (Private Waller); Roger Ewing (Private Swenshoilm); Homare Suguro (L/Cpl Hirano); Kenji Sahara (Cpl Fujimoto); Masahiko Tanimura (Lead Private Ando); Hizao Dazai (Private Tokumaru); Susumu Korobe (Private Goro); Takashi Inagaki (Private Ishii); Kenichi Hata (Private Sato); Toru Ibuki (Private Arikawa); Ryucho Shunputei (Private Okuda); Lariane Stephens (Lorie).
EXECUTIVE PRODUCER Howard W. Koch
ASSOCIATE PRODUCER William H. Daniels
PRODUCER FOR TOKYO EIGU COMPANY/ ORIGINAL STORY Kikumaru Okuda
SCREENPLAY John Twist, Katsuya Susaki
MUSIC Johnny Williams
MUSIC SUPERVISED AND CONDUCTED BY Morris Stoloff
PHOTOGRAPHY Harold Lipstein
EDITOR Sam O'Steen
ART DIRECTION LeRoy Deane
Technicolor
Panavision
RUNNING TIME 105 minutes

Sinatra's attempt at direction is an anti-war tract, in which a group of Americans crash-land on an island held by the Japanese, and reach a mutual understanding until both sides are back in the war, when the killing resumes. Made in Hawaii, it was a Japanese-American co-production. Sinatra was more at home directing the action sequences than the dialogue, which comes across as trite and obvious.

46 Von Ryan's Express
(Twentieth Century-Fox)
DIRECTOR Mark Robson
CAST Frank Sinatra (Col. Joseph L. Ryan); Trevor Howard (Major Eric Fincham); Raffaella Carra (Gabriella); Brad Dexter (Sgt Bostick); Sergio Fantoni (Capt. Oriani); John Leyton (Lt Orde); Edward Mulhare (Chaplain Costanzo); Wolfgang Preiss (Major Von Klemment); James Brolin (Private Ames); John Van Dreelen (Col. Gortz); Adolfo Celi (Major Battaglia); Vito Scotti (Train Driver); Richard Bakalyan (Cpl Giannini); Michael Goodliffe (Capt. Stein); Michael St Clair (Sgt Dunbar); Ivan Triesault (Von Kleist); William Berger (Gestapo Agent); Mike Romanoff (Italian Nobleman); Buzz Henry (US Soldier).
SCREENPLAY Wendell Mayes, Joseph Landon
Based on the novel by David Westheimer
MUSIC Jerry Goldsmith
ORCHESTRATIONS Arthur Morton
PHOTOGRAPHY William H. Daniels
EDITOR Dorothy Spencer
ART DIRECTION Jack Martin Smith, Hilyard Brown
Color by DeLuxe
CinemaScope
RUNNING TIME 117 minutes
PRODUCED BY Saul David

Sinatra plays the lone American officer in a prisoner-of-war camp in Italy who incurs unpopularity. He organises an incredible escape plan which involves seizing a train, and making a desperate run for the Swiss border. It's an exciting standard escape story with good action sequences, a tough climax and a hard-nosed performance from Sinatra.

47 Marriage on the Rocks (Warner)
DIRECTOR Jack Donohue
PRODUCER, PHOTOGRAPHY William H. Daniels
CAST Frank Sinatra (Dan Edwards); Deborah Kerr (Valerie Edwards); Dean Martin (Ernie Brewer); Cesar Romero (Miguel Santos); Hermione Baddeley (Jeannie MacPherson); Tony Bill (Jim Blake); John McGiver (Shad Nathan); Nancy Sinatra (Tracy Edwards); Davey Davidson (Lisa Sterling); Michel Petit (David Edwards); Joi Lansing (Lola); Tara Ashton (Bunny); Kathleen Freman (Miss Blight); Flip Mark (Rollo); De Forest Kelley (Mr Turner); Sigrid Valdis (Kitty); Byron Foulger (Mr Bruno); Parley Baer (Dr Newman); Reta Shaw (Saleslady at Saks); Nacho Galindo (Mayor); Hedley Mattingly (Mr Smythe); Trini Lopez (Guest Star).
ORIGINAL SCREENPLAY Cy Howard
MUSIC COMPOSED AND CONDUCTED BY Nelson Riddle
EDITOR Sam O'Steen
ART DIRECTION LeRoy Deane
Technicolor
Panavision
RUNNING TIME 109 minutes

A tedious sex farce in which Sinatra plays a long-married adman whose wife plans a divorce, and (accidentally) marries his best friend on a second honeymoon. It tends towards the unfunny most of the time, and once again the self-indulgent antics of the senior 'Clan' members interfere with the progression of the film.

1966

48 Cast a Giant Shadow (United Artists)
DIRECTOR, PRODUCER Melville Shavelson
CAST Kird Douglas (Col. David 'Mickey' Marcus); Senta Berger (Magda Simon); Angie Dickinson (Emma Marcus); James Donald (Major Safir); Stathis Giallelis (Ram Oren); Luther Adler (Jacob Zion); Gary Merrill (Pentagon Chief of Staff); Haym Topol (Abou Ibn Kader); Ruth White (Mrs Chaison); Gordon Jackson (James MacAfee); Michael Hordern (British Ambassador); Allan Cuthbertson (British Immigration Officer); Jeremy Kemp (Senior British Officer); Sean Barrett (Junior British Officer); Michael Shillo (Andre Simon); Rina Ganor (Rona); Ronald Barthrop (Bert Harrison); Vera Dolen (Mrs Martinson); Robert Gardett (General Walsh); Michael Balston (First Sentry); Claude Aliotti (Second Sentry); Samra Dedes (Belly Dancer); Michael Shagriur (Truck Driver); Frank Lattimore (First UN Officer); Ken Buckle (Second

UN Officer); Rodd Dana (Aide to General Randolph); Arthur Hansell (Pentagon Officer); Don Sturkie (Parachute Jump Sergeant); Hillel Rave (Yaakov); Shlomo Hermon (Yussuf); Frank Sinatra (Vince); Yul Brynner (Asher Gonen); John Wayne (General Mike Randolph).
CO-PRODUCER Michael Wayne
SCREENPLAY Melville Shavelson
Based on book by Ted Berkman
MUSIC COMPOSED AND CONDUCTED BY Elmer Bernstein
ORCHESTRATIONS Leo Shuken, Jack Hayes
PHOTOGRAPHY Aldo Tonti
EDITORS Bert Bates, Gene Ruggiero
PRODUCTION DESIGN Michael Stringer
ART DIRECTION Arrigo Equini
Color by DeLuxe
Panavision
RUNNING TIME 139 minutes

In this respectful biography of David Marcus, a New York lawyer who fought and died to establish the state of Israel, Sinatra is one of several guest stars, and plays an American soldier-of-fortune and ex-army flier who drops soda syphons in lieu of bombs on the Arabs from his flimsy Piper Cub.

49 The Oscar (Embassy)
DIRECTOR Russell Rouse
CAST Stephen Boyd (Frank Fane); Elke Sommer (Kay Bergdahl); Milton Berle (Kappy Kapstetter); Eleanor Parker (Sophie Cantaro); Joseph Cotten (Kenneth H. Regan); Jill St John (Laurel Scott); Tony Bennett (Hymie Kelly); Edie Adams (Trina Yale); Ernest Borgnine (Barney Yale); Ed Begley (Grobard); Walter Brennan (Orrin C. Quentin); Broderick Crawford (Sheriff); James Dunn (Network Executive); Edith Head (Herself); Hedda Hopper (Herself); Peter Lawford (Steve Marks); Merle Oberon (Herself); Nancy Sinatra (Herself); Bob Hope (Himself); Frank Sinatra (Himself).
EXECUTIVE PRODUCER Joseph E. Levine
SCREENPLAY Harlan Ellison
Based on novel by Richard Sale
MUSIC Percy Faith
ORCHESTRATIONS Leo Shuken, Jack Hayes
PHOTOGRAPHY Joseph Ruttenberg
EDITOR Chester W. Schaeffer
ART DIRECTION Hal Pereira, Arthur Lonergan
Pathe Color
RUNNING TIME 119 minutes
PRODUCED BY Clarence Greene

A thoroughly meretricious film about a Hollywood heel's rise to fame, culminating with Oscar night when the award he thinks is going to him goes to Sinatra instead. A galaxy of stars were induced to appear in this absurd work as themselves.

50 Assault on a Queen (Paramount)
DIRECTOR Jack Donohue
CAST Frank Sinatra (Mark Britain); Virna Lisi (Rosa Lucchesi); Tony Franciosa (Vic Rossiter); Richard Conte (Tony Moreno); Alf Kjellin (Eric Lauffnauer); Errol John (Link Langley); Murray Matheson (Queen

Mary Captain); Reginald Denny (Master-at-Arms); John Warburton (Bank Manager); Lester Matthews (Doctor); Val Avery (Trench); Gilchrist Stuart (First Officer); Ronald Long (Second Officer); Leslie Bradley (Third Officer); Arthur E. Gould-Porter (Fourth Officer); Laurence Conroy (Junior Officer); Alan Baxter (Crewman); Jack Raine (Bartender); Douglas Dene (Assistant Purser); Noel Drayton (Elevator Operator); Donald Lawton (Chief Radio Operator); Robert C. Shawley (Radio Operator); Barbara Morison (Lady with Diamond); Robert Hoy (Executive Officer); Ray Kellogg (Coast Guard Skipper); Walt Davis (Chief).
ASSOCIATE PRODUCER, PHOTOGRAPHY William H. Daniels
SCREENPLAY Rod Serling
Based on novel by Jack Finney
MUSIC Duke Ellington
ORCHESTRAL ARRANGEMENTS Van Cleave, Frank Comstock
EDITOR Archie Marshek
ART DIRECTION Paul Groesse
Technicolor
Panavision
RUNNING TIME 106 minutes
PRODUCED BY William Goetz

The finding of a small sunken German U-Boat off Florida inspires Sinatra and cohorts to attempt an ambitious, if absurd, caper, namely the hi-jacking of the Queen Mary. The light touch is scarcely apparent, and Franciosa and Sinatra are not a happy acting blend, so the result is tepid.

1967

51 The Naked Runner (Warner)
DIRECTOR Sidney J. Furie
CAST Frank Sinatra (Sam Laker); Peter Vaughan (Slattery); Derren Nesbitt (Colonel Hartmann); Nadia Gray (Karen); Toby Robins (Ruth); Inger Stratton (Anna); Cyril Luckham (Cabinet Minister); Edward Fox (Ritchie Jackson); J. A. B. Dubin-Behrman (Joseph); Michael Newport (Patrick Laker).
SCREENPLAY Stanley Mann
Based on novel by Francis Clifford
MUSIC Harry Sukman
ORCHESTRATIONS Herbert Spencer
PHOTOGRAPHY Otto Heller
EDITOR Barry Vince
ART DIRECTION Peter Proud
Technicolor
Techniscope
RUNNING TIME 103 minutes
PRODUCED BY Brad Dexter

A fussy espionage thriller, using modish swinging-Sixties style camerawork which now looks very jaded, in which Sinatra plays an American businessman in London, set up by British intelligence as a pawn in their dangerous game. Sinatra's own company produced the film, and it is the only one he made in Britain.

52 Tony Rome (Twentieth Century-Fox)
DIRECTOR Gordon Douglas

CAST Frank Sinatra (Tony Rome); Jill St John (Anne Archer); Richard Conte (Lt Santini); Gena Rowlands (Rita Kosterman); Simon Oakland (Rudolph Kosterman); Jeffrey Lynn (Adam Boyd); Lloyd Bochner (Vic Rood); Robert J. Wilke (Ralph Turpin); Virginia Vincent (Sally Bullock); Joan Shawlee (Fat Candy); Richard Krisher (Donald Pines); Lloyd Gough (Jules Langley); Babe Hart (Oscar); Templeton Fox (Mrs Schuyler); Rocky Graziano (Packy); Elisabeth Fraser (Irma); Shecky Green (Catleg); Jeanne Cooper (Lorna Boyd); Harry Davis (Henrik Ruyter); Stanley Ross (Sam Boyd); Deanna Lund (Georgia McKay); Buss Henry (Nimmo); Joe E. Ross (Bartender); Michael Ronanoff (Maitre D'); Tiffany Bolling (Photo Girl); Sue Lyon (Diana Pines).
SCREENPLAY Richard L. Breen
Based on novel Miami Mayhem by Marvin H. Albert
MUSIC Billy May
PHOTOGRAPHY Joseph Biroc
EDITOR Robert Simpson
ART DIRECTION Jack Martin Smith, James Roth
Color by Deluxe
Panavision
RUNNING TIME 110 minutes
PRODUCED BY Aaron Rosenberg

Sinatra plays a sardonic Miami private detective who lives on a boat, and is called in to unravel a whodunit as intricate as The Big Sleep, to which it bears more than a fleeting resemblance. An old genre is adequately revived and embellished with a few touches that would not have been permissible in the days of Forties film noir.

1968

53 The Detective (Twentieth Century-Fox)
DIRECTOR Gordon Douglas
CAST Frank Sinatra (Joe Leland); Lee Remick (Karen Leland); Ralph Meeker (Lt Curran); Jack Klugman (Lt Dave Schoenstein); Horace McMahon (Chief Tom Farrell); Lloyd Bochner (Dr Wendell Roberts); William Windom (Colin MacIver); Tony Musante (Felix Tesla); Al Freeman Jr (Det. Robbie Loughren); Robert Duvall (Det. Mickey Nestor); Pat Henry (Mercidis); Patrick McIvey (Officer Tanner); Dixie Marquis (Carol Linjack); Sugar Ray Robinson (Officer Kelly); Renee Taylor (Rachel Schoenstein); James Inman (Teddy Leikman); Tom Atkins (Harmon); Jacqueline Bisset (Norma MacIver).
SCREENPLAY Abby Mann
Based on novel by Roderick Thorp
MUSIC Jerry Goldsmith
ORCHESTRATION Warren Barker
PHOTOGRAPHY Joseph Biroc
EDITOR Robert Simpson
ART DIRECTION Jack Martin Smith, William Creber
Color by Deluxe
Panavision
RUNNING TIME 114 minutes
PRODUCED BY Aaron Rosenberg

Sinatra plays a fierce homicide detective in New York who discovers that he has caused the execution of an innocent man, and what with that and a wife who is a nymphomaniac, cannot retain his credibility. It is a self-consciously 'tough' film, dealing with the seamy underside in a manner impossible before Sixties permissiveness opened up the cinema.

54 Lady in Cement

(Twentieth Century-Fox)
DIRECTOR Gordon Douglas
CAST Frank Sinatra (Tony Rome); Raquel Welch (Kit Forrest); Dan Blocker (Earl Gronsky); Richard Conte (Lt Santini); Martin Gabel (Al Mungar); Lainie Kazan (Marie Baretto); Pat Henry (Hal Rubin); Steve Peck (Paul Mungar); Virginia Wood (Audrey); Richard Deacon (Arnie Sherwin); Frank Raiter (Danny Yale); Peter Hock (Frenchy); Alex Stevens (Shev); Christine Todd (Sandra Lomax); Mac Robbins (Sidney the Organiser); Tommy Uhlar (Tighe Santini); Ray Baumel (Paco); Pauly Dash (McComb); Andy Jarrell (The Pool Boy).
SCREENPLAY Marvin H. Albert, Jack Guss
Based on novel by Marvin H. Albert
MUSIC COMPOSED AND CONDUCTED BY Hugo Montenegro
ORCHESTRATION Billy May
PHOTOGRAPHY Joseph Biroc
EDITOR Robert Simpson
ART DIRECTION LeRoy Deane
Color by DeLuxe
Panavision
RUNNING TIME 93 minutes
PRODUCED BY Aaron Rosenberg

Tony Rome discovers a naked blonde under water, her feet in a block of cement, and investigates. The rapid reprise of the Miami private eye has much the same ingredients as the first film, but mixed slightly more smoothly, resulting in a fashionable blend of sex, cynicism and violence.

1970

55 Dirty Dingus Magee (MGM)

DIRECTOR, PRODUCER Burt Kennedy
CAST Frank Sinatra (Dingus Magee); George Kennedy (Hoke Birdill); Anne Jackson (Belle Knops); Lois Nettleton (Prudence Frost); Jack Elam (John Wesley Hardin); Michele Carey (Anna Hoitwater); John Dehner (General); Henry Jones (Rev. Green); Harry Carey Jr (Stuart); Paul Fix (Chief Crazy Blanket); Donal Barry (Shotgun Rider); Mike Wagner (Stagecoach Driver).
SCREENPLAY Tom and Frank Waldman, Joseph Heller
Based on novel The Ballad of Dingus Magee by David Markson
MUSIC Jeff Alexander, Billy Strange
PHOTOGRAPHY Harry Stradling Jr
EDITOR William B. Gulick
ART DIRECTION George W. Davis, J. McMillan Johnson
MetroColor
Panavision

RUNNING TIME 91 minutes

A crude comedy western with Sinatra as a scurrilous lowlife outlaw. Most critics were offended on its first release, and if the film is not treated seriously, but viewed instead in the spirit with which it was intended, it can be regarded as a spoof of its genre almost in the Blazing Saddles class.

1977

56 Contract on Cherry Street (Columbia)

DIRECTOR William A. Graham
CAST Frank Sinatra (Dep. Insp. Frank Hovannes); Jay Black (Tommy Sinardos); Verna Bloom (Emily Hovannes); Martin Balsam (Capt. Ernie Weinberg); Joe DeSantis (Vincenso Seruto); Martin Gabel (Baruch Waldman); Harry Guardino (Ron Polito); James Luisi (Al Palmini); Michael Nouri (Lou Savage); Marco St John (Eddie Manzaro); Henry Silva (Roberto Obregon); Richard Ward (Jack Kittens); Addison Powell (Bob Halloran); Steve Inwood (Fran Marks); Johnny Barnes (Otis Washington); Lenny Montana (Phil Lombardi); Murray Moston (Richie Saint); Robert Davi (Mickey Sinardos); Nicky Blair (Jeff Diamond); Estelle Omons (Flo Weinberg); Ruth Rivera (Cecelia); Sol Weiner (Paul Gold).
EXECUTIVE PRODUCER Renee Valente
TELEPLAY Edward Anhalt
Based on a book by Philip Rosenberg
MUSIC Jerry Goldsmith
PHOTOGRAPHY Jack Priestley
EDITOR Eric Albertson
ART DIRECTION Robert Gundlach
Made for television
RUNNING TIME 180 minutes
PRODUCED BY Hugh Benson

Sinatra's television movie debut features him as a police lieutenant conducting a private war against the New York Mafia following the shooting of his colleague and best friend. The demands of television to fill a three-hour time slot result in much long-winded and repetitive plot exposition, and the pace is less satisfactory than in some of his later cinema films.

1980

57 The First Deadly Sin

(Filmways/Artanis/Cinema Seven)
DIRECTOR Brian G. Hutton
CAST Frank Sinatra (Edward Delaney); Faye Dunaway (Barbara Delaney); David Dukes (Daniel Blank); George Coe (Dr Bernardi); Brenda Vaccaro (Monica Gilbert); Martin Gabel (Christopher Langley); Anthony Zerbe (Capt. Broughton); James Whitmore (Dr Sanford Ferguson); Joe Spinell (Charles Lipsky); Anna Navarro (Sonny Jordeen); Fred Fuster (Delivery Man); Jeffrey De Munn (Sgt Correlli); John Devaney (John Rogers); Robert Weil (Sol Appel); Hugh Hurd (Ben Johnson); Jon de Vries (Calvin Sawtell); Eddie Jones (Officer Curdy); Victor Arnold (Officer Kendall); Frank

Bongiorno (Nick); Reuben Green (Bill Garvin); Tom Signorelli (Carl Lucas); Richard Backus (Walt Ashman); Frederick Rolf (Judge James Braggs); Carol Gustafson (Matron); Michael Ingram (Bernard Gilbert); Bill Couch (Albert Feinberg); Larry Loonin (Hardware Salesman); Denise Lute (Sports Clerk Girl); Robert Cenedello (Night Doorman); Sherman Jones, Nick Caris, R. Bruce McLane (Detectives).
EXECUTIVE PRODUCERS Frank Sinatra, Elliott Kastner
ASSOCIATE PRODUCER Fred Caruso
SCREENPLAY Mann Rubin
Based on novel by Lawrence Sanders
MUSIC Gordon Jenkins
ORCHESTRATIONS Don Harris
PHOTOGRAPHY Jack Priestley
EDITOR Eric Albertson
ART DIRECTION Woody Mackintosh
Color by TVC
RUNNING TIME 101 minutes
PRODUCED BY George Pappas, Mark Shanker

Sinatra's return to the cinema screen after a 10-year absence casts him yet again as a cop remorselessly tracking down a killer, his anxiety coloured here by the fact of imminent retirement and the imminent death of his wife who has had a bungled kidney operation. It is altogether too much to encompass, and the gloom-laden intensity mars what could have been a straightforward police thriller.